I am honored and pleased to endors[e] ... *into Your Traumatic Memories*. With keen wisdom from on high, Emily uses experiences from her own life and from her work with others to help the reader come face-to-face with hidden and suppressed memories that lead to conflict and heartbreak in relationships. With a soothing grace, she gently guides us to the only solution for healing—the real and living Jesus, Himself.

DON BROWN
Author of 15 books, including national bestsellers
LAST FIGHTER PILOT, TREASON and MALACCA CONSPIRACY

Invite Jesus has given me hope that I will finally be able to overcome those things that have held me back for years.

ROBBIN J. GRAHAM, Emily's long-time friend

Emily Gardner Foppe has a huge heart for hurting people—and the knowledge to systematically dismantle the foundation that Satan has built in people's lives. She doesn't just talk and write about memory healing and deliverance. She does it! This book will show you how to do it, too.

DR. SCOTT BITCON, Deliverance Pastor and Trainer
Phoenix, Arizona

On behalf of those who are survivors of Satanic Ritual Abuse, child trafficking, incest, childhood sexual trauma, abusive homes, broken homes, fatherless homes, and many other situations in which the devil has seized the opportunity to hurt the innocent, I would like to say a giant "Thank You" to Emily for writing this book! She has courageously tackled many difficult topics, and has done it from a place of compassion, having the heart of Jesus. And that heart is one of wanting to help those who have been hurt, to *heal*.

"JOSHUA COLLINS"
Satanic Ritual Abuse survivor and author of *Born into Battle*

As someone with 20 years in the mental health field, I can testify that many providers feel at a loss when it comes to helping patients find true healing and deliverance. All the medications and coping skills at our disposal only go so far. Also, as a society we have had a front row seat to the inadequacy of our mental health system during the Covid pandemic. We have come to a point where we can no longer ignore the spiritual core of who we are. Also, we must understand what the underlying driving forces of suffering are, to know what to do about it. This is exactly why this unique book, *Invite Jesus,* is so timely and the revelations worthy of any effort needed to take hold of them!

ANGELA WHITE, APRN Ph.D.
Board Certified Psychiatric Nurse Practitioner

Emily Gardner Foppe bares her soul again, masterfully linking teachings from the Christian faith to pivotal moments in her life story. Her engaging writing style strips themes that could be considered irrelevant, archaic, or baseless by secularists and Christian believers alike, and renders them applicable to everyday life situations. Furthermore, Emily addresses the issues of mental illness, suffering, and family dysfunction, offering a vital therapeutic solution for all who are willing to embrace it. The message contained within the book can and will save lives.

MARGARET KERN, Coast Guard Auxiliary Chaplain
Master of Divinity in Chaplaincy, Regent University

My story, as told in my book *Bipolar Missionary,* is an example of how even people who love God and want to serve Him can suffer from painful childhood memories that complicate life and ministry. A number of years ago the Holy Spirit spontaneously helped me heal one of my most traumatic memories. The healing presence of Jesus was so real that it changed a lot of things for me, especially how I viewed my earthly father. More recently, I received a prophetic word and "deliverance prayer" at a House Church Meeting that immediately propelled me into yet another significant and life-changing childhood memory healing. This healing has been particularly life altering! My testimony is that healing can occur gradually through many different spiritual mechanisms, such as Bible Study, personal prayer, counseling, etc. But when we engage the Father's heart through the healing of memories, there often comes a surge of transformation that cannot be altogether explained.

Paul Samuels, Author of *Bipolar Missionary*

Emily Gardner Foppe does a masterful job relating the utmost importance of healing traumatic experiences that wound our souls, cloud our minds, scar our emotions, and ultimately deter us from fulfilling our divine destinies. Using interesting, personal accounts, Emily draws her audience into practical, Bible-based solutions. These methods show that "inviting" Jesus to come is often the missing link between bondage and freedom for those seeking demonic deliverance. I highly recommend this excellent work!

ROBERT J. WINTERS, Doctor of Ministry, Senior Pastor
Prepare the Way International Church
Phoenix, Arizona

As I read *Invite Jesus into Your Traumatic Memories,* something quite unexpected happened. Almost immediately, I began having thoughts of unresolved conflict in some of the memories I thought I had taken care of a long time ago! Then I began to see Jesus in my mind, wrapping His arms around me and "rewriting" these memories for me! He was there the whole time. But I didn't see Him until now. Truly, He is our Savior, Healer and Advocate in the Courts of Heaven. Praise God, I have been challenged in this book to ask the Holy Spirit to bring a searchlight into my thought life so I can stay washed in His blood! I am clean!

NORMAN CHEEVER
Arizona Director, Full Gospel Businessmen's
Fellowship International

Invite Jesus into Your Traumatic Memories is an excellent guide for anyone who needs to awaken their repressed memories.

CAITLYN HENNEHAN-FOPPE,
PhD in Conflict Analysis and Resolution

When Emily first introduced the idea of memory healing with Jesus to me, shame prevented me from allowing Him to witness what had happened. But when I finally opened the door and let Him enter my past, I saw in my mind how much He loved me! He had been there with me when I was a child! He had grieved for me! I wasn't alone, and I wasn't abandoned by Him. The surprising revelation that Jesus also loved my father was what helped me to completely forgive him. The forgiveness released me from the bondage and heaviness that those memories had on my life. I finally found freedom! The original memories were erased and replaced with the ones I had experienced in the healing. Those beautiful memories with Jesus by my side are the ones I will always remember.

JODIE S., from Chapter Three

My husband and I read this book together! And we agree that *Invite Jesus into Your Traumatic Memories* will inspire all who read it to go further in their walk with Jesus, no matter how long you have known and followed Him. As Emily explains, through personal stories and other testimonies, all people, including Christians, need to be freed and healed from painful memories. This is the only way the church will be ready for His second coming! We have to be perfected in His love! We also appreciate how Emily tied in stories and passages from the Bible that are parallel to what is happening in our world right now. *Invite Jesus* is a must read for all Christians who believe that we are moving into the end times and whose desire is to be the perfect bride of Christ! "Therefore, rejoice, O heavens and you who dwell in them! But woe to you, O earth and sea, for the devil has come down to you in great wrath, because he knows his time is short" (Revelation 12:12 ESV).

SANDI CHEEVER

Invite Jesus teaches us how to be in His presence so we can get free from the traumas that have plagued our lives and kept us in bondage. Emily Foppe's transparency about her own family struggles makes it easy for readers of any background to connect and feel that this book was written just for them!

KIMBERLY SPARROW
Accra, Ghana

God is using *Invite Jesus* to cleanse and purify me. Also, to deliver me from an orphan spirit! I had no idea that this was how I had been living! In 2016, I read Emily's first book *Finding the Secret Place* and experienced a great deal of healing. Now I realize that what God started then has been unfolding. And I understand so much better the deepest places of pain and the reasons behind my anger and sadness. Living in a place away from His presence brings much fear, sadness, and rejection. Now I know that He is teaching me how to always live in that secret place with Him. I finally feel that He is taking me to the place of ultimate healing and deliverance.

CONNIE BLALOCK, from Chapter Three
Owner of Glory Beans Coffee House
Albemarle, North Carolina

Emily has written about deep and difficult issues in a way that leads one toward the love of Jesus and His healing intentions for troubled hearts and minds. No matter where we have come from, what we have experienced, or even how advanced we might think ourselves, *Invite Jesus* leads us to a deeper walk and understanding of the Kingdom of God.

DIANE PHILLIPS, from Australia, Counsellor and former
School Chaplain, Emily's Prayer Partner in *Sons Arising*

It wasn't until I dove into the first few chapters of *Invite Jesus into Your Traumatic Memories* that I realized that some of my most painful memories had been locked away. I needed to be healed from this pain to be assured I could stop the cycle of life from repeating itself. Emily has an amazing way of guiding you towards the root of your current thought pattern or problem and showing you how to open doors that will allow Jesus to heal you in ways you never thought possible. This is a must read for anyone who feels abandoned or is in bondage from haunting, but perhaps "forgotten," memories.

LISA HAVEN
Conservative Political Commentator, Radio Show Host,
and Alternative Media News Reporter

INVITE
Jesus
into your
traumatic
memories

Let Him heal your divisions
and set your heart free!

EMILY GARDNER FOPPE

Invite Jesus into Your Traumatic Memories
© 2022 by Emily Gardner Foppe
Published by The Secret Place, LLC
Scottsdale, AZ
www.emilygardnerfoppe.com

The Passion Translation, Isaiah: The Vision, © 2018, used by permission of BroadStreet Publishing Group, LLC.

The Passion Translation, Genesis: Firstfruits, © 2019, used by permission of BroadStreet Publishing Group, LLC.

The Passion Translation, New Testament with Psalms, Proverbs, and Song of Songs, Second Edition, © 2018, used by permission of BroadStreet Publishing Group, LLC.

The Amplified Topical Reference Bible, copyright © 2006, used by permission of Zondervan, Grand Rapid, Michigan 49530. All rights reserved

Scriptures marked "NLT" are taken from the New Life Translation of the Bible.

Scriptures marked "NIV" are taken from the New International Version of the Bible.

Scriptures marked "KJV" are taken from the King James Version of the Bible.

Scriptures marked "NKJV" are taken from the New King James Version of the Bible.

Scriptures marked "AMP" taken from the Amplified® Bible, Copyright © 2015 by The Lockman Foundation. Used by permission. (www.lockman.org)

ISBN: 978-0-578-36575-6
Printed in the USA
Cover design by Robin Black, Inspirio Design

I dedicate this book to all God's people,
who love Him and are moving forward on the path
to a future that is good, not evil, the perfect day.

I would like to thank my friend Patricia Sweatte for all her devotion, encouragement, and help during the writing and development of this book. Her technical and graphic design skills (which include the design of my new Secret Place logo, the diagrams inside the book, and the creation of my new website) have been such a tremendous blessing!

Many thanks to my good friends and assistant "proofreaders" Celeste Ross and Deb Jenkins for their conscientious efforts!

To my editor, Teresa Crumpton: Teresa, I love your "teaching" approach to editing and will recommend you to anyone who needs such work done! teresa@authorspark.org

In addition, I am so happy with the creative genious of my graphic artist and typesetter, Robin Black, who created the covers for both of my books. I have gotten so many compliments on them both. Thank you, Robin! robin@inspiriodesign.com

Last, but not least, a big thank you goes to my husband, Larry, who always believes in the work that I am doing. He is my best cheerleader. I love you, Larry!

Table of Contents

A Note from the Author 15

Chapter One, Realize 21

Chapter Two, Reroute 41

Chapter Three, Receive 56

Chapter Four, Release 76

Chapter Five, Renew 96

Chapter Six, Redirect 123

Chapter Seven, Rejoice 147

Chapter Eight, Repeat 177

Afterword 205

Endnotes 209

A Note from the Author

"Herein is our love made perfect, that we may have boldness
in the day of judgment. Because as He is, so we are in the world"
(1 John 4:17-18 KJV).

I find most humans are dysfunctional, as in "divided," to one extent or
another— even believers in the Lord Jesus Christ! Even church leaders!
Also—whether it's a dysfunction with God, self, or others—these things
keep us distracted, unproductive, ineffective, and dissatisfied. This book
provides a biblical roadmap for getting out of this trap.

Let me say upfront that I feel compelled to use my family dynamic
as one of the main illustrations in this book because it is the story I know
best. For any reader who knew my parents, please don't be alarmed.
They are now in heaven and have the advantage of seeing me from that
perspective. One day, when I see them again, I believe they will tell me
how happy they are with the work that I am doing to help people heal
from within. They will be proud that I am able to tell this story.

My dad was a minister in a mainline Christian denomination for over
more than fifty years and served five churches. He was humble and faithful and served as best he knew how. But he was not a perfect man. And he
was hindered in many ways, just like other people who suffer from childhood traumas and never receive deep inner healing, (memory healing), and
deliverance—the ministry I've been involved with for the last five years.

While I know and have ministered to many people who have endured
evil, such as molestation, incest, physical abuse, and even Satanic Ritual
Abuse (SRA), my family-life experience was largely untouched by these
kinds of trauma. Still, the relationships in my family were dysfunctional. My mom and dad needed inner healing and deliverance. As much
as I loved them, I have had to face the unpleasant reality that they were

15

in bondage to a form of religion that did nothing to help them resolve their major issues.

WHAT DOES IT MEAN TO "BE DIVIDED?

God's intension is for every person to live with a "whole" soul, that is, an "undivided" one. Because it is this "wholeness" that allows us to live in perfect alignment with Him. However, when a person suffers a traumatic wounding, a "part" of him often separates from the whole, creating a "division." As a result, some wounded "parts" carry negative emotions tied to the trauma they have experienced. When a person's individual parts are healed, their negative emotions are dissolved. Then the parts are "assimilated" back into the "whole." The soul is no longer fractured.

WHAT IS MEMORY HEALING?

Memory healing involves an inner-healing process, whereby painful or traumatic memories are revisited. However, Jesus is "invited" to come into these memories. There, He enables the person in need of healing to feel His presence. Often, He is "seen" and "heard."

Experiencing the Lord's presence releases an abundance of love, peace, and freedom, and provides a sense of safety and security. The result is a supernatural ability to understand and embrace God's ways—and to forgive self, and others. Afterward, when this same memory is recalled, it comes forth in its "rewritten" form!

WHAT IS DELIVERANCE?

Deliverance is the act of dissolving a demon's "legal right" to attach himself to a victim's "soul" wounds. This is accomplished when a complete memory healing has occurred.

Sadly, I do not recall any touching, kissing, hugging, or sincere words of affirmation between my parents—except once when my dad first entered the hospital about a year before he died. Even worse, at a family gathering a mere few months before his death at age 87, Dad blurted out a statement about an old girlfriend who "made me the man I am today." Think how my mom felt!

Over the years, there were always problems and issues. One of the most significant was the dysfunctional bond Dad had with his mother. Another was the countless hours he spent away from the home, pastoring and studying. These caused him to fall very short at building and supporting his own family and loving his wife the way Christ loves the church.

It bothers me to admit this, but Mom was often depressed, humiliated, hopeless, and angry. Dad was passive, ill-equipped, distant, and down-trodden. I was helpless, embarrassed, confused, and fearful. Even though we were God's people, we were laden with dysfunction and hopelessness that was a result of living our lives apart from the power of the Holy Spirit to change things.

In other words, it was, in many aspects, a vain religion we practiced.

This book is about waking up to the fact that there are adjustments we all can make to right the wrongs in our lives. Also, we must also wake up to the fact that we have an enemy who is opposing us in our efforts—Satan, that is, the devil.[1]

We can get him off our backs through memory healing and deliverance. With that done, we can move beyond the legal aspects of the heavenly courts[2] to the intimacy of God's Presence. This is where the fullness of healing takes effect, our minds change radically, and we begin to embrace God's thinking.

But this is the hitch. Because our minds have been corrupted by the enemy, at least some things we *know* to be *right* at the beginning of this journey could be *wrong*. Proceed no farther in reading this book unless you are willing to consider what God has to say about it. You *may* have to get rid of some of your preconceived ideas. If this proves to be the case, you will be touched by a revelation of *rightness*[3] which will prepare you for the days ahead.

Follow the protocol as outlined in this book, and get rid of divisions within so you can be more effective, focused, prepared, and ready. In so

WHO IS SATAN?

According to the Bible, Satan is our greatest adversary or
antidikos—a legal term in the Greek language meaning "an
opponent in a suit of law." Once an archangel, he rebelled
against God in heaven, because he wanted to be higher than
God.[1] Presumably, this happened before man was even created. Immediately, Satan and other rebellious angels were
cast "down" from heaven to "the ground"[2] where they would
remain separated from God's presence. Eventually Satan
found his way to the Garden of Eden, where he had no power
or "authority."[3] However, that changed when man disobeyed
God and ate from The Tree of the Knowledge of Good and Evil.
With that regrettable event, man, in effect, yielded the authority God had given him to Satan.

doing, you will enjoy the perception and development of new spiritual
realities and live the life that God had in mind for you since before the
beginning of time. You will experience the gradual healing of unpleasant,
dysfunctional relationships with other people. Your God-ordained destiny
will be fulfilled, and your life will be more satisfying and fun.

But there's more: It's not all about us. The church has a destiny which
needs to be fulfilled, too. Our individual restoration,[4] strong participation,
and support within the Body of Christ will allow God's love to find its full
expression through the Church.[5] This expression will enable Jesus' "bride"
to fight Satan, bring in the harvest, and stand strong for His return.

Restoration and the Messiah's Return

Before He ascended into heaven, Jesus commanded His disciples to go to
Jerusalem and wait for the power to come. That power was the Holy Spirit.

Now, we must apply the power He sent like never before. In fact,
until widespread healing and restoration within the Church occurs, the
Messiah's return to earth will be delayed.[6] This fact alone makes the
pursuit of individual and relational healing in one's immediate sphere of

WHAT'S WITH THE BOXES?

In many conversations I had with my husband Larry while writing this book, he thought the concepts and truths found here may not be familiar to all readers. So I created the boxes. These boxes represent many of the questions, issues, concepts, and truths that Larry felt were never fully addressed or explained in his own upbringing, which was Catholic. So, we did this for the benefit of hurting people who are seeking solutions, irrespective of their biblical training.

influence one of the most significant contributions a Christian can make in today's world.

My hope and prayer is that many souls who have been opposed by the enemy will find the inspiration needed within these pages to do the necessary work.

Start with the light that already shines within you:

> "The spirit God breathed into man is like a living lamp, a shining light searching into the innermost chamber of our being" (Proverbs 20:27 TPT).

Then *lean* into His love—the Mighty Flame of the Lord Most Passionate:

Fasten me upon your heart as a seal of fire forevermore. This living, consuming flame will seal you as my prisoner of love. My passion is stronger than the chains of death and the grave, all-consuming as the very flashes of fire from the burning heart of God.[7] Place this fierce, unrelenting fire over your entire being. Rivers of pain and persecution will never extinguish this flame. Endless floods will be unable to quench this raging fire that burns within you. Everything will be consumed. It will stop at nothing as you yield everything to this furious fire until it won't even seem to you like a sacrifice anymore (Song of Songs 8:6–7 TPT).

This passionate, fiery love will propel you to the end of the path. May God bless you in the journey.

—Emily Gardner Foppe

Chapter One

REALIZE

"And whoever shall call on the name of the Lord
shall be delivered and saved" (Joel 2:32a AMP).

Summary: The first key to getting the divisions within us healed is REALIZING there is a war going on in the *unseen* realm.

The problem is this: we are largely unaware of the war because the enemy of our souls has obscured our ability to see. It is he, our opponent in the heavenly court, who has stolen our divine mindset and vision, our purpose, and our power. Consequently, we live in dangerous territory with no supplies, no equipment, no direction. We need a Savior and Deliverer!

The Good News is this: When we purpose to meet with God first in His Heavenly Courtroom[1] and then beyond it, in the intimacy of His presence in the Secret Place,[2] the Throne Room,[3] the Sanctuary,[4] or the mountain of God,[5] we get our stolen property back. In other words, under the protection of the Father's love and intimacy, we get direction and help about how to fight and win in our struggle against Satan, who is the source of all our chaos and dysfunction.

I was a PK, a "preacher's kid." My dad was the minister at the Presbyterian church across the way from the church-owned house our family called home.

This particular day I was home from college and trying to find my mom. She wasn't in the kitchen or on her usual perch, the den sofa. "Mom, where are you?" Whatever I needed to ask her couldn't wait.

"Mom?" The house was quiet. Oddly, the TV was not turned on, and my brothers were nowhere around.

There came a faint voice from the master bedroom beside the den, a sound I could hardly distinguish to be her voice, yet it had to be. "I'm in here, honey."

That was strange. Was something wrong? My heart picked up as I opened the unlocked bedroom door and bolted through. She was in the bathroom. "Mom, are you OK?"

I was shocked to see her, sitting on the toilet with a scrunched up red face, eyes shut tight, hands clasped in her lap. She was trying to mask her emotions; but as I knelt on the floor to throw my arms around her, she let go and began sobbing out loud.

"Mom, what is wrong?" I was in a panic to find out. Had someone died? But the bellowing continued. I had never heard such distraught-sounding emotion coming out of her. Not even when my grandmother had passed away ten years prior. I just held her tight and kept repeating "I'm so sorry" until the sobbing subsided.

My mom was the one person in my life who had always been there for me. My dad was in and out, but aloof—caught up in his own world and didn't talk much. Mom, on the other hand, was generally available when I got home from school and eager to hear about my day. Most everything about her was relaxed versus uptight and formal, and everything she said came out "Georgia southern."

But my mom was no push-over. She was strong minded and always had an opinion. I witnessed many times her angry, even furious, outbursts toward my dad, who was passive, ethereal, non-combative and had a hard time getting around to things, especially if it involved stepping on someone's toes. Despite all that, my mom was never selfish when it came to helping my dad with the church work. She was especially generous with her time and talent as artist and "unpaid secretary." That's how she would refer to herself!I think my dad picked her to be his wife because he was well into his thirties when they met and entered his first pastorate, and he needed someone like her to offset his quirky, reserved, sometimes discombobulated style. He wanted to be successful in the ministry.

Since high school, my mom had wanted to be a minister's wife. That's when she read Catherine Marshall's book, *A Man Called Peter*, the heart-warming story of Peter Marshall, the Scottish-born Presbyterian preacher who became chaplain to the US Senate in the 1940s. It was the perfect inspiration for a young, noble-minded woman like my mom, herself raised in the Presbyterian church.

My parents, Mary Ann and Charles, married within a year of meeting on a blind date after mutual friends set them up. The initial meeting was less than exciting, she always said. But soon after, she was invited to a family gathering put on by my Great Aunt Margaret. A good-looking eligible man like my dad needed a date, and she insisted he bring the new gal who taught art at the local high school.

Mom decided to give him the benefit of the doubt and went along, though the first half of the party was dismal. Dad just wasn't the social type. Then to show him she could have a good time, with or without his notice, she cozied up to a few of the other guests. That's when he perked up and took an interest that led to almost immediate engagement and marriage the following March—seemingly, "a match made in heaven."

When I bounded into the bathroom that day and found Mom in such distress, I knew in my spirit that something was terribly *wrong*. And I figured the turmoil involved a problem with Dad, with Dearest (my Dad's mother) or with something going on in the church. It was always one or several of those combined. It had been that way my whole life. A surge of helplessness swept through me. I was at a loss.

In the last year I had begun reading and studying the Bible fervently. But I had no clue what to do or what to pray in a situation like this. And I sensed that Mom's issues were worse than usual—that she was, in fact, in some sort of danger. I had heard her speak of individuals having nervous breakdowns. Was she having one now?[6]

All these years later, I cannot recall exactly what transpired prior to this encounter with Mom in the bathroom. But I know it had something to do with what my dad did or didn't do, as the case might be. In other words, there was a *trigger* [7]—and this time, it sent Mom into a downward spiral of disappointment, hopelessness, and bitterness that changed the course of her life.

I was also affected by this incident. I distinctly remember standing there, helplessly wringing my hands and thinking *There is absolutely nothing I can do to help this. These people will never change! Lord, what am I to do?*

Who is Lurking Outside Your Tent? [8]

As you can see from my family story, Satan and his minions are always lurking around, especially when life is lived apart from the holy protection and direction of the Holy Spirit. That's when demons seize the opportunity to kill and destroy.

How do they do it? They routinely and adversely manifest in the lives of those around us. And don't be fooled. They also manifest in *us*, having come to us through genetics, the atmosphere, or traumas inflicted upon us. In other words, the evil around us and in us works to *affect* our minds, our wills, our emotions, and our physical bodies.[9] And the greater evil's influence, the thicker the web woven around our spirits; for evil's objective is to keep the human spirit tied down and unable to experience union with the Holy Spirit.

It would be many years before I would understand the truth and the severity concerning the purposes and methods Satan uses to *oppose* our souls. This revelation would come through decades of my own trials and errors. In addition, a great deal of personal re-study of the Bible was required. I also spent much time *inquiring* of God—at the same time believing that He does have solutions—and that He will share His solutions, if only we have ears to hear.

"So everyone who hears these words of Mine and acts upon them [obeying them] will be like a sensible (prudent, practical, wise,) man who built his house upon the rock" (Matthew 7:24 AMP).

What God showed me through this process is that all human beings have been affected by evil forces, that is, evil spirits or demons.[10] Some are affected more than others. These demons, emanating from an unseen spiritual realm, manifest through our dysfunctional attitudes, motivations, and prejudices. These include fear, depression, shame, guilt, greed, pride, hate, self-hate, and lawlessness. A major point of entry for them is created when physical, mental, or emotional pain is inflicted upon us by others.

Most psychologists agree that the most serious woundedness in a person surfaces early in life through one or both parents—or another family member. Often, a childhood incident is so severe it is *forgotten,* that is, locked away in the brain. Called *dissociation*, this coping mechanism is designed by God to protect a child until he can process it through more mature eyes. However, these forgotten wounds must be remembered and then healed for a person to be unaffected by them in adulthood. This is what my process does.

Regardless the situation, all traumatic wounds hinder in various ways, especially in relationships. The repercussions are often carried for a lifetime, unless inner healing and deliverance is received. Through my ministry, I have seen these influences come to bear repeatedly, even among those who have believed in the Lord a long time.

I believe my findings explain why strong Christians—even people engaged in fulltime ministry—often exhibit very dysfunctional behaviors. Let's admit it. Churches split due to strife, greed, adultery etc., and the divorce rate among those in the church is just as high or higher as that of the unchurched. I am a prime example of one who went to church her whole life, knew God, studied the Bible, tried to seek God's way—and still ended up miserable and divorced.

The questions I have asked myself and God are to be discussed in this book. What is it that keeps so many people, especially Christians, from getting life and relationships right? Aren't we supposed to know better? Is there anything we can do about these problems? If so, what? And what will happen if we don't?

To answer these and other questions, we must go back to the very beginning of creation itself. What really happened when the human race *fell?*

What in the World is Really Going on?

The Bible tells us that Satan was lurking about in the Garden of Eden, near The Tree of the Knowledge of Good and Evil—the one tree God had designated *forbidden*.

To Adam and Eve, "God said, 'You shall not eat from it nor touch it, otherwise you will die'" (Genesis 3:3 AMP).

Now prior to Eve's encounter with Satan, the atmosphere in the Garden of Eden was full of harmony, peace, fluidity, and light. It was

HOW MANY DEMONS ARE THERE?

It is impossible to know the number of demons that exist. But we do know there is a demon hierarchy[1] of some sort, with the one Jesus identified as the *"dark ruler"* of this world[2] at the top. Also, we know that demons were once-upon-a-time angels. They rebelled against their Creator and were cast down from heaven—about one third of them removed.[3]

On the flip side, Revelation 5:11 speaks of the *"myriads and myriads"*[4] of good angels who encircle the throne of God. According to *The Passion Translation* notes, *"myriads and myriads"* could be interpreted to mean "ten thousands of ten thousands, and thousands of thousands"—or more than 110 million angels!

right. However, when Eve opened the door to this enemy by allowing herself to get involved in a dangerous conversation, in which twisted questions were posed and lies were told, things quickly turned sour.

"Can it really be that God has said, 'You shall not eat from every tree of the garden?'" the serpent queried, at which point a seed of doubt slipped into Eve's unsuspecting mind, where it settled and developed a tiny root. Was God withholding something from her that she needed? Was it possible to get something needed from this tree?

> But the serpent said to the woman, "You certainly will not die! For God knows that on the day you eat from it your eyes will be opened [that is, you will have greater awareness], and you will be like God, knowing [the difference between] good and evil" (Genesis 3:4-5 AMP).

Rebellious Satan[11] knew just what to say. He suggested to Eve something along these lines: You can be like God, but you need "all the information" to do so. When Eve heard this, the root in her soul grew and a sprout appeared. Suddenly, she felt *less than, not-enough*. But eating of this

WHAT ARE THE DEMONS' NAMES?

There are many names of demons mentioned in the Bible. But the main thing we need to be concerned about as far as deliverance is concerned is what evil spirits *do* to people— their functions. When a spirit comes up, we ask, "What is your name?" We are really trying to determine what his function is. Shame? Lust? Fear? Humiliation? Affliction? Infirmity? "What have you stolen from this person, spiritually, emotionally, or physically?" When we have evil spirits *bound* in the Courts of Heaven, they must tell us. It's powerful. A slew of actual demons' names are mentioned or suggested in the Bible.

A few of these are Legion, Lucifer, Beelzebub, Baal, Moloch, and Leviathan.[1] Leviathan[1] is believed by many deliverance ministers to be one of the most powerful evil spirits at work in the world today. The Bible describes him as a water creature, or crocodile, who is hard-hearted, proud, fearless, swift, and fierce. He hides under the surface, waiting for an opportunity to take down God's people through the twisting of the truth. His most dominate characteristics are *pride and distortion of truth.*

tree would make her smarter and wiser, *better than*, she thought. It only took a split second for her to take and eat, the sprout morphing into a large bush—her eyes opening, seeing quite more than she could bear. But the *spirit of unbelief* had already attached, creating a place of darkness in her soul, a spiritual mutation. This meant that her Divine Nature Ability had been altered.[12] Adam, too, was immediately affected by the darkness coming out of her; and the spirit attached to him, too. After that came other spirits from the pit of hell—fear, guilt, and shame.[13] You know the story.

> And they heard the sound of the Lord God walking in the garden in the cool of the day, and Adam and his wife hid themselves from the presence of the Lord God among the trees of the garden. But the Lord God

called to Adam and said to him, "Where are you?" He
said, "I heard the sound of You [walking] in the garden,
and I was afraid because I was naked; and I hid myself."
(Genesis 3:8-10 AMP).

Why didn't Eve call for God's help before succumbing to the ploys
of the devil? If only she had gotten the words to come out, "Lord, help!"
He would have come. Immediately. So easily, He would have *set her mind
and heart straight.* He would have wrapped the arms of His presence
around her and whispered, "Daughter, My love pulls you through and
gives you everything you need—your spirit forever connected to Mine,
your body and your soul nourished by the trees and My words, your relationships and your work successful and prosperous, your direction and
dominion clear, your destiny sure."

I have a friend who served in the military. One of his favorite lines
is, "It's on a need-to-know basis. And you simply don't need to know!"
His point is that when you are in a military battle your commander gives you only what you need to know at the time, nothing more.
Too much information clouds thinking and allows too much room
for moving around the target, which obscures and blurs vision when a
razor focus is needed. The New Testament explains in Ephesians 4:27,
"Leave no [such] room or foothold to the devil [give no opportunity
to him]"(AMP). Certainly, the likelihood of hitting a target decreases
when the focus is off or *wrong.*

In the case of Adam and Eve, God knew best. They already had
everything they needed. However, their sudden awareness of the existence of evil got them and the whole human race into some big, big
trouble. The reason: Awareness of evil had led to an intimate knowledge
of it, that is, participation in it—which ultimately caused their mindsets
to become tainted and confused, fallen.

Evil Intelligence, the Occult, and the Lord of the Dead

"We know that we are God's children and that the whole world lies
under the misery and influence of the Evil One" (1 John 5:19 TPT).

One of my favorite theologians is Oxford-educated Derek Prince, a leader of the Charismatic Movement[14] and author of many books, articles, and teachings about ridding one's self of demons and curses. Prince's teachings reveal how the serpent "controlled" Eve in the in garden. He also explains how these same tactics are being used in today's world through an evil intelligence called "the occult."

In *The Structures of Satan's Kingdom*, Prince explains how the first mention of the occult can be found in Genesis 3:1 when "the serpent," *nachash*[15] in the Hebrew, appeared to Eve. The subtlety is in the verb form, from which the noun is derived. It is *nachash*[16], which means "to practice divination" or "to communicate with the supernatural world"—as it relates to oracles, omens, and *hidden* information. Technically, the serpent in this passage could mean "the diviner" or "the one who foretells the future."

The implication is that diviners seek information from sources other than the One True God.

In his own words, Prince defines the occult as a form of evil intelligence that is used "to control people and make them do what you want—by the use of any spirit that is not the Holy Spirit." [17]

These definitions fit well with what we know about the serpent who encountered Eve. He distorted the truth, offering her what appeared to be divine, *hidden* understanding that would make her "like the gods".[18]

As the story of Genesis 3 ends, we see that deals made with the enemy don't turn out like we think they will. In Eve's case, she had sought knowledge that would make her smarter and give her more *control*. All she had to do to *get it* was become double-minded, that is, *divide* her allegiance—worship someone other than the One True God.

> [For being as he is] a man of two minds (hesitating, dubious, irresolute), [he is] unstable and unreliable and uncertain about everything [he thinks, feels, decides]" (James 1:8 AMP).

> When you are half-hearted and wavering it leaves you unstable.[19] Can you really expect to receive anything from the Lord when you're in that condition?" (James 1:7-8 TPT).

> Everyone who practices sin also practices lawlessness; and sin is lawlessness [ignoring God's law by action or neglect or by tolerating wrongdoing—being unrestrained by His commands and His will]" (1 John 3:4 AMP).

Of course, the serpent failed to explain to Eve (in full) the "contract" he was offering. Eve got what she wanted—the Knowledge of Good *and Evil*. But she also got slavery, shame, guilt, fear, division, and death.

Division began when her allegiance to God was compromised. That's when the doors of her soul opened and allowed the enemy access. Suddenly, Satan had the ability to inflict pain and cause her soul to "divide." As divisions occurred, demons attached.

Eve got death because her spirit had *died unto God*. Her physical body would eventually die, too.

The kicker: she was forced to live in slavery to the authority of the god of this world, the "lord of the dead."[20] Eve's story confirms our present reality: Oracles, omens, or any words of "wisdom" coming from a source other than the One True God are lies — at best or "half-truths" — and are driven by the dark powers, principalities, and rulers of this world, whose only interest is to kill and destroy our relationship with our Creator God, which leads to our spiritual, emotional, and even physical demise.

Disobedience, Disconnection, Displacement, Disenfranchisement, Dysfunction

When Adam and Eve disobeyed God, everything changed. Suddenly, there was a dark, thick cover of tension, discord, separation, and chaos that separated them from the *rightness* they had previously experienced. It could not be thrust away.[21]

Surely Yahweh's arm is not too powerless to save you nor his ear too deaf to hear. Rather, your sinful deeds have built a barrier between you and your God. Your sins have made God turn his face from you so that he does not hear your prayers (Isaiah 59:2 TPT).

It was too late. The experience of sin[22] and a fallen mindset—fear and guilt and shame —had already created a wall of spiritual separation between the first humans and God.

The enemy had hatched a harmful plot and woven a thick death-web of deceit all around Eve's spirit, then Adam's—their only links to God. They were trapped. Now they were afraid to be near Him, afraid He might punish their disobedience. And the ache within! It was a feeling of something being torn or ripped apart or broken, like a fractured part.

Eve could not begin to explain or define what had just happened. Then she heard Adam speaking with God. What? He was blaming her for the whole incident! But that was only half the story![23]

"They hatch harmful plots like snake's eggs and spin their lies like a spider spins its web. Whoever eats their "eggs" dies and a poisonous snake gets hatched!" (Isaiah 59:5 TPT).

In an official courtroom verdict, God characterized the life Adam and Eve would then live on earth.[24] From that point on their spirits would be *disconnected* from HIs Spirit due to *disobedience*. They would live in danger—because the power of evil, which seeks to destroy all beings made in God's image, would loom over them. Also, because they were *displaced* from God's presence with no apparent place to hide, they would have to *seek to find* God's presence, which would be the only *safe* place to flee in the face of evil.[25]

Further, man's ability to dominate the earth would be removed, his purpose, obscured. He would be *disenfranchised*—homeless, purposeless, and powerless to change anything. In a nutshell, everything about his life would be *dysfunctional*, without proper form, disoriented, bankrupt.

"Everyone who practices sin[26] also practices lawlessness; and sin is lawlessness [ignoring God's law by action or neglect or by tolerating wrongdoing—being unrestrained by His commands and His will]" (1 John 3:4 AMP).

Body, Soul, Spirit, and The Tree of Life

Remember, God's heart from the beginning was to create an eternal union with earthly beings "created in His own image,"[27] meaning made from His own Spirit,[28] set apart from the rest of creation, just a little lower than the angels.

> Compared to all this cosmic glory, why would you bother with puny, mortal man or be infatuated with Adam's sons? Yet what honor you have given to men, created only a little lower than elohim,[29] crowned like kings and queens with glory and magnificence. You have delegated to them mastery over all you have made, making everything subservient to their authority, placing earth

WHAT IS HELL AND WHERE IS IT LOCATED?

Satan's rebellion—which presumably occurred before man was even created—got him cast him down from heaven to "the ground"[1] (erets in Hebrew) a place the Old Testament writers called both Sheol and "the pit," that is, the realm of the dead.[2] The New Testament definition of Hell or Hades is also translated "the realm of the dead" in many passages. In addition, the book of Revelation discusses both a temporary place of confinement called the Abyss,[3] or bottomless pit, where Satan will be retained for 1,000 years—and "a fiery lake of burning brimstone," where he will ultimately be tormented "day and night, forever and ever."[3]

The other part concerning the fiery lake called hell is this: *"And if anyone's [name] was not found recorded in the Book of Life, he was hurled into the lake of fire"* (Revelation 20:15 TPT). One of the greatest gifts God gave mankind was the freedom of choice. As you will see in this book, God gives everyone many, many opportunities to choose Him. What we ultimately do with the opportunities He gives is entirely up to us.

The Tree of Life

Eternity
Revelation
Blessing
Healing
Authority

Yeshua on His right hand
God on His Throne
I Am Who I Am
Holy Spirit

itself under the feet of your image-bearers. All the created order and every living thing of the earth, sky, and sea— the wildest beasts and all the sea creatures—everything is in submission to Adams's sons" (Psalm 8:4-8 TPT).

DO ALL EVIL BEINGS EXIST IN HELL?

There appears to be another "unseen" location where evil angels exist. Sometimes referred to as the "second" heaven, this place is ostensibly located somewhere between the highest realm, where God and the good angels exist,[1] and the earth below. This theory is based on the book of Daniel Chapter Ten where an angel was sent from the Lord to encourage Daniel, who has been praying and fasting for 21 days. Upon arrival, the angel reported that he was detained by an evil angel, the prince of Persia. Apparently, a battle had ensued, somewhere between the highest heaven and his destination, earth. It had lasted 21 days!

Why did He do it? Because God is love.[30] He wanted a family to love, comprised of sons and daughters who *could* and *would choose* to love Him in return.[31]

So, God fashioned human beings who could live eternally connected to Him. There were three distinct parts He made. First, He created a form, or a frame, from the dust of the earth; but it was yet to have life. That's when He breathed [32] His eternal Spirit, into the frame,[33]—and in so doing, man became a "living soul." [34] The soul was the seat of the human mind, will, and emotions—and the part that made him distinctly human. But the soul was sparked by the Spirit. God's Spirit was the ingredient that gave Adam's sons *the potential* to be joined to Him and to know Him intimately.

A person cannot *see* his spirit. Some people may not even know they have one. But hear this: Our spirits are *the most important part of us.* Why? When there is no spirit, there is no soul. When there is no soul, there is no living body. When a person opens up his mind, will, and emotions to God through faith, it is his spirit that joins or connects with God's spirit,[35] making him a child of God[36] and an eternal citizen of the Kingdom of God.

Now when Adam and Eve rebelled, God's love for them did not change. But what God said about The Tree of the Knowledge of Good and Evil was true. "If you eat of it, you will surely die!" He was talking about a spiritual death; their spirits would no longer be connected to His Spirit. Eternal separation from His creation was an issue that had to be resolved.

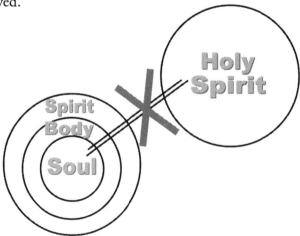

And there was another problem. With no spirit-to-Spirit connection, Adam and Eve's souls had been corrupted! Now they would live in dysfunction—not only in their relationship to God—but in their relationship to self and to others.

And that brings us to the several courses of action God took to work around these issues. First, in an act of mercy, God blocked Adam and Eve from the Tree of Life and drove them from the garden. Why? The fruit from The Tree of Life was *eternal* in nature. If they had been allowed to continue eating the fruit from this tree, they would tragically have lived in a "fallen" state of mind and body forever.

WHAT IS THE SECRET PLACE AND WHERE IS IT FOUND?[1]

The Secret Place is God's supernatural presence, a "hidden" place of shelter[2]—where believers experience the intimacy of God's love through rest,[3] safety,[4] and the secrets of revelation. "There is a private place reserved for the lovers of God, where they sit near him and receive the revelation-secrets of his promises" (Psalm 25:14 TPT).

Clearly, God's presence is a place where secret information is transferred to another, from man to God[5] and from God to man.[6] Also, God equips man there, by exchanging *wrongness for rightness.*[7] Sometimes His work goes unnoticed until much later—when man finally discovers that his destiny is being fulfilled because of what happened in the Secret Place.[8]

In my first book *Finding the Secret Place: 8 Keys to Experiencing God's Presence*, I explain how God used my heartbreak experiences to draw me more deeply into His presence. There, I was able to finally discover the truth about a "stronghold"[9] in my life—one I had never noticed or previously understood, even though I had followed the Lord for more than 30 years! For the first time in my life, I was able to let *Him* meet all my needs and transform me from the inside out.

And the Lord God said, "Behold, the man has become like one of Us [the Father, Son, and Holy Spirit], to know [how to distinguish between] good and evil and blessing and calamity; and now, lest he put forth his hand and take also from the tree of life and eat [its fruit], and live [in this fallen, sinful condition] forever—[37]

Therefore the Lord God sent him forth from the Garden of Eden to till the ground from which he was taken.

So God drove the man out; and at the east of the Garden of Eden He [permanently] stationed the cherubim and the sword with the flashing blade which turned round and round [in every direction] to protect and guard the way (entrance, access) to the tree of life (Genesis 3:22–24 AMP).

WHAT IS THE PURPOSE OF THE HEAVENLY COURTROOM SETTING VS. THE SECRET PLACE?

When we are holding words and attitudes that are *wrong* according to God's standards—or if we are participating in activities that are *wrong*—it's up to us to make those things *right*.[1] So, we go to the heavenly courtroom to meet with God, our Righteous[2] Judge,[3] Jesus, our Mediator,[4] and the Holy Spirit, our Legal Aid.[5] Spending time in the courtroom, as needed, is priority; because we want and need to stay "clean" through the appropriation of Jesus's perfect blood.[6] When we aren't "clean" we can't be effective children in God's Kingdom—because we are living under the legal and emotional constraints of "guilt and shame." However, once we have taken care of our legal issues,[7] we likely want and need the intimacy of the Father's unconditional love, Jesus's friendship, and the Holy Spirit's comfort. Now, we are free to bask in the blissful, restful, peaceful Presence called the Secret Place![8]

Barring man from The Tree of Life was just the beginning of God's plans for man's *restoration*. In fact, God had established long before the creation of the universe plans that would change the outcome of Adam and Eve's error[38] and allow man's spirit an opportunity to be reunited with His Spirit forever. This plan would also give back to humans the upper hand of authority over Satan and provide them with good solutions for solving their many *soul problems* on earth.[39]

Saved, Delivered, and Restored by the Power and Authority of a Name

This was the plan formulated by God: The One Who existed in the heavenly realm[40] with the Father before humans were created, would go to earth to *save* and *deliver* them from eternal separation and the demonic realm. He would accomplish this by the power and authority of His Name.[41]

Referenced in the Genesis courtroom scene as the woman's "Offspring," God foreshadows this Savior's first and second appearance on earth in 3:13, when He forewarns the serpent of his fate: He, the Offspring, "will crush your head, as you crush his heel" (Genesis 3:15b TPT)[42] This eternally existent Savior is the Jewish Messiah, Jesus—in Hebrew, Yeshua, which means "Yahweh is salvation, restoration and deliverance."[43]

Understanding the Hebrew name, Yeshua, helps us see more clearly who this Savior is and what His mission on earth exactly was. It clearly conveys the idea that God not only intended to save us from eternal separation but also to deliver and rescue us from sin's entrapment—and that He would do this through His Son, who bears His Own Name.[44]

Specifically, Yeshua is a shortened form of "Yehoshua," the name for "Joshua."[45] "Yeho" is an abbreviation[46] of God's 4-letter name YHVA, Yahweh,[47] which in Hebrew means "God's Essence Name."[48] "Shua" is a form of the Hebrew verb "yasha" which means "to deliver, save, or rescue from destruction, as in battle."[49] The name of Jesus as seen in this linguistical analysis, "Yehoshua—Yeshua—Jesus," conveys the idea that God intends to save, deliver, and rescue us through His Son.[50]

The implications of this are vast. Not only did Jesus come to save us from eternal separation, but He came to deliver us from the evil dangers we face here on earth—so our corrupted minds could be restored and our *original* identity as God's children embraced. This means that He did

WHY DOES IT REALLY MATTER THAT WE HUMANS GET "HEALED"?

(1) We are each a Spirit. This means God's "inspiration" lives in us. This inspiration is His "stamp." The stamp says "Made in God's Image."

(2) We have a soul, which is our "being"—our mind, will, and emotions.

(3) We have a body which is God's "temple," because it holds the spirit and the soul.

So, we must think of our construction in this way: We are mainly spirit because that is the only part of us that lives forever. Also, when the spirit in us is connected to God's Spirit, we are no longer separated from God. This is how we can live with Him eternally—when our spirits are joined to His. Also, when joined to Him, we can grow "in spirit" and become more like Him here on earth.

what was necessary, so we could have a mindset that bears no shame, fear, guilt, etc. In other words, we can receive all the benefits God bestowed upon men in the beginning, including partaking of The Tree of Life.

First John reminds us, "The reason the Son of God was made manifest (visible) was to undo (destroy, loosen, and dissolve) the works the devil [has done.]" (1 John 3:8 AMP).

As far as inner healing is concerned, having a soul that is whole helps us understand the depth of our spirit connection and growth potential. Having a soul that is broken, or divided, is a painful distraction that stymies our spirit growth—and may prevent us from receiving salvation altogether.

Being whole makes us more productive as "spirit" people, in terms of being able to help others get healed and whole. Last, healing at the soul level helps our bodies heal and stay healthy. Our temples need to be healthy so we can finish the work God has given us to do while we are here on earth.

The bottom line is this: We were made to be healed and fully functioning.

The works of the devil — mind control, confusion, disturbance, fear, chaos, displacement, hate, sickness, death, dysfunction, *wrongness*— began when man lost his intimate relationship with God, his motivation to live according to God's heart, and his authority over creation. Jesus came so we could reclaim what was lost.[51]

As we learn to experience the safety of God's presence once again, by extension having relationship, "heart" motivation and authority in His Courts—and as we gain heaven's perspective, understanding the "legal" aspects of the heavenly realm and the options available to us there—we learn how to make *wrong* things *right*. In other words, the devil's *wrongness* within us is eradicated. We are healed; and the world around us begins to heal, too!

WHAT IS GOD'S "GIFT" OF "AUTHORITY" TO HIS CHILDREN?

It is the ability to *master* evil — using God's power to change things so as to solve the many issues we face due to Satan's influences.[1] This is a move of the Holy Spirit toward the *restoration of all things*[2]—which must manifest in the church worldwide before the Messiah, the Anointed One, reappears.

Since the fall, God has been working to restore His creation back to its original form. For example, one generation after the fall, God offered Cain an opportunity to "make right" his "unacceptable sacrifice." He also tells Cain that he must learn to *master* his sin. In other words, God hints, or foreshadows, that there will ultimately be a way to take back the authority that man had been lost in Eden, so *wrong* things in the soul could again be made *right*.[3]

My Prayer:

God my Father, I acknowledge that I need to receive all the things that You have had in mind for me since the beginning—namely a deep and intimate knowledge of You,[52] and a fuller understanding of Your mysteries and secrets. I ask You to make my heart right, so I can receive all these things.

Personal Questions to Consider:[53]

What "danger" or work of the devil do you currently face?

From what "wrongness" do you need deliverance?

What have you lost in life? Are *you* lost?

Chapter Two

REROUTE

"When I turned to see the voice that was speaking to me, I saw
seven golden lampstands. And walking among the lampstands,
I saw someone like a son of man" (Revelation 1:12–13 TPT).

Summary: To find *right* relationship and intimacy with God, self, and others, we must first enter God's Presence through the heavenly court.

This is where we begin a healing process that touches the deepest levels of our souls—a habit which, when mastered, changes our mindset and allows us to see and filter life through a different lens. Seeing things differently is what allows us to make our *wrong* things *right*.

Bear in mind, dysfunctional habits, relationships, and situations do not correct themselves overnight.[1] Healing at these deep levels must be diligently pursued, but the hard part involves the initial turning from our own thinking and doing.

In other words, we must become convinced that what we have always thought was *right* could be *wrong*. Remember, our souls—which include the mind, will, and emotions—have been controlled, at least in part, by the enemy. Therefore, we must agree to do something different: REROUTE to the courtroom, where we get our legal issues with Satan resolved.

So, we turn to Jesus, our Mediator, the Holy Spirit, our legal aid, and our Father, the Judge who sits on the Throne. But this is just the beginning. Over time, as we become even more deliberate in our REROUTING, we go deeper, always refreshing our mindsets and experiencing greater spiritual realities, which come through our greater intimacy with the Father in a quiet sanctuary called the Secret Place.

But there's more! As REROUTING continues, we ready ourselves for the work of end-time harvest in a heavenly place called the Zion-realm.

WHAT IS THE ZION-REALM?[1]

In the Old and New Testaments, Mount Zion is both a location and a metaphor used to describe a heavenly place called the Zion-realm—the highest realm of God's glory, offering feasting, fellowship, worship, instruction, and healing to the end-time church. From the Zion-realm will come everything we need to overcome the darkness in and around us as we prepare for end-time events. Indeed, from Zion we will "arise and shine." [2]

Early on, my dad developed two unhealthy "soul ties" that he carried until death. One was with his mother. The other, with an old girlfriend he had dated but a few times prior to meeting my mom. Over the years, I always suspected that these emotional ties were anything but normal and were largely responsible for my parent's 54-year-long marriage woes.

Finally, a mere few months before Dad's death at age 87, the suspicion was confirmed at my brother's Thanksgiving dinner. I wasn't present but got the report later. Apparently, the dinner guests were going around the table, everyone sharing the things for which they were most thankful.

Dad, who had been showing some signs of senility in his old age, took his turn. He spoke very thoughtfully and deliberately, with lots of pauses. "I am thankful for my mother," he said. "She made me the man I am today." The family looked around the table, a bit relieved. Not a terrible answer. But he was still tilting his head from side to side, contemplating. My brother leaned in, bracing for the next remark. "And I'm thankful for Ibbie," he continued. "She made me the man I am today."

Ibbie was the old girlfriend.

There was a lot of shuffling about at that point—an urgency to clear the table. Mom told me about it later. She was dejected. But not surprised. Nobody said anything to him about it. He didn't really know what he was saying. Everyone figured his filter was off, due to the senility. The simple truth—at least the truth as he had perceived it in life—didn't have anywhere to go but out.

No surprise to hear Dad praised my grandmother that night. Ibbie was more of a shock, but my brothers and I recognized the name. We had heard about her for decades. She was the gal Dad had been quite enamored with several years prior to meeting Mom—though he didn't date her that many times or even know her that well. At the time, he was in seminary. She was apparently there studying to become a Director of Christian Education.

Ironically, Ibbie was never interested in my Dad and married someone else shortly after they dated. But my dad would bring up her name from time to time even in front of us kids, I think mainly in retaliation to Mom's frustrated outbursts. In Dad's mind, Ibbie represented perfection and light, in stark contrast to my mom, who was anything but—especially when she was angry.

I'm sure Mom's demeaner exacerbated his regrets to the end. He lamented to me but a few years before he died, that, stupidly, he had played the "hard to get" hand with Ibbie. That was why he lost his chance to get her.

It is somewhat hard to imagine a man having an emotional "tie" that strong—to a woman he didn't spend that much time with and never saw again for 60 years. Yet when I heard about the incident at the Thanksgiving table, I knew it was true. The wound created so many years ago from a rather insignificant, nondescript relationship ended up being very deep and wide and long. I witnessed the result of this woundedness over the years and how it affected Dad's relationship with Mom.

Now, I know what soul ties and other traumatic wounds do. They take root in a person's psyche. Then—if they get fed by the forces that seek to kill and destroy—the roots grow deep and manifest fruit that damages and interrupts the normal flow of life, especially in significant relationships. To undo such damage, the bearer of the wound must first become aware that the tie is destructive. Then he must be willing to let it go by deliberately dismantling the power in it, through inner healing and deliverance.

The process is like a GPS system because a person's complete healing can only be accomplished through rerouting—always turning toward Jesus. It's not always easy. And as you might imagine, people who start the process often get off track because the course is not always linear. And there are lots of moving parts, with many adjustments that must be made along the way. But if a wounded person is willing to go through the process, keeping the GPS always set on *Jesus*, he will eventually see his own wounds get healed and likely transform many of his dysfunctional relationships in the process.

WHAT IS A SOUL TIE?

Biblically speaking, a soul tie is a physical, emotional, or psychological bond that is ungodly by biblical standards.[1] Perhaps any obsessive attraction to a person or entity who stymies our spiritual growth and keeps us from depending completely on our union with the Holy Spirit, would be considered a soul tie.

This is the reality: Christians are tied to the Holy Spirit and should think of their spirits as being one with Him, only.[2] Even in marriage two people become one flesh[3]—not one soul or one spirit; and there is no marriage in heaven.[4] So, we definitely fall into a danger zone when we allow ourselves to think in terms of being tied to another person soulfully and outside of covenant boundaries—especially in romantic relationships.

For instance, when we are soul-tied to another, it's easy to view that someone as being more perfect than they really are. How disappointed we become when we discover that they are not the person we idealized them to be. Further, unlawful soul ties can distract us from fulfilling the covenant responsibilities that God has already given us—to spouses, children, grandchildren and/or parents, as was the case with my dad.

Turn, Turn, Turn to Jesus in the Secret Place

To be safe from the dangers of the enemy, a person must learn to turn toward Jesus—in the secret, hidden place where He always is. This is the place where the Holy Spirit shines light into your mind[2] and onto your face, where He wraps His love and protection around you[3] like a security blanket and breathes His life into you.[4] It is the only way to overcome your present darkness and get healed from the heavy burdens of your emotional and spiritual woundedness.

> Jesus said, "Are you weary, carrying a heavy burden? Then come to me. I will refresh your life, for I am your oasis. Simply join your life with mine. Learn my ways and you'll discover that I'm gentle, humble, easy to please. You will find refreshment and rest in me. For all that I require of you will be pleasant and easy to bear" (Matthew 11:28 TPT).

No doubt, Jesus is always wanting us to meet Him in that unseen realm, where He can show us new things, take us to higher levels, and bring those things that have been hidden into our plain view. So, we must continue to Turn, Turn, Turn, Turn, to be with Him there!

I first discovered the value of being with Jesus in the unseen realm around the time that my mom was having her emotional meltdown. At the time, I'm sure I didn't fully understand that I was "finding it." I do remember experiencing a lot of tension between two diametrically opposed worlds, one representing what I now call *rightness*—the other, *wrongness.*[5]

For me, wrongness attitudes and behaviors were manifesting mainly at home. As I said before, my mom was frustrated, irritated, depressed, humiliated, and hopeless. People in the church were arrogant, judging, critical, and blaming. Dad was weak, distant, ill-equipped, and discouraged—though he internalized his discouragement, never discussing it with me or anyone else, to my knowledge. I was helpless, embarrassed, confused, and fearful. Likely, my brothers had these same feelings.

Even though we were God's people, we were laden down in *wrongness.*

The *rightness* manifested at college where I met a number of people through a campus ministry called Inter-Varsity Christian Fellowship.

There was also one very bright and shining light[6] at my home church. Her name was Bernice. She taught the Young Adult Sunday School class, and she exuded the power and love of God like nothing I had ever seen before.

To this day, I'm not sure how Bernice ended up in our church. I tend to think God sent her there just for me, though others will likely argue the same! I do know she was a transplant from Indiana. And she taught me the message of *"Christ in you, the Hope of Glory."*[7] I'm not the one living my life anymore, she would say. Christ lives His life in me.[8]

Admittedly, I didn't really get how that worked exactly. But it sounded *right*. Fortunately, the tension I was feeling between the realms drove me into the Secret Place, where I knew I needed to be to figure it all out.

Repenting is Turning and Being Converted to a New Reality

No one saw me but God. I was crying on my bed, tears of exasperation, disappointment, remorse. I was tired of being a selfish prig![9] I needed to get the heaviness of my sin hanging over me removed! I needed to know the secret of letting this Jesus live His life in me through the power of the Holy Spirit. I needed to be refreshed through heart-felt change!

So, at age 19, I agreed with my accuser,[10] turned and walked through the supernatural door in front of me—the one that separates this "seen" existence from the "unseen" Spirit realm where the Light, Life, and Love of God reside.[11] The barrier lifted, and I rejoiced. I had left behind the idea of living according to my own standards, my own ways of thinking and doing.

In Peter's exhortation to the first church, he said:

"And now you must repent[12] and turn back[13] to God so that your sins will be removed, and so that times of refreshing will stream from the Lord's presence" (Acts 3:19 TPT).

In the book of Revelation, Jesus appears in a vision to the Apostle John and says to the church:

> But this I have against you: You have abandoned the passionate love you had for me at the beginning. Think about how far you have fallen! Repent[14] and do the works of love you did at first. I will come to you and

remove your lampstand from its place of influence if you
do not repent (Revelation 2:2–5 TPT).

The two Greek words highlighted in these verses are closely related—and are critical to what I am talking about in this book. The first word, *repent*, is the Greek word *metanoia*, which means "turn from error" or "take another mind." The second, *turn*, is *epistrepho*, which can mean "be converted."

In my humble opinion, a lot of people in the church have failed to understand and apply the full meaning of these words as they relate to the act of following Jesus Christ. For instance, "turning from error" and "taking another mind" and "being converted" are not one-time events exercised only at the point of conversion.

We should make it our life-long objective to turn and take *Jesus's mindset* on things we encounter in life. Granted this can be accomplished only through the power of the Holy Spirit. But when the Holy Spirit is relied upon, we can always expect to be converted to new spiritual realities. As the Scripture says:

"But God now unveils these profound realities to us by the Spirit. Yes, he has revealed to us his inmost heart and deepest mysteries through the Holy Spirit, who constantly explores all things" (1 Corinthians 2:10 TPT).

"But we have the mind of Christ (the Messiah) and do hold the thoughts (feelings and purposes) of his heart" (1 Corinthians 2:16 AMP).

Repentance Is a Lifestyle of Embracing New Thoughts and Developing a New Mindset

Take the Apostle John as an example of one who turned his whole life. In the Book of Revelation, he turns "to see the voice that was speaking" to him. It was Jesus.

> When I turned to see the voice that was speaking to
> me, I saw seven golden lampstands. And walking among
> the lampstands, I saw someone like a son of man, wear-
> ing a full-length robe with a golden sash over his chest.
> His head and his hair were white like wool—white as

glistening snow. And his eyes were like flames of fire! His feet were gleaming like bright metal, as though they were glowing in a fire, and his voice was like the roar of many rushing waters. In his right hand he held seven stars, and out of his mouth was a sharp, double-edged sword. And his face was shining like the brightness of the blind sun! When I saw him, I fell down at his feet as good as dead, but he laid his right hand on me and I heard his reassuring voice saying: "Don't yield to fear. I am the Beginning and I am the End, the Living One! I was dead, but now look — I am alive forever and ever. And I hold the keys that unlock death and the unseen world. Now I want you to write what you have seen, what is, and what will be after the things that I reveal to you" (Revelation 1:12–19 TPT).

The Greek word used here yet again is *epistrepho*, "to be converted." John is still being converted to new spiritual realities, as many as sixty years after Jesus' crucifixion!

As you can see, the acts of turning and repenting have a lot more to do with embracing a new way of thinking than simply changing a behavior. Unfortunately, I think church people often perceive repentance to have more to do with correcting a behavior than anything. This likely comes about due to inaccurate teaching on the subject. I had a pastor once whose simple definition of repentance was "Stop it!"

Maybe all those years ago, things with my family would have gotten better if I had simply told them to "Stop it!" To Mom I could have said, "Just stop yelling at your husband when he makes you feel rotten! And stop being depressed, biting your nails, and being offended. Just stop it!"

I could have told my dad, "Stop fantasizing about your old girlfriend! It offends God when you do that! It separates you from Him. Stop spending too much time at the church. Stop neglecting your wife! Stop catering to your mother."

And I'm sure my grandmother would have corrected herself if I only I had reminded her that twisting the truth was wrong, and to "Just stop it!"

What about some of the other stories I have heard and observed?

Cutting yourself? Feeling ashamed that your father abused you sexually? Hating him for what he did? Looking at pornography? Being anxious and afraid? Acting like a child? Being a homosexual? Just *stop it*! And do it now, or your sins will not be removed!

I tend to prefer this way of explaining repentance: Turn and look at Jesus. Let His Light, Life, and Love surround you. Don't make excuses. Are you tired of being angry? Are you tired of not loving someone successfully? Are you tired of not having the life that God intended for you? [15] Then just turn.

Tell Him you want to take another mind—His mind. Tell Him you want to experience a new reality. Tell Him you want to embrace His will. Then sit and desire and anticipate His response. He will deliver His thoughts and instructions, in due time. You will see. And you will see that His yoke is easy, and His burden is light![16]

So true repentance is more than just being sorry about something in the moment. It's more than agreeing to stop doing something, cold turkey. It's about being willing to embrace God's will by turning to Him over and over again—then trusting that He will allow His thoughts, feelings and purposes to enter into your heart.

WHAT IS A STRONGHOLD?

A stronghold is a thinking pattern based on lies and deceptions. Over our lifetimes, we have listened to many dark voices that have shut out the Voice of the Father of lights.[1] And our wrong thinking has caused emotional problems, spiritual hang-ups, and physical disease. Our negative, dark thinking has proved harmful to ourselves and others.

But our God is the author of all that is not darkness! We must change our thinking! How? We do it by going on the offensive to tear down these wrong thinking patterns with the spiritual weapons God has provided, namely His Word,[2] His Power,[3] His Spirit,[4] and His Presence. The use of memory healing and deliverance from the courtroom of heaven is a good use of these tools.

What God Did for Me in the Secret Place Was More Than I Imagined

So many things have happened to me in the Secret Place. My life would never be what it is today if I had not spent time there. If I had known the result, I would have gone there more often, especially during times of crisis! But God is good. He took my mistakes and the mistakes of others and recreated them for good, there, in the Secret Place.

More than forty years ago, Jesus redeemed my helplessness, in the Secret Place. This was around the time of my conversion, or soon after, when the incident with my mother in the bathroom occurred. At that time, I was limited in my understanding, and I'm not sure that I was even aware of Jesus's presence there with me that day. But that was the day I cried out, "Lord, please help me to help my mother!"

Now I know that He did hear my cry for help. But His answer came in a most mysterious way. In fact, I was totally unaware of it until recently. What I discovered is that Jesus planted seeds of empowerment in me that day in the bathroom. However, the seeds would not bear fruit until much later in my life—at a time when I was earnestly seeking the power of the Holy Spirit.

But that day in the bathroom was when my desire to heal emotionally wounded people like my mom began. It was the very beginning of the fulfillment of the call on my life, my destiny! I *know* this to be true because the Holy Spirit revealed this to me last year—when I was with Him in the Secret Place.

About ten years after the bathroom incident, the Holy Spirit gave me a special revelation about how the blood of Jesus applied to me personally. Again, there was no one around when I "heard" what He said and "saw" what He did. I was in the Secret Place, crying out to Him for answers to some difficult questions. I write of this in *Finding the Secret Place: 8 Keys to Experiencing God's Presence*. It's called "the lipstick story."

When I remember stories like this one, I am still so amazed by how much God wants me to fulfill my destiny. He will go to any length to give me what I need or to tell me what I need to know—to push me farther down the path toward *rightness*. All I have to do is ask!

Another story I write about in my first book is the one about how the Father God satisfied my loneliness during a time of heartbreak, as only He can do—in the Secret Place. This was the time when I needed to feel

His passion and receive His joy more than ever before; for I had suffered a very difficult breakup with a man I thought I was to marry.

During that year, I learned to embrace what I called "the training program." Mine was the "loneliness" training. But yours might be the "difficult marriage" training, the "wayward child" training, or the "no money" training, or some other.

God is not the source of your angst, but He is using it to drive you into the Secret Place. Embrace the training! The sooner you embrace it, the more quickly He works. I married that same man one year later!

Meet with God in the Secret Place, and you will develop an incredible intimacy with Him as a result. Not only that. He will teach you how to make "the great exchange." You will learn how to hand over to Him your problem or negative emotion so He can redeem it. Then He will give you the opposite quality in exchange.

For example, I learned to give Him my helplessness, and He gave me back empowerment. I gave Him my loneliness, and He gave me back intimacy.[17]

The Story About the Atheists

My husband and I owned an international tapas restaurant in Scottsdale, AZ for about three years. My job there was hostess. One night, I had a very interesting conversation with a few atheists. I had seen them there three or four nights in a row. And so, having greeted these fairly jovial fellows night after night, I finally asked what they were up to in town.

One grimly replied that their mutual buddy from grade school was dying of cancer at the Mayo Clinic, and they were there to pay their last regards. My immediate response was "I'm so sorry to hear that. What is your friend's name?"

He told me the name and I said, "Well, I speak healing now to so-and-so, in Jesus's name." Well, this guy—who before acted like I was his best friend in town—lit into me with "Don't say that!" His face was stern and getting redder by the second. "One, it's not going to happen. And two, I'm an atheist! I believe in science! I liked you until you started talking like that!"

Whew! I must admit I was shocked. Typically, people visiting the restaurant would thank me for something like that, even if they didn't subscribe. I know when someone is placating me. And that's fine. I never try to argue a point. But every now and then, someone will be most appreciative and want to discuss further.

I came back this time with one of the most Holy Spirit-directed responses I can ever remember giving someone whose views were so sharply opposed to mine. I said, "I am so sorry I have offended you. I certainly did not intend to do that." I was earnest in my statement.

What came next was so amazing I knew it came straight from God's heart—through *my* mind: "The reason I said that is because my experience tells me God heals. And if there is anything I can say that would help heal your friend, I want to say it. As far as science is concerned, God *made* science. He certainly *uses* science." I noticed the atheist started softening, though his friend had that anxious look that said, "I can't believe you are getting yourself into this."

I paused for a second and continued. "But God is much bigger than this science He made. The science part of God is this big— like a quarter of a pie." I held up my fingers to show him. "The rest of the pie is the supernatural part of Who God is. That's the part you're missing."

I finished with, "I wrote about this in a book." That was all I needed to say. I was done.

"Well, where is this book of yours?" I was surprised to hear him ask. And his tone wasn't even sarcastic. Had my remarks won back some of his approval?

"I keep a stack of them over there," I said, pointing toward the hostess stand.

"What's the name of it? How much is it?"

I nonchalantly answered his questions, to which he replied, "Well, I want to buy one, but only if you will sign it."

I wrote a note in the book to my new friend. It was something totally illogical like "God loves you! Run to Him in the Secret Place and let His love pull you through!"

Well, if that wasn't enough, the guy's friend, who was humped over at the table listening to our conversation the whole time, started talking to me. "You know," he said, "I've tried to believe for so many years. I have really tried. My son is a preacher at one of those big churches. I've heard him preach. I just can't do it. There is a block."

The guy was literally about to cry right there on the spot. He had his elbows propped, with his head in his hands.

"Maybe you have just tried too hard to figure it out, logically speaking," I interjected. "Like I said, God is mainly supernatural. Give Him a chance to identify Himself to you supernaturally. 'Ask' Him to identify Himself to you this way! One day you'll just be walking down the path, struggling, not believing, and then suddenly, you will. And you won't be able to explain it logically to anyone."

"You got another one of those books?" he asked.

I have to say I was so pleasantly surprised by the interaction I had with these guys. Later, they left with their books in hand—but not before giving me lots of big hugs and thank yous! I did not see or hear from them again. But I will always remember this story, the outcome of which is in God's hands. But I'm believing, that in time, I will hear from one of them!

One More Supernatural Story

Every morning, I go to the Secret Place. It's where Jesus is—and where the Power of the Holy Spirit is. Because my soul is screaming out to me, "Get refreshed and cleaned!" Every day, I live apart from His Light, Life and Love to one degree or another. So I must go there to get *right*.

First, I just sit there and enjoy basking in His love. I acknowledge His love for me out loud. "Lord, you love me! You *love* me! You love *me*! You loved me *first*![18] You are the greatest lover of my soul![19] I am so sorry I have not lived in Your Presence completely. Please exchange my *unawareness* of this mistake for a never-ending *awareness* of my need for Your Presence!"

I continue to acknowledge Him as He covers me, surrounds me.[20] "Thank you Lord! You cover me. No harm can come against me. No offense can overwhelm me."[21]

His Love is so lavish. So complete. "Thank you, Lord. Your love is all I need. Thank you that I can utterly depend on your Love to pull me through and give me everything I need."[22]

Then, I'm ready to receive the fullness of His Light and Life.[23] I visualize the Light shining down upon me. If there is a place in my body that needs a touch, I *see,* or *imagine,* the beam of His most intense Light shining there. At the same time His Light touches my soul, my inward parts. All darkness, all *wrongness,* is exposed and driven out—all fears, anxieties, and disappointments.

Then there's room for His Life, His nature, His *rightness,* to come in. His nature replaces my darkness, my flesh.[24] This is when the Light gives me new thoughts, new revelations. And my joy is full. I am eager to transfer His Light, Life, and Love to others! [25] This is *rightness.*

One day I was lifting some of my people up to the Throne Room in the spirit realm—so the Father's Light, Life, and Love would surround them. I had my eyes closed when, suddenly, I got a picture in my head of a bed. This time, it was a literal picture I saw. It was revolving around in a circle. I saw a headboard and a pillow on it. It kept going around and around. I said, "Lord, what is it?" He said, "A bed!" I was baffled as to what this meant.

Ten minutes later, I picked up my Book of Isaiah, *The Passion Translation,* which had just been published. I had been reading it every day and had gotten to Chapter 28. So, I started at the beginning of that chapter and read through to verse 20 which said, "Your bed is too short to stretch yourself out on, and your covering is too narrow to wrap your-self in" (Isaiah 28:20 TPT).

The footnote for this verse explained, "The bed is a metaphor for their [the people trusting in something or someone other than God] confidence in lies—resting in illusions, not in the truth.[26] Those who trust in lies will not be comfortable. The covering being too narrow means their naked-ness (like hiding behind fig leaves) will still be exposed. They will be too cramped and too cold. Every resting place and shelter will fail them."[27]

The Holy Spirit had given me the *picture* of the bed to confirm this word. He was saying to me, "I see you! Keep lifting your people up to Me! When you do, My Light, Life, and Love really do affect them, espe-cially their thinking.[28] They are realizing that the things they have relied upon are not reliable[29]—and that they are missing out on the abundant Light, Life, and Love that only I can give. Believe it!"

I was so encouraged by the vision and complementary word God gave me that day. And I pray you are encouraged by it, as well, whether for your own benefit or for the benefit of some other people you love! Remember, the Light, Life, and Love of God found in the Secret Place do change things—for you and the people you are bringing before the Lord! It's supernatural.

My Prayer:

Lord, thank You that I can turn and enter into your Presence through the blood of Jesus.[30] Thank You that Your light exposes my darkness and takes away its power to harm me.[31] Your life changes my nature.[32] You give me Your nature through the Essence of Your Name![33] Your love gives me calm and drives out all my fears.[34]

Personal Questions to Consider:[35]

Which of the following is the Holy Spirit currently speaking to you (convicting and convincing you) about? Explain.

1. A need for salvation (through confession of personal sin and faith in Jesus, which produces "right" standing or "innocence" before a holy God).

2. The need to be made righteous (right, pure, holy, taking on His nature so your love for others can be "perfected" and you can be used more effectively to fight the enemy.)

Chapter Three

RECEIVE

There is no fear in love; but perfect love casteth out fear: because fear hath torment. He that feareth is not made perfect in love" (1 John 4:18 KJV).

Summary: Satan has blurred the lines between evil and good. Consequently, we tend to blame everyone but him when it comes to the bad things that have been inflicted upon us. We blame other people. We even blame God. But inviting Jesus to come and be with us in our traumatic memories—that is, RECEIVING Him there—helps us understand that God is always good.

Satan and his minions are the impetus behind all the *bad* things—and all the fear and torment that enters our souls, as well. So when we *see* Jesus from the vantage point of a bad memory and then RECEIVE His words to us about it, we develop faith that God is good and that He supplies all we need to redeem the losses incurred.

My grandmother was born just after the turn of the century. She was a prissy, showy kind of person who spoke in a rather affected manner. I recall that she wore only dresses covered in lace, and hose with heels, every day. And when she answered the phone, she would pick up the receiver, compose herself for what seemed like an eternity and finally say, "Helllllloooou?" There was always an emphasis on the second syllable. She called herself "Dearest."

Early in her life, Dearest was trained through a conservatory to become a concert pianist. Likely her ambitions were quashed when she married into money at around age twenty. Unfortunately, my grandfather was an alcoholic, a philanderer—and a physical and verbal abuser. As a young boy, my dad often witnessed his father's abuse. More than once, Dad remembered seeing his mother thrown to the floor, her husband in a state of drunkenness, kicking her as hard as he could.

When Dad was twelve, she divorced him, and he died four years later of rather bizarre complications somehow related to tuberculosis, my mother confided to me. These things were always considered "family secrets" and were never discussed. As I recall, Dearest would often try to change the story line a bit by telling people she was just "a little old widow."

There were lots of issues with Dearest, but the main one seemed to be her need to manipulate and control people or situations. From my limited, child perspective, she mainly enjoyed driving a wedge between my parents by saying derogatory things about my mom—and controlling my dad by playing the victim.

For example, her constant chatter about Mom, behind her back, was like a game to Dearest. She was syrupy sweet to Mom's face, but then she said the worst things about her to my aunts in the kitchen, such as, "If Mary Ann would lose weight, Charles could get a bigger church." It would always be said at a time when everyone could hear, and it would always get back to Mom. When confronted, she would insist that she loved my mom so much and that "Mary Ann is being overly sensitive."

I don't mean to give the impression that I didn't love my grandmother, because I did—though more so because she was my dad's mother, and I was just supposed to love her. As I got older and discovered the truth about the things she had tried so hard to cover up, I understood why she acted the way she did. I was able to see her through more compassionate eyes.

But during my formative years, those things were never explained. I just remember that even though we lived five hours away and saw her two or three times a year at most, she somehow managed to create and spread a fire of tension and animosity between my parents that was not only disheartening but downright frightening.

The Jezebel, Ahab, and Legion Spirits

Through my own journey into memory healing and deliverance, I have learned quite a bit concerning the characteristics of the most dominant Satanic spirits and how they work in the affairs of men. These will be emphasized in later chapters, but I want to introduce them here as a preamble to this section on memory healing.

The biblical character Jezebel, Queen to King Ahab, represents a demon which ministers of deliverance find most disturbing. The reason: Jezebel is a "religious" spirit who runs rampant in the church. It should come as no surprise that people who operate in the spirit of Jezebel often have a veneer of spirituality that covers over an unrepentant heart, where mastery, power, control, manipulation, and superior *religiosity*[1] are present—all used to *divide and conquer*.

Jezebel is also a *sexual* spirit. So, improper sexual inuendoes and advancements are often used by this spirit to take down leaders and divide churches. In the Bible, Jezebel bowed to the demon idol, Baal, and had many of the true prophets of God murdered because of their allegiance to the true God, Yahweh. Therefore, the most extreme manifestations of Jezebel are cases where Satanic "witches" infiltrate the churches of Jesus Christ to do damage.

Jesus warns the church of Thyatira about the Jezebel spirit in the Apostle John's revelation:

He says, "But I have this against you: that you tolerate the woman Jezebel, who calls herself a prophetess [claiming to be inspired], and who is teaching and leading astray my servants and beguiling them into practicing sexual vice and eating food sacrificed to idols. I gave her time to repent, but she has no desire to repent of her immorality [symbolic of idolatry] and refuses to do so" (Revelation 2:20-21).

The manifestation of the Ahab spirit is the opposite of the Jezebel spirit—the epitome of weakness, limitation, and powerlessness. "For there was no one who sold himself to do evil in the sight of the Lord as did Ahab, incited by his wife Jezebel" (I Kings 21:25 AMP). The Ahab spirit is symbolic of moral tolerance and compromise.

In the case of my grandmother, it is apparent to me that she was plagued to a degree by a spirit of Jezebel, with a secondary Leviathan spirit at work. Leviathan, as you may recall from an earlier chapter, is also a dominant spirit who is very prideful and works to twist the truth.[2] Nelson Schuman confirms that Leviathan most often works in collaboration with the Jezebel spirit. He also confirms that a dominant Jezebel spirit will often be in a marriage relationship or other strong relationship with a dominant Ahab spirit.[3]

In the case of my dad, he was ironically designated the "man of the house" at an early age. I believe this allowed Jezebel plenty of time to develop an already existent generational[4] Spirit of Ahab—which would rule him for the rest of his life. It was like he could not get past this strong, psychological need to kowtow where Dearest was concerned—to the point that he revered her in a delusional way. "She is the kindest, most considerate Christian I know!" he would argue of her, time and time again.

As you can see, a demon's main purpose is to perpetrate wrong, or negative thoughts and emotions in a person—which in turn control his outlook on life. Ultimately, victims are controlled and torment-ed—the trajectory of their lives detrimentally altered—until demons are stopped, or cast out, through a deliverance process in the courts of heaven.

Demons enter victims in one of several ways—either through the generational bloodline, as in a generational "curse,"[5] or through "core wounds." One way a core wound can form is when an outside party inflicts wrongness on the receiving party, who then develops a negative emotion or reaction to the event, such as unforgiveness, fear, hate, etc. Cases like these are the norm for most people.

I'm sure my dad had core wounds that developed in the abusive family environment in which he lived during his formative years. But I am convinced the "generational curse" of Ahab's weakness was the main culprit where it came to his marriage.

No doubt, this curse and the spirit attached to it had caused much confusion in my dad's thinking. It also worked in tandem with Dearest's Jezebel spirit to create core wounds in my mom.

Mom's core wounds were points of entry for bitterness, unforgiveness and victimization—spirits that often work together and are considered synonymous with the spirit of Legion as described in Matthew, Mark, and Luke.[6]

Whether or not these same spirits had already entered my mom through core wounding in childhood, I'm not positive. I do know that my maternal grandmother was extremely shy and somewhat depressed and reclusive her whole adult life. She died of cancer at age sixty-nine. It stands to reason my mom may have had an existing generational spirit of bitterness or a childhood wound that had already developed due to my grandmother's odd behavior, or both.

WHAT IS A GENERATIONAL CURSE AND HOW IS IT RELATED TO A GENERATIONAL SPIRIT?

A generational curse is an *evil force* that is passed down into the third and fourth generations. Generational spirits are attached to these. The impetus for a curse is idolatry and unrepentance. Repentance for a specific sin committed in a family line breaks the related curses. This will be discussed further in later chapters. "You shall have no other gods before or besides Me. You shall not make yourself any graven image [to worship it] or any likeness of anything that is in the heavens above, or that is in the earth beneath, or that is in the water under the earth; You shall not bow down yourself to them or serve them; for I the Lord your God am a jealous God, visiting the iniquity of the fathers upon the children to the third and fourth generation of those who hate Me" (Exodus 20:3–5 AMP).

Hope Deferred Makes the Heart Sick

I'm sorry to say my mother would be plagued with spirits of bitterness, unforgiveness, and the like for the rest of her life. Further, I sincerely believe that a dismal outlook caused her body to manifest disease at age sixty-seven in the form of a major stroke—at which time she lost the use of her left side, walked with a quad cane, and allowed herself to become a virtual recluse until her death at age seventy-eight.

As the Word of God reminds us, "Hope deferred makes the heart sick, but when the desire is fulfilled, it is a tree of life" (Proverbs 13:12 AMP).

Dr. Henry Wright's book, *A More Excellent Way,* explains the connection between the negative emotions we carry and the many diseases of the body and mind.[7] But as we learn to exchange our *wrong*, negative emotions for healthy, *right* ones, we tap into The Tree of Life!

If only I had really understood about these scientific and psychological connections and the supernatural healings that can occur through memory healing and deliverance. I would have been prepared and equipped to help my mother before—and certainly after—this time in her life when she needed it most.

The reality is that I had been given many opportunities to receive the *right* mindset. But I allowed my thinking to remain prejudiced, distorted, and *wrong*, for far too long. I consider this delay in understanding the deep workings of the Holy Spirit to be one of the greatest losses in my life. As a result, I lost the opportunity to be involved in what could have been my mom's healing *on earth*.

In other words, early on, I could have developed a *vision* of her healthy mind and emotional makeup, a strong body, and a strong spirit, riding out the later years of her life with purpose and satisfaction. I also lost the opportunity to develop vision for what could have been a strong, healthy first marriage and family life. As we will discuss later, keeping the vision that God gives us "front and center" brings the power of the Holy Spirit into the equation and gives us the ability to speak to those things that "are not" as though they already "were." This was the case with Abraham:

> That's what the Scripture means when it says: "I have made you the father of many nations." He is our example and father, for in God's presence he believed that God can raise the dead and call into being things that don't even exist yet. Against all odds, when it looked hopeless, Abraham believed the promise and expected God to fulfill it. He took God at his word, and as a result he became the father of many nations. God's declaration over him

came to pass: "Your descendants will be so many that they will be impossible to count!" (Romans 4:17–18 TPT).

The Spirits of Fear and Religion Widespread

The spirit that I battled at an early age was a subtle form of "fear." There are many forms of this spirit, I have found. And many people suffer from it.

I would describe my fear in life as "I have made a mistake, and now I must suffer the consequences." This is the same fear I can now trace through Dearest and my dad, a generational fear manifested in me. As I recall, this fear first surfaced from a sense I felt early on that my parents only tolerated one another.

As I previously explained, my parents were not very affectionate toward one another; and in my adolescence, I feared that they would get a divorce. As I got older and realized that divorce, for them, was not an option, the fear took the "I must learn to suffer the consequences" form.

Now, as I look at the spirit of fear through my mature spiritual eyes, I am convinced that this demon rises up when there is an ongoing "drought" or scarcity of God's unconditional love. Don't get me wrong. God's love is real and available. But when people are not deliberate about *receiving* it, fear comes in and *torments* the mind. As the Scriptures say, "There is no fear in love; but perfect love casteth out fear: because fear hath torment. He that feareth is not made perfect in love" (1 John 4:18 KJV).

Another spirit that took root in me at an early age was *false humility,* which I think stemmed from a generational *spirit of religion.* For me, this spirit manifested when I developed the habit of *keeping secrets* to protect our family reputation.

I remember thinking that my parent's issues were a secret that no one else could know—especially people in the church. If someone found out the truth, Dad could get thrown out of the church, and we would have nowhere to go. So, even at a young age, I tried hard to put on a veneer of goodness.

As a result, I was an overachiever in school, and my reputation all through grade school, high school, and college, and beyond was probably something like a "goody two shoes."

Unfortunately, my fear of failure, with the suffering that was attached to it, along with the need to always look *right*—even when not—carried over into my first marriage. I, too, had an Ahab type spirit, constantly giving in and covering up, enabling. Everything was good. Everything was fine. I tried so hard!

But the harder I tried, the more rejected I felt. My fear of facing a loveless marriage for the rest of my life—reliving my parent's unhappiness—was becoming my reality. I remember vividly the dread of "hope deferred." That's when I knew I had to "beat the system" I was born into and get out.

With that said, I do have regrets. I realize now I could have "beaten the system" another way. Part of the reason I am writing this book is because there are a lot of people out there—even Christians—who have lost all hope that relationships can be restored. I realize this is a tricky problem for those people who are being battered or abused physically. Do I stay, or do I go? Get someone to counsel you if this is your situation. You cannot live under the same roof with a person who is physically abusing you. No amount of "counseling" will fix that kind of problem in the short term.

With that said, a marriage relationship can heal if the person who is doing the abusing is willing to receive inner healing and deliverance at the deepest, deepest levels. Ideally, both parties should receive it.

The problem is, most people, even church people, even Pentecostal people, have no idea what I'm talking about when I speak of these mechanisms. One of the greatest hindrances to healing in the church is that people plagued by religious spirits do not think they are the problem!

As you can imagine, healing and deliverance at this level, especially in the church, is not easy; and it is certainly not a "quick fix." True healing that lasts involves a process of peeling back the many layers and allowing Jesus to heal the deep, deep hurts in a person. All the core wounds must be healed. *Then* all the demons attached to them must go!

Last, there must be a constant infilling of God's truth to fill in all the now-empty places. This comes from the Word of God, both written and spoken. From start to finish, this entire process is not something the church typically teaches.

WHAT IS A SPIRIT OF RELIGION?

A person's need to impress others concerning their *superior spirituality* is born out of a spirit of religion. This spirit drives him to perform repetitive dead works and traditions that will make him look good and feel important among his peers. This is but a *form of godliness, a false veneer,* that expresses no real joy and does not know the power of the Holy Spirit.[1] Religious spirits nailed Jesus to the cross!

The mindset of this spirit is born out of The Tree of the Knowledge of Good and Evil, as all fallen mindsets are. The New Testament word for evil is *poneros*, which means "toilsome, bad, pain-ridden, emphasizing the inevitable agonies that always go with evil."

The Mirror Translation notes that "The Tree of the Knowledge of Good and Evil represents mankind's lost sense of identity and righteousness, where the global pursuit of mankind would now be their constant effort to achieve righteousness by means of their own works. This inevitably leads to disappointment where shame replaces innocence, and union and fellowship are lost."[2]

The opposite of a religious spirit is the spirit of freedom that comes from intimacy with God. This is a natural outpouring of life born from union with the Holy Spirit.

"But the fruit produced by the Holy Spirit within you is divine love in all its varied expressions: joy that overflows, peace that subdues, patience that endures, kindness in action, a life full of virtue, faith that prevails, gentleness of heart, and strength of spirit. Never set the law above these qualities, for they are meant to be limitless" (Galatians 5:22-23 TPT).

Memory Healing in the Secret Place is the Foundation Needed for Court

In later chapters I will introduce dissolving of curses and the process for effective deliverance from demons. For now, I want to introduce the foundation for the healing method I use in my ministry—memory healing.

This is the message I want to give to the world: It is possible for relationships to change radically when traumatic memory "blocks" are removed using these methods. The block is removed when the negative emotion associated with the memory is dissolved. In other words, the emotion the person is "holding" in the memory is given to Jesus. Many of the people with whom I am currently working are getting blocks removed and seeing breakthrough results.

Such is the case with my married friends Lisa and Ricardo. Both Lisa and Ricardo are strong Christians. But both carried emotional blocks of disappointment and rejection due to severe abandonment in early childhood. Lisa was pushing for separation when my pastor recommended that she come and see me for inner healing and deliverance.

In our session, Lisa had a supernatural encounter with Jesus in several memories. One of her main takeaways was the fact that He spoke to her concerning a parallel between an adult life experience and something that happened to her at age two. She had never seen this before, and this one simple thing made a big difference in her emotional outlook. But she still wasn't ready to reconcile. Her husband needed the same healing.

A few weeks later, through Lisa's urging, Ricardo came. My pastor sat in on his session. Three and a half hours later, this tall, stocky man of color bawled like a baby when Jesus showed him things about his mother he had never realized before. That week Ricardo called his mom. Though they had been estranged for a long while, their relationship turned around in that conversation and is now healed. And Lisa and Ricardo have also reconciled!

"For with God nothing is ever impossible and no word from God shall be without power or impossible of fulfillment" (Luke 1:37 AMP).

Inspired by a Story of Healing

The first real experience I ever had with memory healing happened quite by accident. My friend Bess told me she had a spiritual block she could not figure out. It was restricting her intimacy with God and needed to be removed.

I had heard Bess's story several times. Her father was a dictatorial attorney. Nothing she did was ever good enough. She had been sexually abused by a neighbor, but her father never intervened to defend her. One day after church, she reiterated about the block. I said, "Let's pray now about this. I believe God will show you what is blocking intimacy with Him."

As I started to pray, the only memory healing story I had ever heard flashed into my mind. It was the story of a person who had been ridiculed at school because he was poor and didn't have "cool" clothes, only outdated hand-me-downs. A prayer minister had encouraged this individual to go back to the memory in junior high when he had on the plaid "high-waters" and "ask Jesus to come."

"Do you see Him?" the minister asked—at which point the guy broke down and cried uncontrollably. "Yes, I see Him!"

"What is He doing?"

"Well, He's just standing there. But He's got on the same pants as me!"

So, I decided to try a memory healing with my friend Bess. Mind you, I had never tried this before.

"Bess, you know how you have told me that your father shunned you during your childhood?" I asked. "Let's just go back to one of those memories and see what happens."

She agreed. We went into God's presence; and she recalled a situation, a very basic one. She was about five years old. Her father was home from work, sitting in the recliner, reading the paper, and watching the news. She was trying to tell him something, but he pushed her away and said he was busy. He didn't even turn his head to look at her.

That was it. Little five-year-old Bess, who was "holding" fear and anxiety at the time, was devastated.

At the height of the emotion, I prompted Bess to invite Jesus into this memory. She got very quiet. Within a few seconds, her lip starting quivering. Then she broke down and didn't recover for at least ten minutes.

The next thing I got out of her was, "I thought I had forgiven him! But this is the first time I have ever seen him through Jesus's eyes!"

Receive His Fiery Heart of Unconditional Love

We can't go wrong when we allow God to come and speak with us in our memories about the things that matter most to Him. What matters most to him? Intimacy. And along with that, the removal of anything that blocks our intimacy with Him. These things matter because His heart for us is like a fiery flame of passion. He wants to *engage* with us!

Perhaps God's fiery heart is best described in the story of Moses—to whom God first appeared in a "burning" bush and to whom He gave the first "valentine."

In this case, God's "burning" heart sought Moses because He was seeking relationship with the entire world. But His initial plan of action was to make contact with one family—so He could make known through them what He wanted His relationship with all mankind to be like. He would do this through Moses's people, the Jews.

So God arranged a private meeting with Moses on Mount Sinai to discuss the things that mattered to Him most. For more than a month, they met "face to face, as a man speaks to his friend" (Exodus 33:11 AMP).

Now the Hebrew word for "speak," *dabar*, suggests the conversation was not casual, but intimate—the sharing of hearts between two people, such as a husband and wife. Also, the Hebrew word for "friend," *ra'ah*, connotes a "consuming passion." So when Moses and God were speaking to one another, they were doing so as beloveds—sharing passion one for the other.[8]

It was after God finished His conversation with Moses that He presented to him and to mankind the first "valentine"—a list, written with His own finger on two tablets of stone. It described His heart for people—defining what intimacy in His relationship with mankind would look like. In a nutshell, the valentine message was, "Be Mine!"

"And He gave to Moses, when He had ceased communing with him on Mount Sinai, the two tables of the Testimony, tables of stone, written with the finger of God" (Exodus 31:18 AMP).

The Valentine God Gave to Us

Let's analyze this valentine message further. According to Hebrew scholar Chaim Bentorah, the phrase "when He had ceased communing with him" has lost its true meaning in the translation. The entire phrase is one Hebrew word, *kekalotho*, taken from the root word *kalah*, a homonym that can mean both "complete" and "bride."

Because Jewish literature states that man is not *kalah*, complete or "finished," until he gets married, or "takes a bride," the phrase "when He had ceased communing with him" should be translated as both "complete" and "bride."

What does all this mean? God spoke to Moses intimately, as His bride. When He was "finished," or "had ceased" speaking with him, He gave him two tablets, the Ten Commandments, as a gift to His bride. God was, in essence, revealing the deepest desires of His heart to Moses—and by extension to His people.[9]

This commentary emphasizes the fact that God's heart is to have a relationship with us based on principles promoting intimacy and protection.

What did the valentine say? Perhaps this is the essence of it:

"I love you more than anyone one else possibly could! My greatest desire is for our relationship to be always full, never lacking. Hear me, My love. I don't want you to lack any good thing or miss out on any blessing! But there are certain things that you must hold sacred for this to be reality.

"You cannot let any 'thing' or person become more important to you than Me. You cannot use My name in a derogatory manner. Also, please have one day every week reserved just for Me. And don't commit adultery against Me or lie to Me or steal from Me. Honor Me and our relationship! Last, honor all the other people I made in these same ways. But go out of your way to honor your family members, especially your parents. Also, make a special effort to help and honor those who believe in Me. When you do all these things, everyone will know that you are mine![10]

"Don't forget, I am the Greatest Lover of your Soul! And I will always love you, regardless. However, if these things are disregarded on your part, it will hurt My heart. Ultimately, it will hurt your heart, too. So, be aligned and in accordance with the Divine Principles I have set in place, by holding our relationship sacred! Then I will see you and bless you and honor you and protect you. This is My Promise."

God's heart grieves when we lose our intimacy with Him. Has

something in your past blocked intimacy with this God of fiery love, Who wants nothing more than to honor and protect you and have relationship with you?

Don't Be Afraid to Receive Him There

Jodie wanted to heal her memories of mother and father abuse but was hesitant to let Jesus come into the worst memories. We had several sessions, where she healed other memories. One occurred after her junior-high-school graduation.

All the parents were gathering around the graduates for hugs and pictures. Jodie kept looking around for her parents, who had been in attendance, but for some reason could not be located. She waited and looked, but there was no sign of them. Did they leave without telling her, figuring she could walk home alone?

Jodie departed for home, holding "disappointment," "embarrassment," and feelings of "less than." She was wearing her new pink dress; it would have been perfect for pictures. Her head was hanging low. But Jesus was there with her, holding her hand. His reminder to her was: "I will never leave you or disappoint you."

He walked with Jodie all the way to the front porch. She stopped. Would she let Jesus enter the house? No, there was too much going on in there. She would be embarrassed to let His pure eyes see.

I knew Jodie was still holding a lot of anger about the things that her father had done to her, though she repeatedly stated that she had forgiven him long before. I kept encouraging her to go to a father memory. She did not want to relive it.

"But what if you go to heaven and your dad is there?" I wondered. "What will you do? What will you say to him?" I probed.

"How could that be?" she argued. "God would not forgive him for these things."

Jodie knew the truth about repentance, but where it came to her father, she had never allowed herself to believe God would forgive that much. Or that her father would have repented. But memory healing forces these kinds of things to the surface. Would she take a chance on another encounter with Jesus? It would require her to get as real and up close and personal as anyone could with the One whose mission is to get those blocks of unforgiveness removed.

A few weeks later, Jodie was finally ready to let Jesus to come in and see all the stuff she had been hiding. In the memory, she saw the love Jesus had for her father, despite all the things he was doing. And she was able to understand how her father's own wounds had affected him in life.

As a sidebar, Jodie was able to see both her parents looking directly into Jesus's eyes and receiving His forgiveness. They held one another and walked away with Jesus. Jodie's need to correct and be perfect in everything, along with her feelings of inadequacy and insecurity, have been healed as a result. Her healing has lasted more than three years.

With God there are so many possibilities!

"Vengeance is Mine," Sayeth the Lord![11]

Jesus does not come into our memories to punish the people who are hurting us. According to the Bible, their final judgment won't come until the last days.[12] Nor does Jesus come into our memories to prevent wrongdoing, because He adheres strictly to the free-will principle God placed over us in the beginning.

But when we invite Jesus to come and be with us in our dark places, He can show us what He sees. And we can understand how He feels. And He can help us forgive.

And when we forgive the perpetrators, Jesus gives us the power of the Holy Spirit, diffusing the negativity that has come forth from that memory. Yes, the negative power that has followed you and affected you all this time, no matter how early in life it occurred, is suddenly *dissolved* by Him. It's almost as though it never happened.

> Jesus said, "I have told you these things, so that in Me you may have [perfect] peace and confidence. In the world you have tribulation and trials and distress and frustration; but be of good cheer [take courage; be confident, certain, undaunted]! For I have overcome the world. [I have deprived it of power to harm you and have conquered it for you]" (John 16:33 AMP).

When my friend Connie gave Jesus all her worst stuff, He diffused the power that had come to her from the worst thing that ever happened. At age four, Connie had suffered physical and possible sexual abuse from her father. As an adult, she had no memory of the sexual abuse but "sensed" that it had occurred.[13] She does remember much of the abuse he inflicted upon her mother, sister, and brother.

One day a few years ago, Connie decided to pursue further healing of her worst memories. When she went into God's presence and recalled a particular memory, this is what she saw and experienced supernaturally: Connie's father and mother were arguing in the car. It didn't take long for her father to become enraged at her mother, who was yelling back at him from the front passenger seat. The tension between them was escalating fast, the car swerving from one side of the road to the other. Terrified of what would happen next, Connie and her sister and brother huddled in the back seat. "Come Jesus!" Connie cried out.

When she got the nerve to look, Connie saw Jesus sitting in between her parents on the console of the car. He was turning His head from side to side, looking back and forth between them, tears streaming down His face. Suddenly, her father veered off the road and drove at a high speed into a field, where the car came to a crashing stop. He was yelling, "Give me that screwdriver out of the glove compartment. I'm gonna use it to kill every last one of you!"

Everyone was crying and screaming. But Jesus was there. Now, He was in the back seat holding Connie and her sister and brother very close. Tears of agony continued to spill down His face. "I died for this!" He shouted. No one heard but Connie—the irate man shoving his wife against the car door during all the terrified chaos, still clambering to open the glove box to find his weapon.

Then, just as he was about to thrust the door open, the unthinkable occurred. From under her seat, Connie's mom wielded a handgun a friend had recently given to her. Desperate to save herself and her children, she raised the shaking gun and pulled the trigger, shooting her husband in the chest.

The result for Connie was a life plagued by terror, sadness, fearing for her life, running—and eventually, cancer.

Find Healing in His Wounds

He wants it all. The worst stuff you are holding. Your fear, anxiety, anger, sadness. Your loss of childhood innocence. Your cancer. Your suicidal thoughts. He died for all of it. Hand it to Him when He comes.

Then forgive. Because when you forgive yourself and others, there is power to change things.

Connie had been on a healing journey for about ten years when this memory encounter with Jesus occurred. But when she finally completely forgave her father, many things began changing very quickly. Today, she is cancer-free and no longer plagued by the many negative emotions that had previously tormented her.[14]

Last, be forgiven. Be forgiven for any part you may have played. Be forgiven for your unwillingness to hand over these things until now. Then look. Look into His wounds. You will see all your soul wounds, your sins, your losses, there. From the moment Jesus said upon the cross, "It is finished,"[15] your wounds and mine were there, in His wounds.

> For he was the one who carried our sicknesses and endured the torment of our sufferings. We viewed him as one who was being punished for something he himself had done, as one who was struck down by God and brought low. But it was because of our rebellious deeds that he was pierced and because of our sins that he was crushed. He endured the punishment that made us completely whole, and in his wounding we found our healing. Like wayward sheep we have all wandered astray. Each of us has turned from God's paths and chosen our own way; even so, Yahweh laid the guilt of our every sin upon him (Isaiah 53:4-6 TPT).

The passage says, "in" his wounding we found our healing. "Wounding" is the Hebrew word *chaburah,* which is taken from the root word *chabar. Chabar* means "to join together, to unite, to have fellowship, to become a couple." *The Passion Translation* notes suggest a nuanced meaning: "In the fellowship of being one with him is our healing."[16]

Redeem Your Losses

> He has rescued us completely from the tyrannical
> rule of darkness and has translated us into the kingdom
> realm of his beloved Son. For in the Son all our sins are
> canceled and we have the release of redemption through
> his very blood (Colossians 1:13, 14 TPT).

You shouldn't be surprised to hear me say that memory healing is really about "setting you straight" so you can be more effective and productive while on earth. This is what Jesus does when He comes into your memory. Going in, it's all about you—getting your hurts healed so the pain will go away. But this can't happen until you "give up" or "hand over" your stuff—your losses and the weakness or *wrongness* attached to each one—so Jesus can redeem them.

To "redeem" something, in this context, is to regain possession of *a lost thing* in exchange for a payment of equal value. Jesus became our Redeemer when He shed his perfect blood. The value of his blood was the price required to win us back from Satan's ownership.[17]

> But now [in spite of past judgments for Israel's sins],
> thus says the Lord, He Who created you, O Jacob, and
> He Who formed you, O Israel: Fear not, for I have
> redeemed you [ransomed you by paying a price instead
> of leaving you captives]; I have called you by your name;
> you are Mine (Isaiah 43:1 AMP).

> For while we were enemies we were reconciled to
> God through the death of His Son, it is much more
> [certain], now that we are reconciled, that we shall be
> saved[18] (daily delivered from sin's dominion) through
> His [resurrection] life (Romans 5:10 AMP).

In Romans, Paul says that even though we were once God's enemies, He saw to it that we could be reconciled back to Him through the death of Jesus. In other words, Jesus's life was *exchanged*[19] for ours. That sacrifice of life, and the bloodshed that came from it, was the payment.

There is yet another mysterious exchange that takes place when a penitent person asks the Savior to forgive his sins for the very first time. This is it: The sinner *gives his life* to Jesus, and Jesus *gives His life* to the sinner, in return! As believers in the Messiah-Savior,[20] we have *exchanged* our life for His! However, we may not have received *revelation* of what this really means quite yet. Sin's dominion has been holding up the process. Sin's dominion is the *wrongness* we are *holding onto*—and the thing for which Satan is constantly *judging* and *accusing* us. *What* are we holding still? Grief, sadness, unforgiveness, anger, guilt?

What we must realize is that we cannot get these things exchanged for Jesus's life of joy and peace because we are still *letting Satan be our judge*! To get the process of exchange completed, a wounded person must trust Jesus to make his wrong things right.

This means *he must allow Jesus to be his Judge* instead of Satan. Also, he must *understand* that Jesus *wants* us to feel His passion and be made whole. He *wants* to redeem *all* our stolen property. He has already paid the redemption fees!

Satan wants us to feel his torment and be fearful!

So let Jesus be your judge in the heavenly courtroom. Don't delay. He will gently reveal how the wrong things are still dominating your life. In that moment, when you acknowledge Him as the only person in the universe who can redeem them, He will quickly exchange whatever you have been holding for *rightness*. This is when the process of redeeming all your mistakes and losses in life begins!

Set into motion all the good things God wants for you now by receiving Jesus into your life and into your memories. Let Him remove the blocks that have kept you separated or distanced, terrorized, fearful, and sad. You will feel an immediate rush of peace—and assurance that far greater things are destined to come.

Then your Redeemer will love you through your current issues, so you can get on with your destiny—the vision He has had for you since the creation of the world. Embrace the vision He is giving you. His *rightness* will give you the ability to fulfill it!

My Prayer:

Lord, thank you for showing me how to restore my heart to *rightness*.[21] Jesus, I affirm now the belief that Your blood shed for me was enough to free me from the power of Satan. And I declare that when I acknowledge this truth in faith, I can give You my *wrong* things, and You will make the "exchange" for me.

So, I apply Your blood to my mind, my will, and my emotions now, supernaturally, through faith. And I give these things to You now: My Fear. My Offense. My Shame. My Anxiety. My Guilt.

I RECEIVE back, right now, in "exchange," the mighty flame of Your passionate LOVE, the DEFENSE of the Holy Spirit, the HONOR You give me as Your child, Your PEACE and a CLEAN CONSCIENCE. Thank You for loving me so much!

Personal Questions to Consider:[22]

Has anything from your past "blocked" your intimacy with the Father?

How do any of these opposites relate to your personal experience? (Darkness vs. Light, Wrongness vs. Rightness, Bondage vs. Deliverance, Condemnation vs. Mercy, the Natural Realm vs. the Spiritual Realm, Fear vs. God's Love)

Have you allowed Satan to judge you instead of just letting the Father of Lights[23] be your Judge? Can you trust Him now to remove the "blocks" that are keeping you from grasping the next step toward *rightness*?

Chapter Four

RELEASE

"A stream of fire came forth from before Him: a thousand thousands ministered to Him and ten thousand times ten thousand rose up and stood before Him: the Judge was seated [the court was in session] and the books were opened" (Daniel 7:10 AMP).

Summary: A covenant is a legal agreement establishing relationship between two parties, spiritual in nature and based on trust and promises.[1] The very first covenant, initiated by Yahweh, the Father God, was considered a permanent bond between Himself and all of creation,[2] especially humankind.[3] It was established within the highest judicial system in the universe, His Kingdom.[4]

As Christian believers, we are bonded to Yahweh through a *second* covenant, which comes to us through Jesus Christ, Yeshua, Son of the Father.[5] Jesus is also our heavenly courtroom Mediator.[6] This covenant of grace is available to all human beings—meaning any who will accept it. And God always keeps his promises.[7]

One such promise is that believers can win over the enemy, Satan, whose self-appointed job on earth is to find *legal* reasons to oppose human beings.[8] His accusations against us can include sins we have committed of our own free will and those we have inherited through generational sin.[9]

But Satan is subject to the Kingdom's judicial system, so we have a *legal* recourse *against him*. We can go to the heavenly court,[10] satisfy his accusations, and then trust the heavenly Judge to render a verdict against Satan, in our favor.[11] Our full participation in this judicial process, RELEASES us from Satan's bondage and sets us free to fulfill our role or destiny within God's Kingdom.

I sensed that something was not going according to plan when Justin suddenly slumped over in the worn leather chair he'd been sitting in for the last two and a half hours. During our session, he used a hand towel to wipe perspiration from his forehead. Now he was using it to cover his entire head, as though he thought he might be able to hide. I could tell something odd was happening, because his head was shaking under the towel, trembling as though about to erupt into an uncontrollable emotion—a definite switch from the numbness he had displayed in the previous memory-healing attempt.

Suddenly, I heard a loud, but high-pitched, hissing voice coming forth: "Justin? You want Justin? Well, you can't have him! He's mine. He needs me!" This was followed by an eerie cackle, which startled me completely! A demon was manifesting right in front of my eyes! He had been hiding under the surface of Justin's personae the entire session, distracting him with all kinds of extraneous thoughts, ranging from pornographic pictures to lists of items he needed to buy for car repairs.

Now, this demon was mocking me. He came out from under the towel. Justin's eyes were closed, his forehead, furrowed and tight. His head was still bobbling about. I was thinking fast, trying to regroup. I had not planned to deal with a demon directly, at this point. And rarely had a demon manifested exactly like this one! I had been involved in this level of healing and deliverance ministry for less than a year, so I still didn't know entirely what to expect.

I had gotten nowhere with the first memory we tried to heal. There were too many distractions and blocks. So, I had gone to this one—Justin's most suspicious early childhood memory—and to no surprise, the one over which the demon was most territorial.

Justin had been concerned about this memory for decades because he knew something awful happened in it, but he could not remember any of the details. He did remember that he was about six years old. It involved a boy down the street, a bag of snacks, and a dark shed off the carport at his house. He also remembered that the boy came by often—and always with the snacks, which they shared in the shed that was lined with green shag carpet.

Other than these details, Justin drew a total blank—until he invited Jesus to come, exchanged his childhood confusion for confidence and supernatural understanding, broke the curse of sexual perversion, forgave the young teenage boy, forgave himself, and then demanded that the demon go, in the name of Jesus.

Justin's story is a common one. He is a good man. He has been a believer in Yeshua since age eight; and he comes from a long line of Christian believers, on his mom and biological dad's sides. However, Justin has suffered from guilt, condemnation, abandonment, shame, and self-hatred most of his life.

He also hates his biological father. Of course, he knows he needs to forgive him but can't seem to get there. It's hard to forgive a man who walked out on a mom with three young boys. Combine that with more recent occurrences. There are just too many reasons why Justin cannot let the unforgiveness go. He thinks about it constantly, replaying stories about his father's deceit over and over in his head. He has tried many times to rid himself of these detriments. He also feels strongly that his efforts are somehow always being sabotaged.

WHAT IS INIQUITY?

Iniquity is considered the most egregious level of sin in the Bible and is generally tied to "unrestrained," "deliberate," and "intentional" forms of idolatry, sexual perversity, bloodshed, and the occult. In Hebrew, "iniquity"[1] can be interpreted to mean "twisted or crooked."[2] Therefore, it is easy to see how iniquitous sin corrupts the human's Divine Nature Ability capacity. Then this corruption or limitation "passes" through generational lines, into the third and fourth generations. It is also easy to imagine how iniquity has shaped the human identity, having caused him to live "without portion or form."[3]

Satan Still Seeks to Sabotage with His Bag of Curses and Afflictions

Satan's modus operandi has always been to find and take out people who threaten his work and existence. One way he does this is with curses. Curses are recurring sin "traits" or "instances" that come from unconfessed, iniquitous sin.

Biblically speaking, anything that is clearly not a blessing is probably a curse of some sort. In other words, *patterns* in one's life—or in one's generational bloodline—that do not promote or reflect honor, blessing, and acknowledgment of God as the only true God are considered a curse form representing disobedience, disconnection, displacement, disenfranchisement, dysfunction, that is, a bankrupt identity.[12] These include:

- Tendency to harm self and others through sexual perversion, addictions, lying, cheating, manipulation, control, power-mongering, vindictive behavior, unforgiveness, jealousy, hatred, and physical abuse
- Tendency to be a "magnet" for bad or harmful occurrences, such as divorce, murder, suicide, abortion, illegitimate birth, premature death, accidents, sicknesses that don't heal, miscarriages, infertility, dysfunctional family relationships, financial ruin, bad reputation, incarceration, abandonment, poverty, debt
- Tendency to live in a constant state of personal turmoil and languishing spirit—including fear, anxiety, no assurance of life, disappointment, hopelessness, sadness, and unanswered prayers
- Tendency toward rebellion with no regard for the sanctity of life, no regard for God's laws or ways, inability to hear God speak, inability to know God—full of doubt, disbelief, pride, selfishness

Maybe you know someone plagued by a pattern of sin, sickness, tragedy or "things constantly going awry." Seemingly, many of these individuals don't deserve to experience such *curses* or afflictions. But the Bible teaches that Satan has a legitimate reason for placing a curse or affliction on them. This legitimacy is based on God's operational principles of the universe.

It's disturbing to think about, but Satan's curses don't "land" unless they are *deserved*—either directly, through volitional sin, or indirectly, through generational sin. Proverbs 26:2 teaches, "An undeserved curse will be powerless to harm you. It may flutter over you like a bird, but it will find no place to land" (TPT). In other words, a deserved curse will land.

When a sin becomes a generational curse, it can extend into the third and fourth generations.

> The Lord is long-suffering and slow to anger, and abundant in mercy and loving-kindness, forgiving iniquity and transgression. But he will by no means clear the guilty, visiting the iniquity of the fathers upon the children, upon the third and fourth generation (Numbers 14:18 AMP).

"He will by no means clear the guilty," the passage reads. Such was the case with Job (sounds like "oh"), the righteous and blessed Old Testament character, whose reputation was impeccable, by most standards.

"There was a man in the land of Uz whose name was Job, and that man was blameless and upright, and one who [reverently] feared God and abstained from and shunned evil [because it was wrong]" (Job 1:1 AMP).

Yet we find that Satan *cursed* Job in almost every way possible, taking his wealth, his family, and his health. As the story continues, we see that Satan also thwarted Job's ability to hear God speak—and to get his prayers answered. I don't know about you, but "poor" Job's story was always disheartening to me—until I understood more than just the bits and pieces. Growing up, I could not imagine how God would allow such horrible things to happen to such a *good* man. It just didn't make sense to me, and as time wore on, and I experienced my own afflictions in life, I would think of Job and say to myself, "Oh well, Job couldn't do anything about his situation, either." That's when I completely gave up trusting that God could or would change things in my life.

Then, finally, after about five years, I began to see things differently. Even though I had known God for a very long time, I realized that His work in the universe was, in fact, based on principles that I had not yet fully understood. Then I decided to do something about my losses. I decided to take responsibility.

The story of Job in the heavenly court helped me understand how to do just that.

The Heavenly Courtroom, the Center of the Universe, and God's Judicial System

Before Satan met up with Job, he had been going *"to and fro on the earth,"* at which point he and all the other angels *"presented themselves"* to the Lord in the heavenly court.[13] This is the center of the universe[14] where Jesus, the Anointed One, has existed with God in His Kingdom since before the beginning of time.[15] God Himself was and still is the Judge in this Kingdom, where He is Good, Just, and Righteous.[16] And He is the Judge of all.[17]

In this courtroom scenario, Satan presented himself to God the Judge because he had found a *just cause* to land a curse on Job.

In his book *Operating in the Courts of Heaven*, Robert Henderson says the word *judge* speaks of a judicial system with judicial activity.[18] The Apostle John reminds us in the book of Revelation that Satan is one of the key players in this judicial system. His chief title is *accuser* of God's children—the one who "keeps bringing before our God charges against them day and night!" (Revelation 12:10 AMP)[19]

Another of Henderson's premises is that Satan, in addition to being *the accuser*, is a *legalist*. He is compelled to enforce his *legal rights* against those on earth who have not taken responsibility for their sins. These are the people who have not experienced heart-felt repentance concerning a sin or sins in question.

As we consider Satan's legal rights and our need for repentance, it is important to remember our study of the word *righteousness* from Chapter Two. In the Bible, *righteousness* is used in two different contexts, to describe two different levels of *righteous* being. The first level is considered "right standing with God." This state of being comes about when a person is first convicted of sin that leads to repentance and salvation. This is called *justification* in many Bible versions.[20] The Greek word is *dikaioo*,[21] meaning "to render righteous, to declare innocent." God declares even the worst of sinners "innocent" when he sincerely repents for the very first time.

> And that through Him everyone who believes [who acknowledges Jesus as his Savior and devotes himself to Him] is absolved (cleared and freed) [dikaioo] from every charge from which he could not be justified and freed by the Law of Moses and given right standing with God" (Acts 13:39 AMP).

The second level of righteousness is the result of conviction of sin that leads to repentance and "uprightness of heart." This second state is one we develop over time as we conform to the image of Jesus through the Holy Spirit's conviction leading to purity of life and correct thinking, feeling, and acting. The Greek word here is *dikaiosyne*.[22]

"How enriched you are when you crave righteousness [dikaiosyne]! For you will be surrounded with fruitfulness" (Matthew 5:6 TPT).

> Do not continue offering or yielding your bodily members [and faculties] to sin as instruments (tools) of wickedness. But offer and yield yourselves to God as though you have been raised from the dead to [perpetual] life, and your bodily members [and faculties] to God, presenting them as implements of righteousness [dikaiosyne]. For sin shall not [any longer] exert dominion over you, since now you are not under Law [as slaves], but under grace [as subjects of God's favor and mercy] (Romans 6:13–14 AMP).

Righteousness in these passages refers to a process of *becoming right*, or righteous, and is often associated with *sanctification*.[23] To be *sanctified* in the Greek is to be "purified internally by the renewal of the soul."[24]

In this chapter, when I speak of the need for repentance, I am speaking to myself and any other believing persons, who have already received initial salvation. We are the people in God's Kingdom who are now being convicted of sin that leads to repentance and *uprightness of heart*.

In the case of a believer, when Satan sees an error in us, even a generational one that has not been addressed or made *right*, he has the legal right to go before God and ask permission to deliver a punishment for the *wrongness*—just as he did with Job and Peter.[25] Again, this has nothing to do with a forgiven, believing person's *position in Christ*, as regards his eternal salvation. He has already been declared "innocent" as far as salvation is concerned. But it does have to do with his *quality of life* and his level of intimacy and relationship with the Father.

"Simon, Simon (Peter), listen! Satan has asked excessively that [all of] you be given up to him [out of the power and keeping of God], that he might sift [all of] you like grain" (Luke 22:31 AMP).

Satan's *asking* here means "to beg for oneself, to ask that a person be given up to one from the power of another."[26] If Satan's request proves to be legitimate, he might be freed to deliver a curse or affliction—at which point the recipient feels the negative effects—fear, anxiety, guilt, and the like. He may also notice evidence of Satan's curse in the form of an adverse circumstance or a repeating pattern—for example, plans are always foiled or relationships are always sabotaged.

The Reputation of Each Courtroom Participant Precedes Him

As the heavenly court convenes in Job Chapter One, the text doesn't tell us everything about the characters. But as Bible readers, we can certainly compare other revealing passages of Scripture to this one. Then we can piece the whole story together and make sense of it. In other words, we are allowed to read between the lines!

Certainly, we can rely on any facts that support the reputations of all the key players—of God the Father, who is always good, loves us, and has our best interests at heart; God the Judge, who is always just and right; Jesus, the Mediator; and Satan, who never gives up trying to mar, corrupt or destroy humans made in God's image. Even Job has a reputation that precedes him.

Let's start with Job. We can't know for sure exactly what blemishes Satan found to hold against him, but likely it had something to do with his religious pride, dead works, and fear of the unknown, as these passages would suggest:

> Job's friend asks, "Is not your [reverent] fear of God
> your confidence and the integrity and uprightness of
> your ways your hope?" (Job 3:6 AMP).

> His sons used to go and feast in the house of each on
> his day (birthday) in turn, and they invited their three
> sisters to eat and drink with them. And when the days
> of their feasting were over, Job sent for them to purify
> and hallow them, and rose up early in the morning and
> offered burnt offerings according to the number of them
> all. For Job said, It may be that my sons have sinned and
> cursed or disowned God in their hearts. Thus did Job at
> all [such] times (Job 1:4–5 AMP).

> For the very thing which I greatly fear comes upon me,
> and that of which I am afraid befalls me (Job 3:25 AMP).

Though "good," we can presume that Job was a man with hidden
weaknesses that had not been resolved. In other words, Job had *a fallen
state of mind*, just like everyone else born of Adam. As the text says, he
feared bad consequences. Likely, he struggled to find inner peace. The
fear in his mind told him there was something *wrong*—and that if he
tried desperately enough, he could "fix it." So, he performed rote sacrifices over and over to rid himself of the fear and to appease the apparent
"wrath of God" against his children's immoral behavior.

With all this, you might say that going into these courtroom pro-
ceedings, Job had *missed the mark*. At a minimum, his *wrongness* caused
him to fall slightly off the course God intended.

The Hebrew word most often associated with this level of sin is
chata'ah,[27] meaning "to miss the mark, not share in the prize" or "an
offense, sometimes habitual." This usage would be associated with more
unintentional sin.

The next character in this courtroom scene is, Satan, a *fallen* arch
angel.[28] He is evil, and therefore opposite to God in character. But he
is not the antithesis of God, meaning he is not *equal* to Him in stature

and strength. He is still subject to the Judge's heavenly courtroom procedures, just like all the rest of us. For example, he must always tell the truth in court. And he must follow court orders. Violation on either count means the Judge will throw him out of court!

On earth, Satan is a liar and a thief, who masquerades as an angel of light.[29] He especially loves to pick on people like Job, whose God-ordained destinies are most threatening. Such a person's slightest move toward full surrender to God's Ways, totally unnerves him. He will lie, cheat, steal, kill, and destroy to keep someone like this out of alignment with God's plans!

God is the Righteous Judge in our heavenly courtroom, the governmental center of the universe. He has final say over what Satan can and cannot do. But He will always allow Satan to act according to his *legal rights*—based on the operational principles of the universe already set in place. He is also Omniscient,[30] knowing everything about His subjects.

At the same time, God is a loving Father. To fully understand the heavenly court and why it is pertinent to this story of Job and to our lives here on earth today, we must also understand this dual reality. As our loving Father, God is always driving us toward repentance. He wants us to view our freedom *to choose* repentance as one of His greatest gifts, for it is the act of repentance and God's ensuing forgiveness that moves us to a place of truth.[31]

And let's not forget Jesus. He is present in the story, because we know from other scripture that He has existed in the heavenly realm with God the Father since the beginning.[32] We also know that He is an active Participant and Messenger in many passages throughout the Old Testament, where He is most often depicted as The Angel of the Lord.

Then [the guiding angel] showed me Joshua the high priest standing before the Angel of the Lord, and Satan standing at Joshua's right hand to be his adversary and to accuse him" (Zechariah 3:1 AMP).

Satan Steals Our Blessings, God Drives Us to Repentance, Curses Dissolve

We are the onlookers concerning this story of Job, and we need to understand what God is trying to tell us concerning its principal theme: *repentance dissolves curses*. As discussed in Chapter Two, the act of turning and embracing God's mind, ways, and purposes, effectively allows us to escape Satan's snare. God's blessings are restored. We are no longer used for Satan's purposes. We *discover* (that is, "become") our true selves![33]

I have a hunch that many Christians, same as me, have sidestepped this revelation. So, lean into a fresh understanding! Now is the time for individual believers to know and apply this truth. Our lives, our relationships, and the second coming of Jesus all depend on it!

To reiterate, God's assessment as Judge is always based on the courtroom findings, which are based on the judicial principles He set in place before the foundation of the world. So, when Satan got God's permission to "wreak havoc" in Job's world, be assured that Satan had good enough reasons, or God would not have "withdrawn" His blessing.[34]

Likely, Satan had already identified Job's destiny-potential long before his initial meeting with God. And he had accessed Job's unrepentant fear, guilt, and spiritual pride based on dead works. Perhaps he had some generational sin, as well. We can't know for sure. But we can assume Job had unrepentant sin of some sort, and Satan knew it. He had a *legal* reason to land a curse on him.

In Job, Chapter One, when Satan appears in court, God knows Satan has a *legal* reason to be there. He knows of the *hidden* weaknesses and sins of which Job has not been relieved.[35] And long before anything is said, God knows Satan is looking to stir something up with Job.

At some point in the conversation, I think Satan said to God something like this: "Job is not for real. He has an air of pride and moral superiority. He thinks his good works are more than sufficient to win your favor. Yet he has an underlying fear issue, increasingly. The fear grips him so much that he does not trust you as a loving father. This fear is driving him to perform empty sacrifices with no inward reality. The truth is his heart is divided—between You, his kids, his reputation, his material blessings, etc. It's not a completely *upright heart*. In fact, it's far from You![36] Give me my legal right to take away all the blessings You have so graciously bestowed upon him, and he will curse Your face."[37]

As Judge and Father, God's decision-making in Satan's case against Job is based on two things. From a legal perspective, God will not override Job's freewill. To do so would undermine the principle of choice He has already established in the universe. In other words, He will not *make* Job change his ways or trust Him. Nor will He say "no" to Satan's request, because he has a valid legal claim.

God Issues a "Divine Restraining Order" On Satan's Activity[38]

As Job's Father, God's desire is to help him find an inner abundance of life and restoration that he had not yet experienced. And God knows exactly *what* blocks Job from this! He also knows that giving Satan *permission* to go about his business, will change Job's status quo for the worse. But God will work with Job—to help him *see* and *hear* the truth about things. Then his inner man will change for good, and the blessings of fully functioning relationships with God, himself, and others will flow.

Based on all the facts here and elsewhere in the Bible, I suppose God responded to Satan something along these lines: "You speak correctly. I release you to do the measure of justice you are allowed, based on My Kingdom Laws."

God does, however, issue a Divine Restraining Order on Satan, prohibiting him from taking Job's life. "Behold, he is in your hand; only spare his life" (Job 2:6 AMP). This dictate will allow Job more time, which he needs to get to a place of sincere repentance. Does God, in His foreknowledge, know that Job will eventually confess and repent—and that Satan will be forced out of his way once and for all? I believe He does!

As Job's story continues, true repentance is slow coming. "I am clean, without transgression; I am innocent, neither is there iniquity in me," he insists (Job 33:9 AMP). The more Satan squeezes, the more underlying, curse-related "stuff" comes out of him—word curses, lies, bitterness, hopelessness, stubbornness, and pride.[39] Job even accuses God of not giving him a fair trial! He laments:

> For [God is not a mere man, as I am, that I should
> answer Him, that we should come together in court.
> There is no umpire between us, who might lay his hand

upon us both, [would that there were!] That He might take His rod away from [threatening] me, and that the fear of Him might not terrify me] (Job 9:32–35 AMP).

Job's diatribe is in response to the counsel of three friends who come and go. They sit by his side, doing the best they can to provide comfort, which comes mainly in the form of unwanted advice.

Job refutes his friends throughout, clearly irritated by what he perceives to be meaningless chatter. Nothing they say empowers or inspires him. He accuses them of making things worse. Also, he falsely perceives that God is responsible for his misery. He has no clue that Satan is a player in this performance and the cause of all his turmoil. Job has no understanding of what is really going on! He is going deeper and deeper into a wrong pattern of thinking based on lies coming from the occultic forces of evil at work in the world around him.

And that is why, at this point in the story, Job's sin can be described as a stronghold or transgression—*pasha* in the Hebrew. It means "revolt or rebellion," "to break away from authority" and "to expand into activities that lead to much wickedness and evil." This is obviously a level of *fallen thinking* that is much more vigorous and intentional than the previous level of *chata'ah*, to miss the mark.

And it was for this reason that Job's friends "cease(d) to answer him, because he was [rigidly] righteous (upright and in right standing with God) in his own eyes" (Job 32:1 AMP).

A Fresh Revelatory Vision Helps Job See the Truth

Enter an "unknown" friend—one who has been listening in on Job's lengthy discourses with his friends from a distance, though he has been deliberately silent. He is a younger man, but one who, unlike the others, acknowledges a dependence on "the breath of the Almighty" which "gives men understanding." He says, "[It is] the Spirit of God that made me [which has stirred me up], and the breath of the Almighty that gives me life [which inspires me]" (Job 33:4 AMP). Undoubtedly, for this man, the Holy Spirit is not an entity to be discussed, but a force to be relied upon!

Ironically, what Job's new friend tells him is not altogether different from what the other friends have said. But these new words come forth like a fountain of fresh revelatory vision[40]—with a prophetic foreshadowing of Jesus's blood shed for the remission of Job's sin.

"Then, if God's voice can be heard, [God] is gracious to him and says, 'Deliver him from going down into the pit [of destruction]; I have found a ransom[41] (a price of redemption, an atonement)!'" (Job 33:24 AMP).

The young man continues speaking under the unction of the Holy Spirit, uninterrupted. Is Job finally *hearing* a new message? A message of hope—about a Savior, Redeemer, and Deliverer?

"For with God nothing is ever impossible and no word from God shall be without power or impossible of fulfillment" (Luke 1:37 AMP).

Suddenly—out of a *whirlwind*—Job hears God's voice for the very first time.

God asks, "Who is this that darkens counsel [questioning my authority and wisdom] By words without knowledge?" (Job 38:2 AMP).[42]

God speaks to Job as his Heavenly Judge: First, He chastises him for pridefully condemning His *judgments* and making his own self out to be righteous and justified.[43] Then He reminds Job that He is the Maker and the Judge of all; and He is to be acknowledged as such.[44] Further, God reveals that He is the Supreme Ruler of the Government of the World and that He looks on everyone who is proud and brings them low. He also treads down the wicked where they stand.[45]

Job finally utters a humble response,

"Behold, I am of little importance and contemptible; what can I reply to You? I lay my hand on my mouth" (Job 40:4 AMP).

Continuing to listen, Job demotes and lowers himself, under the mighty hand of God, his Just and Righteous Judge.[46] Then by an act of his will—he confesses: "I had heard of You [only] by the hearing of the ear, but now my [spiritual] eyes see You. Therefore, I loathe [my words] and abhor myself and repent in dust and ashes" (Job 42:1-6 AMP).

Perhaps Job's repentance experience was like that of Saul of Tarsus, who after years of persecuting those who believed in Jesus's resurrection from the dead, met Jesus face to face on the road to Damascus:

> Jesus appeared to him and said, "I am Jesus, the
> one you are persecuting. Get up and stand to your feet,
> for I have appeared to you to reveal your destiny and to
> commission you as my assistant. You will be a witness
> to what you have seen and to the things I will reveal
> whenever I appear to you. I will rescue you from the
> persecution of your own people and from the hostility of
> the other nations that I will send you to. And you will
> open their eyes to their true condition, so that they may
> turn from darkness to the Light and from the power of
> Satan to the power of God. By placing their faith in me
> they will receive the total forgiveness of sins and be made
> holy, taking hold of the inheritance that I give to my
> children!" (Acts 26:18 TPT).

Likewise, Job has now "turned," recognizing the face or *presence* of his Maker. But did he see the face of Jesus, also? Remember, in Chapter Nine Job had longed for a courtroom Mediator, who could help him through the process!

> For [God is not a mere man, as I am, that I should
> answer Him, that we should come together in court.
> There is no umpire between us, who might lay his
> hand upon us both, [would that there were!] That He
> might take His rod away from [threatening] me, and
> that the fear of Him might not terrify me] (Job 9:32-
> 35 AMP).

Like Saul, Job has finally turned into the face of God to see his true condition—pride and fear of judgment. Now he is ready to change his life and embrace God's good and perfect will.

Now Job's Enemy, Satan, has no legal right against Job. His conscience is clear of dead works, guilt, fear, and pride.[47] God's blessings flow to him, as well!

What took so long for Job to repent and reverse Satan's curses? Why couldn't Job *hear* God speak? What was blocking him from the fullness of God's presence and the blessings that ensued? The final part of God's discourse to Job in Chapter 41 reveals the answer: the controlling power and pride of Satan, also known as Leviathan in this passage, "the fierce and fearless monarch over all the sons[48] of pride."[49]

To explain the Evil One in terms Job can understand, God uses an analogy of a sea creature, Leviathan, who has kept himself *hidden* from Job as though in the depths of the sea. But Job has seen and felt Leviathan's ill effects: "He makes the deep boil like a pot; he makes the sea like a [foaming] pot of ointment" (Job 41:31 AMP).

Leviathan is illusive, appearing suddenly. Then he swiftly snares his unsuspecting prey, dismembering it piece by piece with twisting and turning, downward. Further, no one can get to him. He's too tight to penetrate. His heart is too hard to crack. No one battles him. Only God, his Creator, can master him.[50]

Job contemplates what God has revealed to him: In the earth, there is a created being turned evil, a player who is full of pride, manipulation, control, torment, and lies. He is also the source of human suffering and related curses. Has he been the source of Job's suffering? Has Job been played and manipulated by this creature—to carry out his purposes?

At the end of the story, Job finally realizes that he must allow the God of the Universe, the Creator of all things, to *master* Satan's power, on his behalf, so he can be *released* from bondage:

> For [the Father] has rescued us and has drawn us to Himself from the dominion of darkness, and has trans-ferred us to the kingdom of His beloved Son, in whom we have redemption [because of His sacrifice, resulting in] the forgiveness of our sins [and the cancellation of sins' penalty] (Colossians 1:13–14 AMP).

The Initial Steps to Dissolving Satan's Curses Against Us

It only took me a short time of helping people get healed and deliv-ered from demonic spirits and the curses they bring before I understood completely the following profound realities:

- Satan's contract with God in the court of heavenly law allows him the legal right to curse—per God's permission and within His *restraining orders.*
- Curses flow down into the third and fourth generations until Satan's legal rights have been dissolved through a person's sincere confession and repentance. I have found, based on my own experience and the testimonies of others, that a person cannot break a generational curse until he repents on behalf of someone else.
- Satan is a liar and a deceiver. He wants you to think there is nothing you can do to get rid of your shame, your guilt, your fear—and your negative, controlling memories. He doesn't want you to understand his legal rights against you, that is, that he is the source of your ills. He doesn't want you to know how the heavenly courts operate. He certainly doesn't want you to know that God has mastery over him!

What are the initial steps one must take to get Satan's rights *dissolved*—to get him off your back and out of your way, so you can get your mindset straight, and get on with fulfilling your God-given destiny? I believe these are key initial steps:

- ASK God to tell you the truth. Do not lean on your own understanding.[51] If you are plagued by something that you can't quite put your finger on, that is, something is just not *right*—chances are Satan has a legal right against you for some reason. And it is your legal right as a child of God to know what that reason is!
- ASK God to help you see the truth about the order of the universe and the courts of heaven. Do so with intense desire! He has given us access to the courts, so we can clear the way, remove the blocks, and trust Him to master Satan on our behalf. God told Job: As fierce and unmastered as any created being in God's creation may be, "only God Who made him and can bring near His sword to master him" (Job 40:19 AMP).
- ASK God to help you see the truth about your sin and your

pride. Again, desire it intensely. Remember, pride keeps you from repenting. Repentance is one of God's greatest gifts to us. And it is the only way we can get saved, healed, and delivered. It is the only way we can truly know ourselves!

- In addition, ASK the Holy Spirit to give you a fresh revelation about this: that your hope to get free cannot rest in anything or anyone other than Jesus's blood and righteousness. The Hebrew word for *hope*[52] means "ground of hope, expectation, things hoped for, outcome." But it also means "cord"—the thing to which you are attached, or the thing to which a desired outcome is attached. In the beginning of Job's story, we learned that his hope and respect[53] rested not in God as his personal Savior and Deliverer, but *in Job's own goodness and rightness.*

- BE WILLING to go through the healing and deliverance process. It is an act of humility to do so—but it is helpful on so many levels. I don't know anyone who has done it and then regretted having done so. For starters, it helps you understand the hurts, habits, and hang-ups of the people who have hurt you. This means that the hurt *parts* of you can now truly forgive these people. This is when the healing occurs—and when these parts of you can finally *let go* of the debilitating negative emotions they have been *holding,* and the memories to which these are attached.

The bottom line: *Memory healing and deliverance in the courts of heaven get rid of the divisions within you that have prevented wholeness.* By going through this process, you *see* your sin[54] and move to a place of repentance, which purifies your heart, your mind, even your hands—and leaves you clean, so blessings can flow.

> Come close to God and He will come close to you. [Recognize that you are] sinners, get your soiled hands clean; [realize that you have been disloyal] wavering individuals with divided interests, and purify your hearts [of your spiritual adultery] (James 4:8 AMP).

Applying the Principles of the Heavenly Judicial System *Releases* Us from Curses

The Book of Job, the very first written book of the Bible, describes the central principles of God's universal system—a judicial Kingdom that applies to us as believers, even today. What worked in Job's world to get him aligned with God's purposes and *released* from Satan's curses and legalistic requirements will work for us, as well.

How long did Job's battle with Satan last? My guess is it took decades for Job to finally realize who his real enemy was—and then repent for this glaring error. But once he did, everything quickly changed; and then God was able to fulfill his destiny.

Interestingly, one of Job's annoying friends had prophesied Job's destiny long before repentance even occurred. He said:

> You will make your prayer to Him, and He will hear you, and you will pay your vows. You shall also decide and decree a thing and it shall be established for you; and the light [of God's favor] shall shine upon your ways. When they make you low, you will say, There is a lifting up; and the humble person He lifts up and saves. He will even deliver the one [for whom you intercede] who is not innocent; yes, he will be delivered through the cleanness of your hands (Job 22:21-22, 27-30 AMP).

Just as Job's friend prophesied, he did hear God speak; ad, soon after that, he repented fr trying to be a god unto himself. Repentance, being truly sorry for trying to do life contrary to God's way, is what it took.

Then, true to His promises, God lifted Job up. He saved and delivered him. And true to the prophesy, Job prayed for his friends. They, too, were delivered—"through the cleanness of his hands." After Job prayed for his friends, the Lord gave him back twice what he had previously lost!

> And my servant Job shall pray for you, for I will accept [his prayer] that I deal not with you after your folly, in

that you have not spoken of Me the thing that is right, as M servant Job has. So Eliphaz the Temanite and Bildad the Shuhite and Zophar the Naamathite went and did as the Lord commanded them; and the Lord accepted [Job's prayer]. And the Lord turned the captivity of Job and restored his fortunes, when he prayed for his friends; also the Lord gave Job twice as much as he had before (Job 42:8b–10 AMP).

My Prayer:

Father, I apply the blood of Jesus to my mind, my will, and my emotions, now. In so doing, I am asking You, Holy Spirit, to please help me to see the truth about my sin and my pride. Drive out all the darkness from my mind. Alin my will with Yours Give me Your nature. If there are "legal" blocks to receiving what You desire to give, please show me how to go tocourt, so I can defeat the enemy's rights against me—that all the rights I have as an heir to your Kingdom can be released to me, in me, and through me, in Jesus's mighty Name, I pray. Amen.

Personal Questions to Consider:[55]

Are you aware of any "legal rights" that Satan could possibly be holding against you?

Have you noticed any negative "patterns" in your life that may be an indicator of any such rights?

Would there be any reason that you would choose NOT to participate in a memory healing and deliverance session, given the opportunity, such as the one described in this book?

Chapter Five

RENEW

"And the tempter came and said to Him, If You are God's Son,
command these stones to be made [loaves of] bread. But He replied,
It has been written, Man shall not live and be upheld and sustained by
bread alone, but by every word that comes forth from the mouth
of God" (Matthew 4:3–4 AMP).

Summary: Jesus characterized the tempter as the evil "father" of this world—unseen, with no human body, yet very present in the affairs of men—always speaking to them, always seeking to engage them for his purposes.[1] So when a person becomes a Child of God, he enters the Kingdom with a fallen and corrupted[2] mindset[3]—due to his own bad choices, trauma inflicted upon him by outside forces, and generational sin.[4] To live free of the fear, agitation, discontent, falsehood, discouragement, and all of Satan's entanglements, this child must develop a new way of thinking, a new mindset. In other words, he must get Satan's words "out" of him and get God's words "into" him! [5]

One of the most effective ways to accomplish this is by way of deliverance in the courts of heaven. However, a person's success in this endeavor depends largely on his level of personal *engagement* with the Father, the Son, and the Holy Spirit. This is why memory healing becomes such a vital part of this formula.

Through memory healing, one *hears* what God Himself is saying in a traumatic memory[6] through Jesus.[7] Then through the power of the Holy Spirit, the person engaging with Jesus gives Him all negative emotions associated with this memory. He also forgives his perpetrators, forgives himself, receives the Father's forgiveness—and breaks Satan's word curses.

The result is this: Satan's lies—along with all associated negative thoughts and traumatic memories—are uprooted, crushed, smashed, and destroyed. Also, the traumatized "parts" of a person held captive by Satan—are set free. Restoration and "wholeness"[8] occur when the fullness of the Holy Spirit enters and rests within.

Simply stated: through this process, Satan and his minions are "bound" and sent to a place of God's choosing—and the negative, tormenting words that have come from them subside. Now, with no mind clutter, the believer can receive into himself the incorruptible and eternal "Words" of God the Father.[9] His mind is RENEWED.[10]

My friend Lisa sidled up to the Costco display stand, where there was a promotion for a new brand of chips. She exchanged a few pleasantries with the lady distributing them, took a small handful and proceeded to nibble. I lagged behind, scoping out the small group of customers munching down on their chips in front of the stand. I wasn't interested in eating anything, and I'm pretty sure Lisa wasn't either. But her style was more "organic." She preferred "blending in" and appearing to be really shopping. Which we were doing. Sort of.

"So, how are they?" I asked the guy standing closest to me. He looked to be about mid to late 50s, nicely dressed. By this time Lisa joined in with her two cents worth concerning the munchies.

I could tell immediately that this guy wasn't the shy type. So while we had him somewhat engaged, I said, "Hey, I'm Emily, and this is my friend, Lisa. Believe it or not we decided to bless some people today while we're here shopping."

I spoke calmly and smiled and acted like this was a standard thing people do from time to time. (I did sell encyclopedias door-to-door in college; so maybe I have a knack for this kind of thing, I dunno.) I continued, instinctively, "Do you need one—a blessing?" I said it with a somewhat serious tone and then broke into an almost impish grin.

I guess you could say this guy, Mark, seemed somewhat surprised by my question. Most people are, at first. But he didn't indicate he was the least bit irritated by it. In fact, his whole face lit up.

Then he blurted, "Well, what I really need is a girlfriend!"

Lisa and I looked at each other and chuckled. assuring him we were both taken—but that we were very serious about the blessing part.

So, with a little hesitation but still an agreeable air about him, he said, "Ok, but I'll warn you. I'm a heathen!"

I replied, "Aww, we'll bless you, anyway!"

Mark's eyes told me he wasn't going to resist. Then he shifted his weight a little and braced himself. "Ok," he said.

His lips were slightly pursed, but his cheeks and eyes were grinning. My eyes were open, but I was concentrating on what I was about to do, putting on my quiet, blessing voice—at the same time focusing on Mark, who was looking straight ahead, still grinning in almost disbelief that this was really happening at the chip stand in Costco. "Mark, I bless you, in the name of God, our Father. Who loves you, so much! Who wants to bless you—with so many things." I spoke slowly like I always do, then paused. Now his eyes were concentrating. His silly grin, somewhat diminished.

"Who has given you an ability to know Him intimately, and to hear His voice—and to feel His passion." I continued, emphasizing all the key words.

"And Who wants you to see yourself as He sees you, one *dearly* loved. And Who wants you to be successful and prosperous in *all* things— especially in your relationships." I stopped. Then I added, "You know, like with your mother and your sister." That's what I heard, so I said it.

Now Mark's face was clearly serious, his eyes, slightly squinted. He had that look of not wanting to miss a word I was saying.

"And Who wants to heal all your bad memories, your sicknesses, and your addictions. And Who wants to help you fulfill your destiny. I bless you, Mark, in His Name.

"And I bless you in the name of Jesus, His Son, who is your Redeemer. That means He will take all the dark things you hand over to Him," I explained, "and then He will give you back the opposite thing, in return. Like if you give Him all your heaviness, He will give you back His joy.

"And I bless you in the name of the Holy Spirit. Who is your Comforter. Your Legal Aid![11] Your Helper. Your Peace."

"And I speak all these things to you, Mark, in Jesus' Name."

That was it. I was finished, but Mark continued looking straight ahead. His stance had been perfectly still the whole time, like a soldier. I was sure he hadn't missed one detail.

Lisa and I withdrew, standing back a tad. Finally, after a few seconds, Mark relaxed, letting out some air. Lisa and I didn't say anything else. He needed a second to adjust to what must have been a very strange encounter.

"Humph," he uttered. "That was really nice. Thank you for that."

"Sure thing!" I said. We didn't really want to say much more, unless there were questions.

We felt like God had said, "Let some people I show you *hear* some of My words—so they can perhaps sense that they are loved by Me—that I want to have fellowship with them and bless them."

Lisa and I said goodbye to our Costco friend and departed for the check-out line. Moments later, as we were walking across the parking lot, we saw him again, from a distance, raising his arm high and waving enthusiastically from side to side, yelling, "Goodbye, ladies, and thanks again!"

Too Many Corrupted Thoughts Lead to Death and Darkness

Before we go further, let's try to understand a few basic spiritual concepts about the power of words. The most powerful words in the universe are the ones we *hear* and then *speak* out loud. By this I mean the ones we ingest, internalize, and carry with us, then speak. They are close to us, in our minds and hearts. Then they become part of our "conversation." These are the words that either "make us" or "break us," depending on the source.

God's words, ingested, are good for us. They create light, life, and love in us. They attract blessings to us. Bear in mind, we may not always hear them! But the book of Revelation confirms that they are being spoken, perpetually—through Yeshua, the Christ, the Messiah, who is *testifying* about the Father's heart and about our destinies in the heavenly courts. For instance in the book of Revelation, an angel explains to John concerning the words that Jesus is speaking:

> Then I fell prostrate at his feet to worship (to pay divine honors) to him, but he [restrained me] and said, Refrain! [You must not do that!] I am [only] another servant with you and your brethren who have [accepted and hold] the testimony borne by Jesus. Worship God! For the substance (essence) of the truth revealed by Jesus is the spirit of all prophecy [the vital breath, the inspiration of all inspired preaching and interpretation of the divine will and purpose, including both mine and yours] (Revelation 19:10 AMP).

The words Jesus spoke on earth and the words He is still speaking in the heavenly realm are alive, powerful, and effective. When our spirits *hear* them, our minds get blessed, changed, and renewed! And when we repeat these words, out loud, into the natural realm, they are especially powerful. Speaking God's words out loud to ourselves and to others, that is, declaring into the atmosphere what He is saying in the heavenly realm can change lives and turn dire situations completely around.

"But the word is very near you, in your mouth and in your mind and in your heart, so that you can do it" (Deuteronomy 30:14 AMP).

On the other hand, negative and antagonistic words we *hear* in the mind are also powerful and do much harm, especially when spoken or acted upon. Many psychological studies confirm that such negative "mind chatter" has grown to epidemic proportions in modern society. The consensus is that of the 12,000 to 80,000 thoughts modern people "think" per day, about 80% of these are considered "negative," or in some way detrimental to positive emotional and spiritual growth. Further, about 90% of these negative thoughts are repeated, verbatim, over and over again, day in and day out. It is a vicious death cycle that never ends.[12] Many of these thoughts do escape into our conversations!

One of my main objectives in this chapter is to convince readers that, from a biblical perspective, the mind chatter people typically describe represents the voice of Satan—the "father" of this world, who is a liar, deceiver, and murderer. He is also "the lord of the dead"[13] and works to keep all humans caught up in a death cycle, spiraling downward. Jesus referred to this counterfeit father when he said to some of the religious Jews of the day:

> Why do you misunderstand what I say? It is because you are unable to hear what I am saying. [You cannot bear to listen to My message; your ears are shut to My teaching.] You are of your father, the devil, and it is your will to practice the lusts and gratify the desires [which are characteristic] of your father. He was a murderer from the beginning and does not stand in the truth, because there is no truth in him. When he speaks a falsehood, he speaks what is natural to him, for he is a liar [himself] and the father of lies and of all that is false (John 8:44 AMP).

Unfortunately, this counterfeit father is working furiously, even among Christians, in just this manner—to minimize the impact of anything the real Father is saying. Paul says to the Corinthians:

"But now I'm afraid that just as Eve was deceived by the serpent's clever lies, your thoughts may be corrupted, and you may lose your single-hearted devotion and pure love for Christ" (2 Corinthians 11:3 TPT).

Remember, we are born into the world with a "fallen" mindset. Then we are "born again"[14]—through the living and eternal Word of God. However, at this point, nonproductive, and often harmful "chatter" has dominated most of our thinking and speaking. Our real Father "has not gotten a word in edgewise!"

But His words will live forever, continually saving, healing, and delivering us. This is why we must "replace" or "exchange" our negative thoughts and emotions, moment by moment, with thoughts and words being spoken directly to us from His throne.So, this is why we abandon everything morally impure and all forms of wicked conduct. Instead with a sensitive spirit we absorb God's Word, which has been implanted within our nature, for the Word of Life has power to continually deliver us (James 1:21 TPT). [15]

For through the eternal and living Word of God you have been born again. And this "seed" that he planted within you can never be destroyed but will live and grow inside of you forever. For: "Human beings are frail and temporary, like grass, and the glory of man fleeting like blossoms of the field. The grass dries and withers and the flowers fall off, but the Word of the Lord endures forever!" And this is the Word that was announced to you! (1 Peter 1:23–25 TPT).[15]

Demons Are Persons Who Distort Our Thinking

Oh, how our true Father God wants to help us settle our *legal disputes* with the counterfeit father of this world, so we can stop the flow of negative, false, hurtful, and even tormenting words coming at us—once and for all. Then, the Words of God can freely flow, become implanted in us, and then *come out* of us.

Now we have already established that Satan is responsible for a deluge of negativity and associated manifestations and curses—lies, theft, murder, fear, anxiety, depression, lust, pride, sickness, weakness, and poverty, to name a few.

We have also established that Satan is a *father*. But we must take this concept one step further. A father is a person. Therefore, Satan is a "person," *a being*, though we can't see him. Likewise, his family of *demons* can be characterized as spiritual "persons" or "beings."

Derek Prince had good reason to describe demons and the conditions they manifest as "persons without bodies."[16] In his forty-plus years of ministry, he found that eighty percent of a person's total deliverance and healing was complete when he had revelation of this fact: the condition of fear, anxiety, hopelessness, despair, lustful thinking, etc. is, in fact, a "person."

To use Prince's terminology, fear is a person. Sickness is a person. Poverty is a person. Therefore, these manifestations and others like them should be treated as such.

In "How to Be Delivered from Demons," Prince explains how this revelation came about. He tells the story of his early years in ministry when he fell prey to a severe depression that would not dissipate. There appeared to be no logical reason for the depression. In other words, he could determine no root cause or circumstantial reason for the problem. Also, there had been no amount of fasting or praying that would remedy it. Exasperated that he could not shake it off, he had begun blaming himself. Then one day he read in Isaiah 61 that the Lord would give him "a garment of praise" in exchange for a "spirit of heaviness."[17]

Suddenly, the Holy Spirit revealed that the heaviness oppressing him was in fact a "person"—that is, someone other than himself. The remedy, Prince discovered, was treating the depression—not as a condition, or an "it"—but as an actual person. Thinking of the depression in these terms allowed him to reckon with "him" appropriately and get rid of "him" quickly.

Can a Good Christian Really Be Tormented or Cursed by a Demon?

If you have read this far, perhaps you have become convinced that demons can plague even committed Christians. Perhaps you are plagued by a demon yourself. But many people in the church argue that "good" Christians cannot have demons or be tormented by demons and their curses. I'm not going to argue with them one way or the other.[18] But look around. People everywhere—including many staunch in the Christian faith—are plagued by darkness.[19]

Like Justin from Chapter Four, they are "born again," saved, and going to heaven. But they are not fully delivered from Satan's oppression. Their lives are still distorted, constricted, "without the proper form." Many are tormented by secret fears, anxiety, bitterness, unforgiveness, depression, addictions, and mental or emotional disorders of all types. Some suffer from character flaws resulting in more noticeable patterns of extreme anger, violence, and other abusive behaviors toward themselves or others.

Consider all the suicide cases you hear about, even among those who believe. Consider the "fall" of many pastors and other leaders in the church who break their marriage vows through involvement in extra-marital affairs and/or pornography. Consider the states of apathy, depression, and loneliness in which many people in our modern age of technology are purported to live.

Many ministers of deliverance agree that when a believer in Christ is "demonized" there are parts of his personality over which he is not in complete control. It is true that the believer is God's "possession" or "owned" by God because his spirit is joined to God's Spirit.[20] However, he can still be "afflicted" by Satan. This is the point: Somehow Satan has managed to catch "a part" of him in a trap—to use him for his purposes.[21] His mind is yet to be transformed.

Derek Prince espoused this belief:[22] He and others like him agree that "demonization"[23] causes a believer's soul—his mind, will, and emotions—to be fragmented, divided. James was referring to believers in the Lord Jesus Christ when he said, "[For being as he is] a man of two minds (hesitating, dubious, irresolute), [he is] unstable and unreliable and uncertain about everything [he thinks, feels, decides]" (James 1:8 AMP).

This almost goes without saying: Until a believer's fragmented soul is restored to wholeness, his life is on a trajectory that is to some degree "off the course" God intended. And this is an unsafe place for a believing person to be—or any person for that matter—as Satan is inclined to take advantage of "weakness" in a person's soul and stir up trouble as often as he is able.

Demons Attach in Places of Weakness

There is a Gospel account in which a woman's place of weakness is the entry point for a demon—in this case, a demon of infirmity. After Jesus healed this woman, He explained to onlookers that the source of her physical problem was a "spirit of bondage," which can be translated as a "spirit of weakness."[24] The intimation here is that a "weakness" within this woman's soul had attracted the spirit associated with the physical infirmity from which she suffered:

> One Sabbath day, while Jesus was teaching in the synagogue, he encountered a seriously handicapped woman. She was crippled and had been doubled over for eighteen years. Her condition was caused by a demonic spirit of bondage that had left her unable to stand up straight. When Jesus saw her condition, he called her over and

gently laid his hands on her. Then he said, "Dear woman, you are free. I release you forever from this crippling spirit." Instantly she stood straight and tall and overflowed with glorious praise to God! (Luke 13:10-13 TPT).

Along these same lines, you will remember that Satan found a "weakness" in Job, fear, which prompted him to take a legal action, resulting in a string of curses and related afflictions.[25] When we allow it, either through ignorance or rebellion, Satan's demons do take advantage of our weaknesses. They come, find a weakness, enter, attach, then "speak" to our minds.

But how can a person know for sure if he really has a demon or demons?[26]

For starters, we can identify the existence of demons in us by inquiring of the Holy Spirit concerning our traumatic life experiences and the "weaknesses" or "soul wounds" they have left behind. Here are two examples of how demons can enter a person based on Justin's experience.[27]

1. A "demon-motivated" person inflicts pain upon an innocent, helpless victim—which forcibly *opens* a gate to the innocent person's soul, creating a place of weakness, an easy entry point for demons. This occurred when six-year-old Justin was molested by the older neighborhood boy. Upon forced entry, the demons said to Justin, "You are worthless, fat, weird, no good!" These curse words created a demonic presence in Justin, a "person" called "self-hate." Over time, the demons' accusations caused Justin to become his own stumbling block, opening doors to yet other demons.[28]

2. An already weakened person opens more doors to the demonic, thereby weakening himself further. For example, Justin's neighborhood friend was likely abused and weakened by someone else. Through his "weakness" he began opening a "door" called pornography that allowed demons to enter and led to fantasizing about having sex with other boys. Then his pornographic thoughts morphed into a *pattern of thinking* that drove him to perverted behaviors against innocent victims like Justin. This twisted behavior ultimately resulted in the young man's own death.[29]

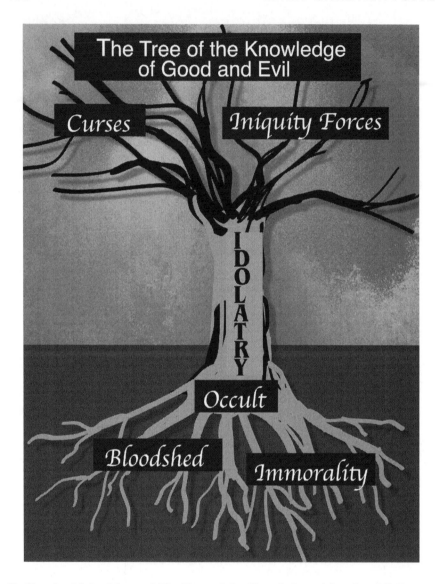

Undissolved Iniquities and The Tree of the Knowledge of Good and Evil

Another way we can identify our demons is by asking the Holy Spirit to give us revelation of any genetic, spiritual "mutations" we may have inherited through our bloodlines. Genetic mutations are generational curses, as described in Chapter Four. These curses begin when a person's unrepentant sin goes unrestrained and then develops into "iniquity."

Iniquities are the most egregious form of sin, so much so that the presence of iniquity in a person can "change" his DNA, that is, minimize his Divine Nature Ability, his ability to take on the nature of God![30] Remember, after the fall of man, our minds became twisted, confused, distorted, without the correct form.[31] Humanity's Divine Nature Ability has been affected ever since.

In the Bible, iniquities are associated with several main categories of lawless behavior—idolatry, witchcraft, murder, and sexual immorality being the main ones. The diagram of The Tree of the Knowledge of Good and Evil shows the relationship that exists between all of these, with the occult as the epicenter.

You may recall from Chapter One, the occult is the dark force used by the enemy to control our thinking, our mindsets, our attitudes. So, think of it this way: Witchcraft, bloodshed, and sexual immorality, the tap roots to the tree, are the tangible proofs that iniquitous, occultic forces are at work. Fear, hatred, greed, pride, manipulation, and control are the result.

The stronger the occultic forces, the deeper the roots and the more pervasive the result. Again, the "result" can *also* be curses that have come to us through the generations—like sickness, recurring tragic events, financial ruin, addiction, suicide, depression, severe allergies, etc., as described in Chapter Four.

The lynchpin of this whole scenario is a person's "posture" toward false, counterfeit gods, as depicted on the trunk of the tree. Go back to the garden, and you will see the truth of this statement. Eve wanted something that she didn't think she could get without allegiance to the false god Lucifer, "the lord of the dead." So, she chose to believe the serpent instead of God and got the hidden knowledge she was seeking, along with all the other curses that came with the package.

To reiterate, when a sin pattern in a person gets to the iniquity[32] level, mutations in one's spiritual DNA occur and the "imprints" are passed on — manifesting as bents, traits, tendencies, sicknesses, or even "recurring tragic events"—into the third and fourth generations. In other words, these manifestations, initiated by the unforgiven sins of an individual, then "follow" his family line—until someone like me or you goes to court and addresses the "persons without bodies" behind them.

When we follow the protocol for heavenly courtroom procedures, we can find out, with the help of the Holy Spirit, who in our lineage gave Satan a legal right to plague us. Then we can settle his cases against us through repentance and forgiveness, dissolving the curses and telling Satan's minions to go.

Let me give you an example of what I am talking about again based on the experience of Derek Prince, regarding his bout with depression. Prince explained that the culprit was a person who had seemingly "followed" his family through the generational bloodline. In other words, a "spirit of depression," a disembodied person connected to his bloodline, had been imprinted into his own spiritual DNA.

Apparently, no other members of Prince's family, likewise affected, had identified the source or root of the weakness. Therefore, due to either ignorance or unwillingness, nothing had been done to dissolve it. Remember, Satan is a legalist. If we don't find the root of a weakness, where Satan is attached—and then get that marginalized place healed through confession and repentance—he will not go away.

Prince testified that he succeeded in being delivered from his "spirit of heaviness" when he learned to deal with the "persons" involved—a demon with legal rights and a distant relative's unabsolved sin. When he went through the confession and repentance process on behalf of the person responsible for the genetic mutation, he was able to rid himself of these "people" who had robbed him of the peace rightfully his as a child of God.

Here is one more point regarding the need to dissolve generational sins: Every young, innocent, helpless person eventually passes a point in life, where he is expected to take responsibility for his "imprints"—and the thoughts and words and actions that flow out of them. This is why the Bible teaches us to "demolish every deceptive fantasy that opposes God, and break through every arrogant attitude that is raised up in defiance of the true knowledge of God."[33]

When we don't go through a healing and deliverance process, these "imprints" are not dissolved, and repercussions can occur. The danger comes when negative or demonic thoughts associated with these imprints are not restrained and a progression of sin follows.

The cycle repeats itself. First, random thoughts ("to miss the mark") become intentions or habits, then strongholds ("to rebel or revolt against God's ways"), then iniquities ("crooked" or "perverse").

Lorena Is Tormented by a Violent Presence Who is Trying to Kill Her

Lorena is a strong Christian in her early 40s with a past deeply rooted in the occult—both generationally and through life experience. Almost two years ago, she came to me for memory healing and deliverance because she had suffered severe nightmares, which she described as "a dark presence" that was "attempting to assassinate" her. The episodes had continued night after night for more than a week—and were so severe and frightening, she had resorted to hiding in the closet with her small son, playing praise music, quoting scripture, and "doing warfare prayers."[34]

Lorena had become a Christian at age eight, through her aunt and uncle, both Pentecostal pastors. But even at that young age, she had already experienced abandonment, neglect, molestation, and the death of her mother. At twelve, she went to live with this same aunt and uncle—because her stepfather, who sexually abused her since age two, had taken a new wife.

Lorena was rebellious, and life in a strict home environment made things difficult. By sixteen, she was homeless, by choice. A life of sexual promiscuity, drug abuse, and witchcraft followed. Then there was marriage, several children, divorce, another marriage, and another child.

Now her firstborn child, a son in his late 20s, is incarcerated. And her second husband is also incarcerated.

When I met Lorena, there were several things about her I immediately recognized. First, she had a sincere desire to be healed and indicated she was willing to do anything to find the root cause of the dreams, so she could "get rid" of them.

Second, Lorena did not have a "victim mentality."[35] This was partly evidenced by her success in business. Despite her past neglect and abandonment issues, homelessness, and drug and alcohol addictions, she had gone to school, taken a good job, and developed skills she later used to establish, own, and operate a successful medical-consulting company.

Also, Lorena never blamed anyone else for the trials she faced. She never said things like "if only this or that had not happened, I wouldn't be in this state." In other words, she had an attitude of "I am going to take responsibility for this situation." This was the same attitude Derek Prince had when he realized that he must be the one to act and "get rid" of the depression associated with a generational "imprint."

The next thing I noticed about Lorena was her earnest desire to "obey" God. Based on her testimony, she could hear God speak; and when He told her what to do, she would do it. Now, don't get me wrong, Lorena's willingness to obey what God said is generally a very good thing. But truthfully, some of God's "instructions" to her did seem a bit odd to me. "Fast for three days. Fast for a month. Repent for this or that. Do not eat lemons! Remember, I said no fruit!" This type of instruction was constant. But Lorena would do everything she was told, and then some.

Lorena also seemed very well versed in the scriptures, having followed the Lord consistently for eight years. She was active in her church. She understood her authority in Christ and was attempting to use it. She had also learned recently about the courts of heaven and the need to dissolve curses. It made sense to her that the dreams were a curse, a serious retribution, for her past rebellion. Of course, she had repented, repeatedly, for all her past wrongs—even for being depressed, fearful, and suicidal. She was especially repentant for being afraid of the dark presence and for feeling the need to hide in the closet.

But despite all her repentance and obedience, Lorena had no joy. She was laden in fear, burdened by heaviness and guilt, depressed, and having suicidal thoughts, in addition to hearing the voices from the "assassin"—all for reasons she could not determine.

The Information I Gathered about Lorena

If you are interested to learn how to help someone through a healing and deliverance you will want to learn to ask a few critical questions up front to get the process going.

"What negative emotion are you holding? Like if you could just get rid of 'blank negative emotion,' your life would be so much better."

"What is the worst thing that ever happened to you in your child-hood, say before age eight?" [36]

For Lorena, the answer to the first question was FEAR. There were others that came up as we went. I kept a running list. The worst memory was her mother's death—which ironically occurred when she was eight.

I usually try to write down about four "worst things" that happened, the younger the better. Lorena had several in her teenage years that I thought were pertinent to her situation, so I listed them, as well.

When I begin a session with someone the goal is always to find the "root causes" of a person's negative emotions, that is, the "things that happened to them." You want the earliest memories because these are typically the ones that have affected them most. I listed the main things I discovered about Lorena in the initial session, which took about two hours. As you can see, I tried to ask about all the main areas of concern: the occult, idol worship, sexual immorality, bloodshed, and witchcraft. I also delved into areas of unforgiveness. To stir the memory, I showed her The Tree of the Knowledge of Good and Evil, the list of curses in Chapter Four, and the Rightness/Wrongness Chart which can be down-loaded from my website.

Lorena's fact-finding information was as follows:

Spiritual Orientation: She has been a very strong Christian for eight years. She has truly forgiven a lot of people. Dreaming is very big. She considers herself prophetic, meaning she "hears" God tell her things. Seems to be very strict on herself as far as obedience to what God says is concerned. Yet her conversations with God do not seem to give her a lot of joy because she is so traumatized.

Occult: She participated in love "spells," horoscopes, and Tarot cards. She asked for the gift of "conscious channeling" and to be given "spiritual guides."

Pharmakeia: She used cocaine and drank heavily in her 20s and 30s.

Sexual Abuse: Her stepfather abused her, ages two to twelve.

Sexual Immorality: She had lesbian relationship and promiscuous relations with men. Most all centered around occult activities.

Biological Father: Mexican/American. She met him once on her birthday. He was a heroin addict. He had been dedicated to Satan as a baby by his mother and grandmother, who were both witches.

Mother: Mexican/American. Died of cancer at age 44. She neglected Lorena. Her death exacerbated Lorena's abandonment issues.

Aunt and Uncle: They were strict disciplinarians and inflicted some physical abuse, which they intended as "discipline." Lorena has forgiven them, and their relationship is now restored.

Negative Emotions: Fear, shame, anxiety, depression, guilt, confusion, self-hate (she has hit herself with a belt), sadness (she didn't get to tell her mother goodbye).

People Who Hurt Lorena: (1) Her stepdad, who was a drunkard and molested her repeatedly, and who, before he passed away, said he wouldn't forgive her for "telling on him." (2) Her first husband and his family, who inflicted word curses. (Lorena cheated on her ex-husband with a cocaine dealer. He and the family won't forgive her for this). (3) Her aunt and uncle, who were angry with her for rebelling, pulled her around by the hair, and hit her with a belt.

People Lorena hurt: (1) Her younger sister, who Lorena abused sexually when she was a child—and who now refuses to forgive. (2) Her first husband.

Word Curses Spoken Against Her: (1) Her aunt and uncle said, "You are dramatic and trying to get attention. Why can't you just be 'normal'?" (2) Her cousins said, "You are an orphan! You will never be first choice. You will always be second." (3) Her first husband said, "You are fat. No one is ever going to want you." (4) Her grandmother said, "You are an orphan."

Worst memories: (1) At twelve–thirteen months old, Lorena's mother dropped her on the floor and left her to cry. She had no expression, no remorse. This scene is a recurring dream and possibly a dissociated, memory.

(2) The night of her mother's funeral, Lorena is age eight. Earlier that day she had been sick with a fever, and the aunt had taken her to the emergency room. Now she is looking at her mother in the casket. She is sad and overwhelmed. Her mother has on a white dress that makes her look like a bride. She also has a white veil over her head, and she is holding a rosary. Lorena feels sick and full of disappointment—because her

mother had been sick in the hospital for three months, and her aunt and uncle had kept Lorena from seeing her. She never got to say goodbye.

(3) At fourteen years old Lorena is sleeping in a bed at her grandparent's house. A dark shadow crawls on top of her, straddling her stomach. Then it tries to strangle her. She wakes up, paralyzed, not able to speak. But finally, she says, "Jesus!" and the presence leaves.

(4) At sixteen years old Lorena is with her grandma. They are sitting on the front porch swing together. Lorena puts her head down on her grandmother's lap. She is feeling guilty for making her grandma suffer—because she had gone out the night before, gotten drunk, and had sex. When she came home at 3 a.m. her grandmother was up waiting for her. Her grandmother is loving and forgiving in this moment, but she says to Lorena "You are an orphan." Lorena is always being reminded that she is an orphan. This day she is holding guilt, rejection, and sadness because she is an orphan.

Generational Observations: Lorena is of Mexican descent on both sides of the family. The Satanism mentioned on Lorena's Dad's side points to the occult, as defined in the previous chapter.[37]

Recurring Themes: Death (mother), suicidal thoughts, fear of death (assassin threats at fourteen and again recently), injury (infliction of pain with a belt by her uncle, self-infliction with a belt, recurring memories of being dropped on the floor by her mother), sexual perversion (lesbian and other), sexual abuse (stepdad, two–twelve years old), addiction (cocaine and alcohol), religious rituals that leave her with no joy (reciting warfare prayers, quoting scripture, following God's instruction on fasting, etc., to a tee).

The Occult: Occult involvement on her Dad's side of the family, for sure. Previously, Lorena sold herself out to gods of sex and love. She sought love through use of "love spells." She sought information through "spirit guides."

Abandonment/Rejection: Lorena did not know her father. Her mother died. Her first husband left her. Her second husband left her to go to jail. Her sister refuses to forgive. Her stepdad refused to forgive.

Orphan Spirit: Lorena is orphaned at ages eight (by her mother), 12 (by her step-dad), 16 (by her aunt and uncle).

Curse Categories: Related to being fat, being an orphan, being unwanted.

General Thought: Lorena has sought love in all the wrong places. Lorena needs to know the love of the Father at a deep level before she can be totally healed.

Learning How to be Loved by God in His Presence

In a successful memory healing session, a person's most traumatized "parts" interface and engage at a deep level with Jesus. This is a huge benefit to a traumatized person, because the inner parts' interactions with Him in the memories immediately minimize any existing inner conflict—then establish peace, and usher in joy.[38] Another obvious benefit of memory healing is that it allows the prayer minister to show a hurting person "how" to enter God's presence in order to establish intimacy with the Father through His Son. This closeness of relationship has very likely been lacking in most people I work with. Many have *never* experienced what it feels like to be loved by our Good Father!

Being "blocked" from God's presence and unable to receive His love is a curse. Learning how to be loved by God in His presence is a blessing and the key to living a successful Christian life.

To get started, there are some steps and prayers I use in the memory healing process. However, the Holy Spirit truly is my "guide." With that said, there is no wrong way to go about this when He is with you; so, I won't go into every detail here. I will give you some of the highlights.

First, I try to establish in the person's mind the love and affection the Father has for them personally. I do this with the blessing I gave "Costco Mark" at the very beginning of this chapter. These are *The Words of God* to the hurting individual, which set the tone for the healing.

I always frame my healing sessions with something like this: "We are going to do three things. We are going to break the curses. We are going to get those wounds healed. And we are going to make Satan get his hands off you."[39]

Next, I take the Sword of the Spirit, another name for *The Word of the Lord*, and I "pierce" between the person's soul (the mind, will and emotions) and spirit. This means I "separate" from the person's soul, any "spirit" persons who may be attached. This step is taken straight out of Hebrew 4:12. I'll be talking about this more in Chapter Seven. But for now, suffice it to say that this is a critical part to the healing. The reason is because the "parts" we are going to be dealing with in the memory healings are "soulish," and the demons are "spirit." We can't deal effectively with the wounded soul "parts" when they are all tangled up with demon spirits.

Another reason this "piercing between" is so important is because we are trying to "free" the hurting person's "true" spirit from Satan's entanglement. Remember from Chapter One, the spirit of a person is the most important part of who he is. It is his "God part." And this is the part that must be "freed" from Satan's entrapment so it can "join" with the Holy Spirit. Only through such a union can the person experience true relationship with the Triune God.

Don't skip the separation of soul and spirit! Just say the words, "I divide soul and spirit." But before you say it, engage with the Holy Spirit yourself, believing in your mind and heart that Jesus has given you the authority to perform this separation on behalf of the person you are helping.

Now let's go to a memory from Lorena's healing session. Usually, I do about three of these, one after the other. For now, I will share the one where Jesus came and spoke to eight-year-old Lorena on a very personal level, after the death of her mother.

"Lorena, let's ask the Holy Spirit to take you back to the time when your mom died, and you were at the funeral home. You were eight. Do you remember what you looked like then?

"Yes."

"Did you have long brown hair?"

"Yes."

"What were you wearing that day?"

"A blue dress."

"Little eight-year-old Lorena, who is feeling so sad because her mom died and left her, little Lorena who is also feeling sick to her stomach and is so disappointed because her mother was in the hospital for such a long time, and she didn't even get to tell her good-by at all. Can you hear me, little Lorena?"

"Yes."

"Can you see your mom there in the casket? She has on the white dress with the white veil around her head. And she is holding the rosary."

"Yes, I see her." Tears.

"What emotion are you holding, Lorena?"

"Sadness. Disappointment. They could have let me go to her."

"Jesus, come! Come and help this little girl who is hurting so bad." I ask Him to come at the height of the emotion. Pause. Lots of long pauses are needed.

"Lorena, do you see Jesus in the room?"

"Yes, I see Him! He's here for me! He is bending over and calling me to come to Him!"

"Where is He in the room?"

"He's under the tree, the one I saw in my dream. I'm going to Him."

Pause. "What's He doing now?"

"He's holding me. And He says He loves me. I'm His first choice!"

"He says she had bitterness that held her back. But she prayed for me. And He is giving me the opportunity to do things she couldn't do."[40]

Pause. "Now she is coming over to us, where we are, under the tree!"

"Awww! What does she look like?"

"She has long black hair. She is young. She's eating a fruit from the tree! Now she's hugging me and kissing me all over!"

"Is she saying anything to you?"

"Yes, she's saying this is a gift. That she is alive. That she is with Jesus now. She is telling me goodbye."

"Lorena, can you forgive your mom for leaving you? And for neglecting you?"

"Yes, I forgive her."[41]

"And can you forgive your aunt and uncle for not letting you see her in the hospital before she died?"

"Yes, I forgive them."

"Lorena, repeat after me. I break the curses of sadness, disappointment, grief, anger, bitterness, and abandonment."

She repeats.

"Jesus, I ask You to take all this little girl's sadness and disappointment from her now! Lorena, will you let Jesus take your sadness?"

"Yes, I'm doing it. It's leaving me."

"Now we have to tell the demons to go. Repeat after me. 'I command all the demons that have been attached to this wound to go, now, to the pit.'"

She repeats.[42]

"Little eight-year-old Lorena you are all healed. You go, now, with Jesus."[43]

Discovering a Generational Root, Then Executing God's Verdict Against Satan

Usually, the memory healing aspect as just described, is the easy part. The hard part becomes figuring out the generational curses, that is, "what happened" in this person's genealogical lines that caused her to carry one or several spiritual imprints from a cursed relative. Figuring this out will explain why a person has always manifested certain negative emotions, such as depression, fear, and anxiety—or why she and others in her family seem to be magnets for accidents or tragic events, or inclined toward suicide, incarceration, or premature death.

First, we go back to that peaceful place in God's presence, where we met Jesus in the memory. But this time we are here for a slightly different purpose—to find out who is responsible for the curses we are battling. So instead of being with Him in a place where there are fruit trees and flowing brooks, we are standing in the courtroom of heaven!

To this point, Lorena has been somewhat aware of all the "parts" of her soul, who needed a supernatural touch. Finding out what iniquitous things her ancestors did to alter her Divine Nature Ability is entirely different.

As the prayer minister, intercessor, I ask the Holy Spirit to help Lorena find the root cause of her problems—so she can get the associated "memories," or imprints, dissolved. This will happen through her own confession and repentance of another person's sins. Remember, the person responsible for the curse did not repent before the iniquity imprint passed to future generations. Now Lorena must do it, so Satan's legal rights against her will be settled.

This is a condensed version of what typically follows. We ask the Father, who is the Judge, to bind up the person's top two demons, according to Matthew 16:19: "I will give you the keys of heaven's kingdom realm to forbid on earth that which is forbidden in heaven, and to release on earth that which is released in heaven" (Matthew 16:19 TPT).[44]

The demons are bound and told to cooperate with our questioning of them. They are told that the prayer minister understands her authority to cast out demons;[45] and if the demon to whom we are speaking doesn't cooperate, he and all the demons in his jurisdiction will go straight to the lake of fire, a final judgment.[46]

Demons are smart. They know when they are "bound" and taken to court that no option for them is good, except to remain where they are—in the human body. So, a demon might lie or hide, or "trick" the person who is conducting the healing session, so there will be no success in casting him out.

But if the person conducting the session believes in the power of Jesus' blood and knows how to "apply" it, the demons know they have no choice but to cooperate. They know they are "caught," so they agree to suffer the lesser of two punishments—being sent to the "pit," a temporary holding ground of sorts, where they will await their "final" judgment.[47]

Further, the demons know they must tell the truth or suffer the consequences. They must identify themselves by name, explain their functions, and tell what they have done to the victim—spiritually, emotionally, and physically.

Most important, they must reveal what sin or iniquity brought about their legal rights over the victim. They must also acknowledge at what point their "rights" to the victim have been dissolved. This occurs when the victim has fully "executed" God's verdicts at a personal level, through repentance.

At this point in Lorena's deliverance session, two demons came forward and identified themselves to Lorena. The number one demon was a disembodied "spirit of fear." The number two demon was a "spirit of incubus."[48] Bear in mind that Lorena was focusing on being in that peaceful place of God's presence. However, at the same time she is "hearing" the demons "confess" these things. I prompted the demons to tell her "what" to say.

"Are you generational?" I asked the spirit of fear. He answered, "Yes."

"When did you enter Lorena's generational line?" Answer: "45 generations ago."

"What was the iniquity?" Answer: "An Incan Indian sacrificed a child to Satan, in exchange for power."

"What other spirits came with you?" Answer: "Depression and suicide."

In all those generations past, no one had broken the curses! But with the information given, Lorena was able to confess, repent, forgive, and break the curses brought into her bloodline through the spirit of fear.

A quick study of history shows that people in all cultures and in all time periods, even in modern day, have made pledges to the "gods" in exchange for riches and/or fame, most often "sealing the deal" with a sacrifice of animal or human blood. And this blood "cries" from the ground, "Vengeance!" Such was the case with the shed blood of Abel, the very first person murdered by his brother Cain's hands:

Yahweh said, "Listen — the voice of your brother's blood[49] is crying out to me from the ground! What have you done?" (Genesis 4:10 TPT).

Since the days of Cain and Abel, man has believed Satan's lies and embraced evil opinions and prejudices which have led to bloodshed. And to this day, when Satan "hears" the "cries" of "bloods" shed, it is his legal right to respond with curses.

Sadly, the "bloods" continue their crying, until someone repents on behalf of the persons responsible. Then, the voice of the blood of Jesus rises up and cries out "Mercy!" and "Forgiveness!"

And we have come to Jesus who established a new covenant with his blood sprinkled upon the mercy seat; blood that continues to speak from heaven, "forgiveness," a better message than Abel's blood that cries from the earth, "justice" (Hebrews 12:24 TPT).

Jesus is Knocking: Open the Door and Overcome Your Demons

When we are constantly exposed to Satan's bad words and attitudes, activities, and word pictures, we live at risk—because we live in or on the fringe of a "danger zone" that disrespects God and clearly goes against His ways. Knowingly or unknowingly, when we embrace a lifestyle of "thinking and doing" that is contrary to the one God intended, Satan has a legal right against us.

In other words, when we don't live within the boundaries God set, or when someone in our past did not, we are susceptible to Satan's words, the "sin crouching at our door"[50]—and the curses that follow these into the third and fourth generations. Satan's words and curses cause us to miss out on God's blessings! We must get rid of Satan's words and curses through the process of memory healing and deliverance in the courts of heaven.

But getting rid of Satan is just the first step. We must replace those harmful words with the words of God. And this must be done on a recurring basis as we listen to the Words Jesus is speaking[51] to us from the heavenly realm. He has been speaking on our behalf since the very beginning of time![52] Likewise, He is speaking to us through the written word, the Bible. So, pick up the Bible and read and meditate on it. When we *really* hear what he is saying, we *overcome* the evil one and keep him at bay!

Now, here is where the rubber meets the road: To receive the words of God, we must be willing to spend the time needed with Him in the Secret Place, over and over again. The Psalmist reminds us that "there's a private place reserved for the lovers of God, where they sit near him and receive the revelation secrets of his promises" (Psalm 25:14 TPT). When we finally *hear* God's words there, written or spoken, letting them settle within us, over and over, we are changed. Then we are equipped to fulfill what He is saying to us about our purpose, our destiny!

This is the truth: People once divided, with souls tormented and opposed by the enemy, can now eradicate the source of that voice so God's voice can come through. These same persons can now know, understand, and apply the purposes of God's mind vs. the purposes of the devil. This is true, because God's verdict against Satan and his minions has already been rendered through the work Jesus did on the cross. Satan is defeated. But we must execute God's verdict. Execution involves coming clean yourself. Forgiving all perpetrators. Releasing wrong things. Receiving right things. Breaking curses. Demanding that demons go to the pit. Refilling your mind continuously with the *right* words—Jesus's words, the Divine Reason that coordinates a changing universe.

"In the beginning [before all time] was the Word (Christ), and the Word was with God, and the Word was God Himself" (John 1:1 AMP).

He is knocking at the door of your heart and mine now.

Go to court now, my friend! "Execute" in your life the verdicts God has already rendered against your enemy; and the things which already *are* in the heavenly realm will *be* in your life here on earth:

- Knowing Him intimately[53]
- Hearing His voice[54]
- Feeling His passion[55]
- Seeing yourself through His eyes[56]
- Seeing others, especially those who seem unlovely or undeserving, through His eyes[57]
- Receiving the Holy Spirit's anointing so you can serve Him effectively[58]
- Being successful and prosperous in all things, especially your relationships[59]
- Being healed in your spirit, soul, and body (memories, sicknesses, and addictions)[60]
- Fulfilling your destiny![61]

Trust in the Lord completely, and do not rely on your own opinions. With all your heart rely on him to guide you, and he will lead you in every decision you make. Become intimate with him in whatever you do, and he will lead you wherever you go. Don't think for a moment that you know it all, for wisdom comes when you adore him with undivided devotion and avoid everything that's wrong. Then you will find the healing refreshment your body and spirit long for. (Proverbs 3:5–8 TPT).

My Prayer:

Father God, thank you for the testimony of Jesus, the only Voice in the universe that always speaks the Truth. And thank you for the blood of Jesus—the redemption Voice that cries "Mercy!" and "Forgiveness!" Father, I ask you to give me revelation light concerning Your words streaming from the courts in heaven. I receive them. Show me now how to consciously "apply" them to my mind, my will, my emotions, my body, and my circumstances through the healing of all my memories and the casting out of all demons and curses attached to them. Thank You for loving me! Thank You for sending Jesus to pay the price required to set me free from all my darkness—so my Divine Nature Abilities can be restored! Amen.

Personal Questions to Consider: [63]

Do you currently battle "danger zone" areas in your life? If so, is this a concern to you?

If God could help you live more "within His boundaries" do you think your life would be better, more satisfying, less stressful?

What can you do now to minimize negative "mind chatter"?

Chapter Six

REDIRECT

"And I sought a man among them who should build up the wall and stand in the gap[1] before Me for the land, that I should not destroy it, but I found none" (Ezekiel 22:30 AMP).

Summary: The Bible says Jesus came to earth to destroy the work of the devil.[2] In effect, Jesus came to "restrain" the devil, sending his demons to places of confinement until the final judgment. To get the job done, Jesus said what He heard the Father saying[3] and did what He saw the Father doing.[4] Then He sent the disciples out,[5] instructing them to do the same.[6]

Today, God's people continue this work. And those of us who are humble[7]—and "agreeable" to what He is still saying and doing—get to participate.[8] We do this until the restoration of all things has occurred, at which point, Jesus will return to earth to claim His church.[9]

What a demonstration of His amazing grace this is, first to us who have received Him and taken hold of His name,[10] next to the people around us who need help getting free from Satan's entrapment, then to the Church at large! Now we, too, are REDIRECTING evil spirits in and around us, by the power of the Holy Spirit, sending them to a place of confinement,[11] just as Jesus and His disciples did.

The result: the Church is being REDIRECTED toward "the full expression" of God's love.[12] And this is of utmost importance because the Body of Christ must become pure and spotless and righteous before Jesus can return to earth to claim it, His bride.[13] As Christians, if we desire to help move this process along, it behooves us to follow

Jesus's lead—watching and listening and applying the very same divine "restraints" He used against evil, so we can extend the ministry He began and continue taking back the ground the enemy has stolen.[14]

Hannah's mother, Pricilla, was not only perplexed, but she was also disheartened. No, that would be the euphemistic way to explain it. She was downright depressed. Hemmed in. Out of options. And exhausted.

She flung herself down on the bed, too tired to think. Yet she had to think. This was her one opportunity to sort some things out with God. Her husband, Todd, a police officer, was on night shift. The babies were down, and the house was quiet. Maybe she could hear herself think straight if she tried.

I'm not really losing my mind, she thought. But how could anyone have a right mind after four years of constant chaos and abnormal behavior? "Lord, I am losing my mind! I need for you to show up here, tonight! I'm gonna sit here for as long as it takes for You to manifest! Because I'm desperate. You gave me this child, now You are going to have to show me how to get through it."

This wasn't the first time Pricilla had prayed a desperate prayer. Raised in the Baptist Church, she knew the command to pray "without ceasing." And that "the prayer of a righteous man availeth much." So, both she and her husband had tried to be faithful in prayer. And they were in church every Sunday. And other people were praying. Yet nothing was happening. Seemingly, Hannah's eight-year-old behavior was going from bad to worse.

At birth, Hannah had been addicted to crack—her biological mother, a prostitute. On top of that, her mother and grandmother, who lived together, were running a prostitution ring out of their house. And the mother was consistently unable to pass her drug-addiction tests. For these reasons, the Department of Families and Services[15] had begun "monitoring" Hannah's home situation through "announced" visits.

For three and a half years, the department threatened to take Hannah and put her in foster care. During this time, the grandmother had even tried to qualify for guardianship. However, she didn't pass the background check. Finally, Hannah was put up for adoption.

Pricilla and Todd had been foster parents prior to getting Hannah. They knew the system—or thought they did. But soon after the adoption, they didn't know what to think.

Early on, Hannah was the most obstinate child they had ever seen. She also demonstrated the most bizarre behaviors, such as going into trance-like robotic states, where she would remain for long periods of time. Sometimes, while in these states, she would talk about very grotesque things and then suddenly "snap" out of it.

Even several years after the adoption, Hannah would go in and out of "imaginary" places, where she was able to describe in great detail the most horrid situations—men dressed in black hooded robes, babies being cut open, blood on the walls, etc. Later, when questioned, she remembered none of it.

At other times, Hannah might become upset about something, fall to the floor on hands and knees, back away from the person trying to calm her—then swat the air, ferociously, like a "mad" dog in a cage. Of course, these types of behaviors were reported to the doctors, but Hannah never manifested them unless she was behind closed doors.

"Lord, you have got to speak to me about this," Pricilla continued. "I'm scared. I don't know what else to do." She was referring to the new thing Hannah was doing—scratching herself, to the point that her skin was constantly oozing blood. Pricilla had just put Hannah to bed—her little hands covered with oven mitts, duct tape tightly wound around each one.

Pricilla's head hit the pillow thinking, "Something is terribly wrong. This is not normal. God, only You could have a possible solution."

Evil's Most Heinous Secrets Will Be Revealed

After Priscilla prayed her desperate prayer, the truth about what had really happened in Hannah's first three-and-a-half years of life did surface. What "really happened" is an example of just "how evil" evil really is.

The uncovering began when Priscilla was researching Hannah's symptoms online. A website popped up—a "deliverance" ministry, specializing in victims of Satanic Ritual Abuse.[16] Priscilla dismissed it, continuing her search for information regarding Obstinate Defiance

Disorder and Reactive Attachment Disorder. A counselor working in collaboration with a geneticist had recently diagnosed Hannah with these two disorders.

But as Hannah's destructive behaviors worsened, Priscilla's mom remembered hearing a lady at church speak about a form of "psychological counseling" that sounded similar to the ministry Priscilla had noticed online. Would this lady's ministry be able to help, Priscilla's mother wondered?

At the time, neither Priscilla nor her mother knew anything about deliverance from demons. "But I was desperate to help my daughter!" Priscilla lamented, so, she took the plunge and called. As it turned out, the ministry was the very same one she had noticed in her online search the year before![17]

"For there is nothing hidden that shall not be disclosed, nor anything secret that shall not be known and come out into the open" (Luke 8:17 AMP).

The first clue about Hannah's history came when the deliverance team discovered she could easily identify and describe the symbols and rituals most often associated with Freemasonry, a "secret society," known to be closely connected to a worldwide "elitist" group called the Cabal[18] and purported to practice Satanic Ritual Abuse.

Not surprising, there was a Freemason Temple located near where Hannah's mother and grandmother lived during the time that Hannah remained under their care. The two could easily have worked out a lucrative arrangement for Hannah to spend time at this location. Also, this could have gone undetected since the Department of Children and Services made only "announced" visits to the home once or twice a month.

Other disturbing revelations soon came to light. Hannah's true diagnosis was Multiple Personality Disorder (MPD), also known as Dissociative Identity Disorder (DID)—stemming from Mind Control,[19] a technique used in Satanic Ritual Abuse. In other words, through multiple, repeated abuses, that is, "ritualistic abuses," Hannah had developed an intricate mental networking system that allowed her to cope—rather "survive"—through dissociation, the forced forgetting mechanism referenced in previous chapters.

To review, a person's wounded psyche will often split off from the core person into another "part," especially in more-severe trauma cases. This split brings about the forced forgetting. However, the "part" continues to "hold" a deep emotion that can be triggered at any time. When triggered, the "part" surfaces and "acts out."[20]

Hannah likely had been abused so many times, that there were thousands of divisions in her mental network. This meant there were thousands of "parts of Hannah" that needed to be healed. To make matters worse, Hannah's wounded "parts" had been programmed to "think" a certain way when triggered. For example, Hannah's database reminded all "parts" that they were "no good, damaged, good for only one purpose—evil."[21]

This type of programming, words spoken continuously over a person during ritual abuse, prevented Hannah's "parts" from having any ability to think for themselves. For this reason, the "parts" were not easily convinced that anyone trying to help was a friend or ally. Someone trying to "be nice" to a part was just "tricking" her into doing something she did not want to do. Hence, when frightened or "triggered," Hannah's "part" might assume the posture of a ferocious dog—or some other incomprehensible thing.

The Macro Message: There Is a Secret, Worldwide Network of Human Traffickers

Over the last couple hundred years the Cabal has penetrated the ranks of influential groups such as The Freemasons to expand their sphere of control and influence. In addition, they are purported to have "hooks" in politicians, businesspeople, entertainers, sports figures, and media.[22] Allegedly, there are thirteen families worldwide who control the Cabal, also called The Illuminati. These are some of the wealthiest families in the world with connections to wealth and power, from Europe to China.

Why am I bothering to tell you about a worldwide network of elitists, you might ask, when the topic of this book involves the healing of dysfunctional, traumatized individuals? Let me explain the connection.

One: Eight million innocent children just like Hannah go missing worldwide every year, 600,000—800,000 of these in the United States, according to a report by the U.S. Department of Justice in 2013.[23] With that said, the numbers could be higher. The National Center for Missing and Exploited Children (NCMEC)[24] confirms that many children are never reported missing, and that there is no reliable way to determine what the actual number would be, either in the U.S. or abroad.[25]

It is true that in the United States, half of the children reported missing each year are recovered within a short period of time. However, of those remaining at large, the NCMEC reports that 91% of these children are considered "endangered." The FBI's National Crime Information Center (NCIC) database reported approximately 386,000 such children in 2019. Also, in 2020, the NCMEC reported that one in six "endangered" children were sex trafficking victims.[26] If these estimates are correct, approximately 64,333 new runaways are being sex trafficked in the United States each year!

Two: There is a connection between these missing children and the reports of ritual abuse,[27] mind programming, and Satanic Ritual Abuse, which started in the 1980s—though the truth about this is just starting to come into the light.[28] The truth is that thousands of survivors' interviews conducted from the 80s through the turn of the century were largely ignored and eventually silenced.[29] As Derek Prince so astutely stated during his years in ministry, "Satan likes to operate in the dark. He doesn't like people to know what he's doing. Or how he's doing it!"[30]

Three: It's been a long time coming, but in the last ten years, the evil atrocities of Satanism and the occult are finally being exposed—and the truth about what was suspected all along is being validated. This is happening through internet-driven testimonies of former Freemasons,[31] film stars,[32] victims,[33] and other whistleblowers[34]—confirming that an evil, worldwide network comprised of big-name pop artists, Hollywood stars, entrepreneurs, sports figures, and government officials has operated secretly and efficiently to commit heinous crimes against young child-bearing women and children for many decades. These include human trafficking, sexual abuse, Satanic Ritual Abuse, and the harvesting of adrenochrome,[35] a drug driven by the black market, Hollywood elites, and the Cabal.[36]

Of course, this topic of child trafficking and the harvesting of adrenochrome are rarely discussed in the mainstream media, and the general public, including the church, is still largely unaware of these things due to the long history of secrecy and cover-ups.

One of my main objectives in writing this chapter is to make you aware of this evil. I also want to encourage you to do your own research. Then determine what you can to help alleviate the pain and suffering of the children and women who have survived these atrocities. Many of the "children" survivors are now adults.

WHAT IS ADRENOCHROME?

Adrenochrome is blood harvested from children, typically under the age of nine, while they are undergoing a "rush" of adrenaline induced by torture. The procedure is performed by an injection made through the pineal gland. Adrenochrome is known as the "Fountain of Youth" Serum, promoting longevity, vitality, and health, and is linked to Satanism and other secret cults.

Many ancient civilizations such as the Egyptians, the Mayans and the Aztecs conducted similar sacrifices to appease the gods, gain power, and receive "the life forces" that come from them. Former Freemason and X Factor winner, Australian Altiyan Childs verifies in his documentary-style film that the secret religion of Freemasonry and many in The Cabal is the worship of Satan, which includes the ingestion of adrenochrome and human flesh. Satanists believe that when children are sacrificed, the gates of hell open, and Satan's powers are released.

The Micro Message: Bring Each Little Child unto Me

The Bible promises that any man who comes to the Father as a little child can escape the authority of the "dark ruler" and his hierarchy of evil beings[37]—then be delivered from the entanglements of the occult, through Jesus's powerful and perfect blood.

This is true of my friend "Joshua" (a pseudonym), age 48, a believer in Jesus for about four years. I heard Joshua speak on a podcast about two years ago, then contacted him. He was eager to tell his story and I was eager to hear about how he had become such a Spirit-directed believer in Jesus in such a short period of time, given his background. Over a two-year period, we became phone friends and had many conversations concerning his recovery from Satanic Ritual Abuse. His life story, as he as personally communicated it, has helped me better understand and recognize the work of the enemy in today's world—and what we need to do to combat it.[38]

Joshua's story of Satanic Ritual Abuse began in infancy—with his own parents being the primary perpetrators of his abuse, which continued until age 21. During this timeframe, he was in and out of therapy, diagnosed with three different anxiety disorders, bipolar disorder, and various phobias. In addition, he suffered his whole life from severe nightmares three to four nights a week, questioned his sexuality, and contemplated becoming transgender. He also became an atheist.

For many generations, Joshua's family had been involved in occultic practices through a mainline denomination with Gnostic/Luciferian[39] ties. Though Ivy-league educated, financially well-off, and seemingly "normal," Joshua's parents were ingratiated to Satan, leading dark, "secret" lives—controlling, torturing, and killing innocent women and children through ritual sexual abuse and perversity. The rituals, typically performed in their church basement, were designed to mock the Father, the Son, and the Holy Spirit, at the same time invoking the power of Satan.

Joshua's autobiography, *Born into Battle*, describes the abuse he endured from infancy as "being sodomized, sexually abused in all conceivable manners, and physically and psychologically tortured on a regular basis. It also involved being made to witness, and even forced to participate in, the brutal murders of other children."[40]

For instance, at age 13, Joshua and a "brown" girl named LaTonya, who likely came out of human trafficking and child sex slavery, were left alone in a single cell, a dark dungeon-like room on the church property. Apparently, the tormentors gave Joshua and LaTonya time to "bond" in

WHAT IS EVIL INTELLIGENCE AND
HOW DOES IT WORK TO DESTROY LIFE?

Evil Intelligence is a mindset transmitted to human beings from the "dark rulers of this world." People who are not consciously submitted to the will of God are most susceptible to this influence, which is predominantly classified as "mind control." All mind control is "satanic" because it goes against God's intention that His created beings enjoy the freedom to choose.[1]

Mind-control techniques come in various forms, some "organized," such as in Hannah's case. Others come in more spontaneous forms. For instance, a degree of mind control is used when a parent manipulates a child's behavior through chronic verbal and/or psychological abuse—or when a child's family member regularly abuses him or her sexually, threatening to hurt someone if their "secret" gets out. Whether these or similar abuses apply to you or someone else you know, the victims of such abuses become "programmed" over time to think of themselves in negative, harmful ways. Many grow into adulthood full of self-hate, nursing "victim" mentalities—mindsets that make life forever difficult for themselves and the people closest to them.

So, whether a person is a victim of organized Satanic Ritual Abuse or some other form of mind control, the solution for healing is the same—because the wounding comes from the same evil source. Keep reading this chapter, and you will better understand how to overcome the influence of evil intelligence[2] in your own life; likewise, you will learn how to intercede for all the people around you, who have been affected by it to one degree or another.

WHAT IS LUCIFERIANISM?

For hundreds of years, the Illuminati has been bound together by a common world view or ideology and shrouded in oaths
of secrecy. The hidden, core belief that fuels all their goals and
objectives is that Lucifer, the "shining one,"[1] is the true creator
of the universe and mankind.[2] Illuminati is the plural form of the
Latin word "illuminatus," which means "enlightened."

So, it comes as no surprise that the people who comprise
this group worldwide believe Lucifer told them to eat from The
Tree of the Knowledge of Good and Evil so they could become
truly enlightened and superior to all others.[3] God, according to
this version of the Bible story, had told Eve a lie.

Another core belief of the Illuminati is that the world population must ultimately be reduced from the current 7.8 billion[4]
to 500,000,000.[5] This must happen to secure quality of life for
the elite going forward. Also, a one-world government—which
the Illuminati will control—is needed to fulfill the stated population reduction and other related objectives.

Believe it or not, these objectives, clearly representing the
Luciferian world-view can be seen in the form of ten "guide-
lines" engraved on large stones—a structure that mysteriously
appeared in 1980 upon a high hill in Elbert County, Georgia.[6]
Many Christians purport this edifice to be a mockery of the
ten commandments God gave Moses on Mt. Sinai. They claim
1980 began a countdown to the New World Order,[7] based on
the 40-year period between the receipt of the ten commandments and their entrance into the promised land, that is, their
"new" order. The first commandment reads: "Maintain humanity under 500,000,000 in perpetual balance with nature."[8]

In summary, the Illuminati has worked for hundreds of
years to maximize occult technology at macro levels worldwide—the highest levels of government, media,

entertainment, etc.—to accomplish their sinister goals and objectives.

Control, power, and monetary supremacy have been required. As by their tradition, they have operated under a cloak of extreme secrecy—binding members by blood oaths and a system that utilizes bribery and fear tactics to keep them loyal to the cause.[9] These tactics—in combination with the dissemination of misinformation, and the deliberate creation of chaos and disorder, have reinforced their ability to advance in our world the stated goals and objectives.

captivity. Later, the captors drugged Joshua, then "forced" him to beat LaTonya to death with a bludgeon.

Joshua confirms in his autobiography that the psychological torture he experienced when he participated in LaTonya's torture and death is a routine "rites of passage" ritual among Satanists. The story is also a good example of how the two evil sides of the Satanic underworld collide—with organized crime rings providing children to the religious institutions affiliated with Luciferianism for purposes of human sacrifice.

It's hard enough to imagine that evil atrocities of this nature really go on in today's world, let alone in "churches." Yet Paul says it should not surprise us, since *"even Satan transforms himself to appear as an angel of light."*[41]

Preparing to Meet with the Real Jesus

Now, let's address how we might combat Satan's schemes as they trickle down from the top management tiers to the *micromanagement* level, where individual people like Hannah and Joshua, and you and me, have been affected.

To begin, I have discussed with Priscilla many times concerning memory healing and deliverance and how she has used these tools to help Hannah heal from the Satanic Ritual Abuse she suffered as a young child. When it comes right down to it, Priscilla's method is no different than the one I have used with people who are not SRA victims, but who have still suffered at the hand of abusive parents, relatives, spouses, and "friends." Traumatic wounds all come from the same destructive source. They are all demonic. Therefore, they can all be healed in much the same manner: The traumatized "parts" of a person must meet Jesus.

One day the Holy Spirit told Priscilla that when a traumatized part of a person encounters the true Jesus, the Redeemer Jesus—not the counterfeit one who appears in Satanic rituals—she is generally drawn to Him. Therefore, Priscilla's objective is to always "arrange meetings" with the Jesus who can redeem Hannah's parts. However, parts will refuse to cooperate in these meetings if they are overly afraid or angry, that is, plagued by spirits of fear, anger, violence, etc. So, the idea is to get them prepped for a meeting.

When a belligerent part of Hannah comes up, Priscilla's first attempt to prepare her might be, "Can we ask Jesus to come and talk with you about this?"

Priscilla's healing sessions with Hannah are rarely planned, most of the time coming forth spontaneously from various family interactions. So, if a healing session is not possible at the time of the eruption, Priscilla might say, "Holy Spirit, I am asking You to come and lay this part of Hannah to the side until we are able to arrange a meeting with Jesus. And Holy Spirit, I ask that You keep this part of Hannah safe and protected in the meantime."

With either scenario, Priscilla might need to get the antagonizing spirits out of the way temporarily. So, Priscilla might at this point shift and use "the sword of the spirit"—the Word of God being spoken through her own mouth—to accomplish this. This is the authoritative prayer tool described in Chapter Five.

We must never forget, God's words are "alive" and powerful, and when we say them out loud with an authoritative attitude, they can be used to pierce between two things—even two unseen things such as a person's traumatized soul and any spirit(s) that might be attached to it. So, Pricilla might say, "I take the sword of the spirit, and I pierce between the part of Hannah who is so angry and the spirits who are attached to her there! And I bind up these spirits now, in the name of Jesus. You all 'go down' now and wait until I'm ready to deal with you."

When the authoritative words of God are spoken over a stricken person—even when driving down the road with five kids in the car—the spirits who empower the fear, anger, depression, etc., are temporarily put down, bound,[42] and laid to the side. Priscilla has had a lot of practice along these lines. In so doing, she has become more and more aware of the authority Jesus has given her. And she has become convinced that He means for her to use this authority, as often as needed, for His great purposes!

Encountering Jesus in the Traumatic Memory

> But He gives us more and more grace (power of the Holy Spirit, to meet this evil tendency and all others fully). That is why He says, God sets Himself against the proud and haughty, but gives grace [continually] to the lowly (those who are humble enough to receive it). So be subject to God. Resist the devil [stand firm against him], and he will flee from you. Come close to God and He will come close to you. [Recognize that you are] sinners, get your soiled hands clean; [realize that you have been disloyal] wavering individuals with divided interests, and purify your hearts [of your spiritual adultery] (James 4:6–8 AMP).

The objective in memory healing and deliverance is to get a traumatized part healed, break the curses, and send the demons away. The administrator of this healing must have "clean hands and a pure heart." In other words, Priscilla must do her best to stay "clean" spiritually, so she can be effective for Hannah's sake. She visits the courts of heaven frequently, confesses her sins as soon as they occur, applies the blood of Jesus, and receives forgiveness and renewal. She also searches and asks the Holy Spirit to show her anything about her past that would give Satan a "legal" right. This is the essence of maintaining "clean hands" and a "pure heart."

"Hannah, where is Jesus in the room?" Priscilla asked.

"He's here. I'm in a bubble. He's protecting me," Hannah said. In her little girl words, she had told Jesus "her story."

"Hannah, tell Jesus how you are feeling now."

"I'm sad."

"Can you give your 'sad' to Him?"

"Yes."

"Did you give it to Him?"

"Yes."

"What is He saying to you now?"

"That it's ok."

"Hannah, do you forgive the bad people?"

"Yes."

"OK, repeat after me. 'I forgive the bad people who hurt me. And I break the curse of being scared and angry, in Jesus's name.'"

Hanna repeats after Priscilla.

"OK, Hannah (that is, the little 'part' of Hannah who was abused) you can 'go' with Jesus now! You are safe."

Then Priscilla commands all spirits once attached to this particular wound to leave. "In the name of Jesus, I command all spirits of fear, anger, sadness, shame, witchcraft, mind control, and any others attached to this part and her wounds to leave and go to the pit, now!" [43]

Six years ago, when Priscilla was first learning these methods of healing, Hannah's wounded parts would surface daily. Some would talk; others would not. Priscilla's daily prayer was, "Jesus, would you please give me a part who is willing to talk?" Also, "Holy Spirit, would you give me the grace and the discernment I need to deal with this part?"

Sometimes, the evil spirits themselves would manifest. This would typically be a show of convulsing, vomiting, or eyes glazed over as in a trance, etc. The Holy Spirit taught Priscilla that this was nothing more than a demonic "smoke screen" that evil intelligence puts up so she can not engage with Hannah's wounded parts. The spirits know that when the traumatized parts meet with Jesus, they get healed! Then the inevitable occurs: The spirits are "redirected" to the pit. [44]

Regarding casting demons out, Pricilla learned from the Holy Spirit that one might be tempted to do this prematurely, but it's better to wait until the healing of a part is complete. So, when the spirit(s) surface, she learned to tell them to "go down"—not "away." In other words, a spirit may go away if the prayer minister commands him to, but if there is no encounter with Jesus, and no healing or forgiveness coming forth from the victim, a demon's legal right to be there still exists. Therefore, the demon will eventually return and reattach to the same wound. But on the second round, he will bring seven more spirits with him. The person being tormented will be worse off than before![45]

Relating Our Stories to the Big Story

Let me relate the stories of individuals like Hannah, Priscilla, Joshua, you, and me to the big-picture story of Genesis 3—where the serpent gained control of the human mind and psyche for purposes of destroying the image of God in people.

This is easy to explain when the New Testament clearly states in 1 John 5:19 that "the whole world lies under the influence and misery of the Evil One." And the Old Testament prophets heard and recorded utterances such as this:

> Thus [the angel] said, the fourth beast shall be a fourth kingdom on earth, which shall be different from all other kingdoms and shall devour the whole earth, tread it down and break it in pieces and crush it (Daniel 7:23 AMP).

So today, when we observe the pervasive fear so many people in the world are experiencing due to (1) an "out of control" virus, plus, (2) the ongoing racism narrative, and (3) the chaos and unrest caused by political division, we know there is still a pervading evil intelligence that exists at the macro level, trickling down.

The Evil One is *still* "controlling" the human mind, the story of Genesis 3. Indeed, his goal remains the same—to destroy the image of God, that is, minimize our Divine Nature Ability through fear and physical death. And he wants to achieve this in as many people as possible and as quickly as possible, because his time is running out![46]

It is not surprising that when Covid-19 first hit and people were being masked and locked down, my SRA survivor friend, Joshua, was grossly and unexpectedly affected. Routinely, while shopping at Walmart or some such location, he would experience sudden panic attacks. It didn't take long to realize why this was happening: the masks on everyone's faces were causing "flashbacks."

He explained to me recently that, in Satanic rituals, the participants are always masked. The victims tortured and killed are likewise masked. Also, all participants and observers in a ritualistic torture and killing stand in a circle six feet apart!

According to Joshua, masking creates a sense that we have become dehumanized. Isn't this what Satan is trying to do? Take away our ability to see ourselves as "who God created us to be"?

Then God showed Joshua other parallels between the macro story of Genesis 3 and the modern story of Covid-19. He continued, "Satan knows what works. He's been doing it for thousands of years! He knew that all he needed to do was *expand what he had been doing in ritual abuse scenarios to all of mankind.*"

Notice here the parallels between Satanic Ritual Abuse and the fear-induced atmosphere under which we have lived for the better part of two years during the Covid-19 pandemic:

- Masks: These are used to dehumanize people involved in rituals. Likewise, the rules of masking since the Covid outbreak have covered up our faces and thwarted our God-given ability to "express."
- Suffocation: Hypoxia, the deprivation of oxygen to the brain, is a physiological effect used consistently in Satanic Ritual Abuse. Due to Covid-19, constant masking can induce "partial" suffocation and decrease rational thinking.[47]
- Repeated "fear" messages: For a ritual abuse victim, there is a level of terror that is apparent at all times. Since the outbreak of Covid-19, the media's messages have been designed to instill a fear level that shuts down rational thinking.

- Isolation: God made people to be in community and relationship with other people. As a child, Joshua's family moved to another city about every two years—an isolation tactic that curbed his development of meaningful relationships with other people his age. In 2021, we should not have been surprised to find the suicide rate among young people up considerably due to Covid-19 isolation and quarantining. In some parts of the world, call-ins to suicide help lines were up as much as 300%.[48]

- Embracing the narrative: The end-game result of all these tactics is that population develops a "herd" mentality whereby the vast majority "embraces" the false narrative. This means they now accept what the enemy has been saying, believing it to be fact, true, normal. They even view the enemy as "on their side" and someone who has their best interests at heart.[49]

Occult forces control and manipulate all humans, to one degree or another. We know the occult is strong when a person or group of people is hostile and rebellious toward the One True God. Instead of worshipping Him, these people worship knowledge, power, and personal satisfaction—and pursue these at any cost, to obtain power and fortune, through Satan, that is, Lucifer.

Worship of Satan can be either a conscious or unconscious practice, that is, many who are in fact controlled by him may not be aware of it. God made us to "worship"; and we worship someone or something whether we realize it or not. Unconsciously we may worship ourselves, things, careers, other people, etc. The important thing to remember is that worship of any person, thing, or entity other than the One True God is idolatry, that is, the worship of Satan.

Practices closely tied to idolatrous worship are witchcraft,[50] divination through horoscopes or mediums, the use of addictive, mind-altering pharmaceutical drugs, sexual immorality, and murder. Participation in any of these things "opens" the doors to a person's soul. Then spirits of bondage, shame, guilt, and fear enter and attach. Continuing in these behaviors results in progressive spiritual decline, which can end in perpetual spiritual death.

WHAT IS SATANIC RITUAL ABUSE?
From *Born into Battle*, by "Joshua Collins," SRA Survivor

It is (1)"passing their children through the fire to Molech" (a very real, and very brutal ceremony which I witnessed being enacted on at least one occasion that I remember, as a pre-teen); (2) sorcery (a very real invocation of very real demonic entities); (3) witchcraft (the entering into contractual relationships with those demonic entities via the use of ritual magic); (4) sodomy (used particularly in ritual ceremony, in order to facilitate demonic attachment to the individual being victimized); (5) pedophilia; (6) incest (my own parents were my two original, and primary, abusers); (7) orgies; (8) torture; (9) murder; (10) the sacrificing of both animals and human beings, particularly children (as part of ritual ceremonies); (11) the drinking of human blood; (12) the eating of human flesh; (13) and the worship of idols ("Molech" of the Old Testament is one of the idols still worshipped quite extensively to this day).

These practices are the very same ritual magic (witchcraft) practices, which we hear of in the Bible, and which are referred to as "idolatry." Biblical Idolatry = Satanic Ritual Abuse. "And they built the high places of Baal which are in the Valley of the Son of Hinnom, to cause their sons and their daughters to pass through the fire to Molech, which I did not command them, nor did it come into My mind that they should do this abomination, to cause Judah to sin" (Jeremiah 32:35 NKJV).

In other words, any of the above states of mind or activities create a situation where our minds can become controlled by spirits other than the Holy Spirit. Remember, at any point in time, a mind controlled by a spirit other than the Holy Spirit is being controlled by Satan's kingdom, which is the occult.

Now the mind of the flesh [which is sense and reason without the Holy Spirit] is death [death that comprises all the miseries arising from sin, both here and
hereafter]. But the mind of the [Holy] Spirit is life and
[soul] peace [both now and forever]. [That is] because
the mind of the flesh [with its carnal thoughts and pur-
poses] is hostile to God, for it does not submit itself to
God's Law: indeed it cannot (Romans 8:6–7 AMP).

When the Desperate Cry for Help, God Comes!

As horrible as Satanic practices are, when a desperate victim of abuse
cries out for help—even if an abuser himself cries out—God shows up!

Prior to true salvation, Joshua told me he was "a zombie, with no free
will, just reacting to a pre-scripted narrative, with no conscious control
over decisions."[51] Once he cried out for help, several pastors/healers he
found online were available to help navigate him through a process that
involved memory healing and deliverance in the courts of heaven. It was
a tedious process, because the complete transformation of a mind once
controlled by Satan takes time. But Joshua stuck with it.

First, the "parts" of Joshua that had been controlling him had to
meet with Jesus. There were three main ones—with other parts under
those, thirty in all. Over time, as Satan's web of subterfuge got ripped
away, the demons controlling these parts "lost" control. At the same
time, Joshua was discovering the truth about who his real Father was.
His corrupted mindset was changing!

What was Joshua's process? For one, he studied the Bible intensely
to discover what God was really saying and doing. Remember, over the
years, he had been told many lies about the One True God—and about
himself—so his thoughts about both had to be corrected. Also, Joshua
learned that, when "triggered," he had to go straight into the Word of
God and the Presence of God, asking the Holy Spirit to help. This was
the greatest secret he learned—to depend on God's words and presence
through the power of the Holy Spirit, as much as he depended on physical food!

I was so impressed and touched when I heard Joshua interject on a podcast, "I'm sorry, but I feel like I'm getting 'triggered' by some of the things we are talking about. Do you mind if I pause here for one minute and ask the Holy Spirit to help me?" He did, praying out loud for all to hear. It took 30 seconds, but it was powerful. He is so humble about his utter dependence on the One True God![52]

Today, Joshua testifies that after meditating on God's words and learning to always ask for the Holy Spirit's guidance and help, he has a new life, a new authority, and a new Father. He has joined a church and developed some relationships based on godly principles. He is also mentoring several young people, who struggle with addiction. His wife and family continue to support him wholeheartedly.[53]

Likewise, when Priscilla pleaded with God to show up and help her with Hannah, "help" came from the heavenly realm that very night. It was "a pervading and restful peace, a presence," she said, that awakened her and filled the room. Then, when she sat up in the bed to see, "it" pushed her, gently, against the headboard!

How long the Presence lingered, Pricilla was not sure. It was long enough for her to become aware that God's presence is vital, near, loving, and real— and that to get through this life as Hannah's mother, she must have it. It was not going to be an easy task. But God gave Priscilla the same assurance He had given Moses: "My Presence shall go with you, and I will give you rest."[54]

Two weeks later, another helpful and comforting presence came to Priscilla in the night. This time her eyes fixated upon a scroll, floating above her bed. It was radiating light and "spinning" slowly, around, and around.

Then she saw the angel whose large hands held the scroll. He was solemn and accentuated in light, his body bending over into the room from the heavens. As the scroll continued to spin, Priscilla noticed Hebrew words rolling off it into the atmosphere!

Then the angel said, "Eat."

Ezekiel, a prophet of the Old Testament, was also instructed to "eat" the words of God from a scroll.[55] After he did it, God gave him two jobs. "Son of Man, I have made you a watchman to the house of Israel; therefore, hear the word at My mouth and give them warning from Me" (Ezekiel 3:17 AMP).

Per God's instruction, Ezekiel was to speak difficult messages of "lamentation and mourning and woe" to the "rebellious house of Israel." In addition, he was to be their "watchman," or intercessor. This message was exactly the one Priscilla received concerning the work she was to do with Hannah—though Priscilla would be speaking "words of woe" to Hannah's rebellious demons!

As Priscilla would discover, being a "watchman" (*shamar* in Hebrew) and an "intercessor" (*paga* in Hebrew) are intricately related—both words describing a person who is engaged to fight on behalf of someone whose life is in danger.

In other words, an intercessor is someone who "goes between" the evil enemy and the person[56] who needs help, "standing in the gap" for the one who is not able to effectively do this for himself. So, the intercessor "meets" the power of darkness on another person's behalf, to turn the evil away, that is, to *redirect* it. He does this with both God's words spoken through him and God's presence manifested in him.

Then, when the evil is successfully diverted or restrained, the person once in danger becomes "safe." He is "restored" in some sense, either physically or spiritually, or both. The intercessor has become the "enforcer" of the victory that Yeshua, the Christ, has already won on the cross![57]

As in Ezekiel's case, faceoff with evil is never an easy task, but all throughout history God called upon ordinary people to step up to its challenges—humble people who were open to his call, had repented of their own striving and self-idolatry, and knew and acknowledged Him as the One True God. Remember Job, who finally repented, and then prayed for his friends? God was quick to answer that humble prayer. He also restored Job's lost fortunes.

"He will even deliver the one [for whom you intercede] who is not innocent; yes, he will be delivered through the cleanness of your hands" (Job 22:30 AMP).

Final Thoughts About the Redirection of Demons

The process of memory healing, deliverance, and the redirection of demons will become more necessary as we approach the end of time. As more hardcore evidence about sex trafficking and crimes against humanity is gathered and disseminated, criminals will be arrested, and victims will be freed. This will be an unveiling of human suffering and wrongdoing in our country and around the world, so severe, that many people in our midst will need emotional, psychological, and spiritual healing to cope with this news. Perhaps you are one of them.

This doesn't even include the number of victims being freed, who will need help—those who have suffered under the hand of traffickers, abusers, and the elitists who have funded these atrocities. I'm talking about people, especially children, just like Hannah.

All Christians are being called to help alleviate this suffering, even if only in some small way. Joshua's call is to bring awareness of Satanic Ritual Abuse to people like you, who know God and who will now learn to "stand in the gap" for suffering children all over the world.[58]

Priscilla is getting a master's degree in Christian counseling. Her goal is to operate a live-in facility that will be equipped to take in trafficked children—and young women who have been used for reproduction purposes. These abused "image-bearers" will need around-the-clock attention to begin the process of overcoming their traumas through memory healing and deliverance.

Figure out what you can do to help! Not everyone will be motivated or able to take on a high level of responsibility in the fight. But everyone can pray for the children who are coming out of trafficking. Many of you reading this book can financially support groups who are already helping these young people. Some of you may consider becoming a prayer minister or counselor to those who need deliverance.

Shatter the Darkness[59]—the ministry that helped Hannah and Priscilla—is looking for people who want to get trained and ready to help. SRA victims already exist in large numbers.[60] They need our help, our attention, our love, our prayers. They are redeemable! They are just like Hannah and Joshua! With God all things are possible!

The bottom line: If you have gotten this place in Invite Jesus, I pray you have gleaned new insights about evil that will motivate you to now help redirect demons to their place of containment—where they will remain, until God is ready to judge them on the last day.

Certainly, I hope I have inspired you to take care of your own demons. We all have them. When we get our selves disentangled from demons, we can help others get free from theirs!

Now, don't forget, God had no pity for the angels when they sinned but threw them into the lowest, darkest dungeon of gloom and locked them in chains, where they are firmly held until the judgment of torment (2 Peter 2:4 TPT).

> In the same way, there were heavenly messengers in rebellion who went outside their rightful domain of authority and abandoned their appointed realms. God bound them in everlasting chains and is keeping them in the dark abyss of the netherworld until the judgment of the great day (Jude 6 TPT).

My Prayer:

Jesus, I say "yes!" to any assignment You have for me[61]—especially where it comes to "standing in the gap" for people who are seemingly trapped by the enemy with no apparent means of escape. Holy Spirit, be my guide in this endeavor. First, show me how to "get clean" so this process can be most effective.[62] Specifically, give me revelation about how Your blood—applied to my own mind, will and emotions—frees my spirit to resume its rightful position,[63] both here on earth[64] and in heaven![65] Through the blood, my mind is free to receive Your thoughts, feelings, purposes, and ideas. My will is conformed to Your perfect will! My emotions are controlled by You! Now I am ready to use the authority You have given me[66] by "stepping in between"[67] a hurting people and the powers of darkness that are coming against them. Then You and I, together, "push back" on this darkness![68] (You do all the heavy lifting,[69] but you desire my participation.)[70] Give me revelation of this fact: Through the cleanness of "our" hands and the purity of "our" hearts (we are entwined),[71] the demons must be restrained.[72] Thank You, Jesus for allowing me to co-labor with You to finish this important work![73]

Personal Questions to Consider:[74]

What prayer assignments have you been given? Are you willing to "help" the people who have caused you the most pain (that is stand in the gap for them, with Jesus at your side)?

How does this chapter's prayer change your thinking about what God would have you do?

Chapter Seven

REJOICE

"The spirit (neshama) God breathed into man is like a living lamp,
a shining light searching into the innermost chamber of our being"
(Proverbs 20:27 TPT).

Summary: Into every person God has deposited a piece of Himself—
His breath, His inspiration, His imprint, His spirit, His *neshama,*[1] and
it is this "deposit" that has sparked man's body and soul "into life" since
the very beginning.[2] In addition, *neshama* is the "inspiration" that sets
humans apart from the rest of creation and gives us the "potential" to
grow up into the image of Jesus.

Paul describes this apparent growth opportunity in 1 Corinthians
6:17 when he says a believer's spirit can in some mysterious way become
"mingled" or joined to the Holy Spirit.[3] Of course the enemy's objective
is to destroy the potential God promises through such union. But the
Holy Spirit is always pursuing us, always providing opportunities that
will increase our awareness of the availability of this connection. The
reality is this: when a believer has revelation of the joining together of his
spirit to the Holy Spirit, a supernatural partnership between himself and
God is manifested.

"For it is not from man that we draw our life but from God as we are
being joined to Jesus, the Anointed One. And now he is our God-given
wisdom, our virtue, our holiness, and our redemption (1 Corinthians 1:30
TPT).

As the believer's ongoing awareness of this union continues, his connection to the Holy Spirit is further supported, stimulated, and strengthened. At the same time his capacity for spirit "growth" expands. When spirit capacity grows, the strongholds of the flesh are diminished. Authority increases. Joy abounds!

Scanning the fairway, Larry approached the tee box with a swagger. He was having a good day—one under par after four holes. Everything about this day was good. Azure sky, 75 degrees. Good cigar. And he was playing alone. No distractions. It was the same reason he liked playing Solitaire. He could tune everything out for an inordinate amount of time and have no real thoughts about anything at all. A good way to destress. He took one more puff of his Padrone and laid it down in a safe spot on the ground and then placed the ball on the tee.

Dog leg to the right. Two-fifty, straight down the middle, he thought, planting his feet. As before, he took a confident swing. Crack! This time, an errant ball went straight up and curved far to the right, 150 yards down the green toward a small grove of trees near the backyard of a course-side home. He squinted to see the landing. Oddly, at that very moment, a figure standing in the distance toppled over like a tin man, falling straight back, face up.

Larry gasped, his club slipping out of his hand and falling to the ground.

"Oh, my God!" It was a desperate cry for help as he took off in the direction of the collapsed figure, leaving his gear, cart, and cigar, behind.

"Jesus, help me!" Larry ran as fast as he could, but it seemed slow motion was all he could muster. In the distance, he could see two bystanders run to the scene.

He pushed to run faster. "Help me!" was all he could think. Then, without warning, a shocking spew of jumbled syllables interspersed with cries and groans erupted from his mouth. What he was saying he did not know. It was gully washer of unintelligible, mumbo jumbo, flowing continuously, uncontrollably.

As he made his way, Larry could see the bystanders hovering over the body, a man. One gestured wildly and yelled across the yard for more help. From a distance, the fallen figure appeared lifeless!

Approaching the scene, Larry tried to shut off the gibber, talk normally, and listen all at the same time. Thank goodness, the people assisting didn't seem to notice his strange tongue. All their focus was on the ashen-faced, seemingly lifeless victim, Chuck, who looked to be in his early 70s. Apparently, he had been struck by the ball square in the middle of his forehead!

Chuck was still stiff and not moving. Was he breathing? By this time Larry's gibberish had stopped, but his heart was still beating wildly. He tried to focus on being calm and engaged, praying silent prayers in his head for the helpless man, so as to get God's much needed attention.

But Chuck was still not moving, and the moments stretched out way too long.

Finally! A stirring!

The medics arrived and went quickly about their business. Now Chuck was talking, though his speech was a bit slurred. In no time he was on the gurney and hoisted into the ambulance.

Larry gave Chuck's friends all his contact info, and they had agreed to be in touch. Then he trudged back to his abandoned golf cart. Thank God Chuck wasn't dead! But would he be ok? What if Chuck did not completely recover? Would Larry get sued?

Larry's thoughts were consuming him as he climbed into the cart and turned back to the clubhouse. No more golf this day. He would nervously wait in his hotel room for updates.

Later, Larry was surprised to hear Chuck himself on the other end of the line, alert, and cordial. He was going to stay overnight at the hospital for observation.

"What can I do to help?" Larry pleaded. "Can I give you some money for the hospital bills?"

"Oh no, no, that won't be necessary," Chuck insisted. "I have excellent insurance. Don't you worry about a thing. It was an accident. I'm just fine."

Larry hung up the phone almost in disbelief. What a nice guy, Chuck. "God intervened!" Larry exclaimed to me later. "For a minute there, we all thought Chuck might be dead!"

Union with the Holy Spirit

But the one who joins himself to the Lord is mingled into one spirit with him (1 Corinthians 6:17 TPT).

To think I touted the union of the Christian's human spirit to the Holy Spirit, as explained in 1 Corinthians 6:17 and other passages, my whole adult life. But I didn't understand completely the practicality and the reality of this teaching until a long time later.

"Why didn't you tell me?" I asked Larry.

"It was just too weird and even embarrassing," he explained. "I was so desperate. It was a desperate prayer of some sort. And I have never been able to explain it until now."

I had purposefully directed the conversation that night to "spiritual gifts," a topic the Apostle Paul discusses in I Corinthians 14 and Romans 8—and one that has been long debated within the Christian church ever since. I mentioned it because I wanted to introduce Larry to the concept of "groaning"[4] and speaking in an intimate prayer language.

I had recently begun this practice, after resisting it my entire Christian life. And I had hesitated to tell Larry about it until then because I was sure it would seem very bizarre to this former Catholic, who at that time, was going to become my husband.

When I did finally tell him, I was surprised to find that he wasn't shocked at all, just relieved.

"Remember Chuck?" he said.

> And in a similar way, the Holy Spirit takes hold of us in our human frailty to empower us in our weakness. For example, at times we don't even know how to pray, or know the best things to ask for. But the Holy Spirit rises up within us to super-intercede on our behalf, pleading to God with emotional sighs too deep for words. God, the searcher of the heart, knows fully our longings, yet he also understands the desires of the Spirit, because the Holy Spirit passionately pleads before God for us, his holy ones, in perfect harmony with God's plan and our destiny (Romans 8:26-27 TPT).

I have to admit, the Holy Spirit manifested in a very unexpected way the day Larry's golf ball hit Chuck in the head. I now believe God's Spirit "spoke" something into Larry's spirit. In other words, He told him "what" to pray on Chuck's behalf.

Otherwise, how could Larry know what to do or say? He had not yet been exposed to or trained in these spiritual happenings. And why Larry? Was he the only willing receptacle around? God knew the answers to all these questions. But the point is, the right prayers for Chuck got "prayed" into the atmosphere "through" Larry—a person who had never experienced the Spirit language or utterances God gives!

In Larry's weakness God's Spirit was strong.[5] Chuck got delivered from who-knows-what and Larry was taught about the practical applications of praying in the Spirit—all in one shebang. God is just full of pleasant and joyful surprises, isn't He?

The Breath of God in Us is a Bridge

In a recent study of the book of Genesis, I came across the Hebrew word *neshama*—by definition "breath" or "blast, spirit, inspiration, that which gives life." Understanding this word has revolutionized my understanding of healing and deliverance.

Now what I am getting ready to explain is, perhaps, the most important teaching in this book as regards our ability to get healed and then turn things around for both ourselves and others. It has to do with the unique way in which God made us—and how this "wiring" allows us to respond to Him and then receive back from Him.

Let me digress for one minute and remind you of my spiritual roots. Remember, I came from a churchgoing, moralistic family. My dad was a preacher, who loved God and was attempting to live a pure life! But we were still dysfunctional! What I know to be true is this: No matter how "moral" a family might be on the surface, if the Holy Spirit is not alive and present, and functioning at a high level, there is dysfunction. As Paul reminds us, life lived by "sense and reason without the Holy Spirit is death [death that comprises all the miseries arising from sin, both here and hereafter]."[6]

Now, in my family, I was always aware that something was wrong— and that we needed to "get fixed." But I had no hope that anyone in my family would change their ways or their thinking. We, like so many families, were trapped. Of course, I didn't know God had designed a way for getting people out of their traps—a plan that involved a connection to the power of the Holy Spirit through the breath of God already in us.

"Yahweh-God scooped up a lump of soil, sculpted a man, and blew into his nostrils the breath (*neshama*) of life. The man came alive—a living soul (*nephesh*)" (Genesis 2:7 TPT).

As you can see from Genesis 2:7, the soul *(nephesh)* and the spirit, or breath *(neshama)*, are two entities, set apart, with distinct functions and contributions. The breath of God, or *neshama*, did two things at the time of human creation. One, it blew in as a creative force and caused the dirt, a "lifeless" form, to be made "alive." Logically, this was the same point at which blood was first created in humans, as "life" is in the blood.[7] In addition, the *neshama* provided the ingredients needed to form the mind, will, and emotions of the first humans, their souls.

So, using this account of human creation in Genesis 2 as the basis for our inner-healing study, we see that the *neshama* gives us the ingredients we need to develop a physical, emotional, and intellectual life. In other words, the breath of God "sparked" into being our "potential" as regards the ability (1) to choose through the will—and then (2) to express life through the mind and the emotions. As our awareness of these realities grows and develops, our "personalities" expand. This means the *neshama* also gives us the ability (3) to "develop" or "grow up."

But there's more! The *neshama* is a God-given ingredient or force, that is, breath, life, and spirit — but it is also a bridge upon which we can "link" to the Holy Spirit. It is in fact the joining together of the *neshama* to the Holy Spirit that allows us to have relationship with God the Father.

"But the one who joins himself to the Lord is mingled into one spirit with him" (1 Corinthians 6:17 TPT).

Our "revelation" of this union with the Holy Spirit is what gives us joy and strength. It is what empowers us to overcome our hurts, habits, and hang-ups so we can "grow up" into the image of Jesus.

You will show me the path of life: in Your presence is fullness of joy, at Your right hand there are pleasures forevermore (Psalm 16:11 AMP).

Then [Ezra] told them, "Go your way, eat the fat, drink the sweet drink, and send portions to him for whom nothing is prepared: for this day is holy to our Lord. And be not grieved and depressed, for the joy of the Lord is your strength and stronghold" (Nehemiah 8:10 AMP).

Jesus said, "I am a sprouting vine and you're my branches. As you live in union with me as your source, fruitfulness will stream from within you — but when you live separated from me you are powerless. (v.14) My purpose for telling you these things is so that the joy that I experience will fill your hearts with overflowing gladness!" (John 15:5,14 TPT).

Again, this understanding of union is critical to our joy growth. However, we can't be so exuberant about activating this connection that we overlook *first things first*. To activate the connection and relationship with the Holy Spirit, we must first "turn." In other words, we must look at Jesus, repent, and embrace His will. (See Chapter Two.)

Only then can we develop an "awareness" or have a "revelation," concerning "union" with the Holy Spirit. This is it: Our human spirits, which God "breathed" into us in the beginning—but which have previously been "dead" unto God due to sin—have now suddenly come to "life." Through repentance, our spirits have been "released" to join or "bridge" over to the Holy Spirit. Our spirits have become "born again."[8] The crux of the matter is that a once-dead spirit has come to "life."[9]

None of this could happen if God had not provided, at our inception, the *neshama*, the breath, the "bridge" we need to connect with His Spirit, the Holy Spirit.

The Neshama is Life's Perfect Filter, Creating Joy, Even in Dire Circumstances

After rebirth, a Christian believer has an incredible opportunity to filter life through his spirit's connection to the Holy Spirit, become "inspired" by God's divine understanding and revelation, and to experience joy.

> But there is [a vital force] a spirit [of intelligence] (ruach)[10] in a man, and the breath of the Almighty (neshama) gives men understanding (Job 32:8 AMP).

> [It is] the Spirit of God (ruach) that made me [which has stirred me up], and the breath of the Almighty (neshama) that gives me life [which inspires me] (Job 33:4 AMP)

> But I have trusted, leaned on, and been confident in Your mercy and loving-kindness; my heart shall rejoice and be in high spirits in Your salvation (Psalm 13:5 AMP).

Of course, in a perfect-life scenario, every created human would choose to join his spirit to the Holy Spirit, become "born again," live in union with Him, and be directed by Him. In addition, every born-again believer would remain "aware" of his connection to the Holy Spirit. Therefore, his spirit would be always in proper alignment, that is, always operating from the "core" of his identity.

With all this said, a human spirit—again, in connection with the Holy Spirit—would be the perfect "filter" through which every-day-life events would pass. In other words, the human spirit would always have the divine understanding and inspiration needed to make sense of life events "coming at him." And his responses to life would always be "God-inspired." He would be full of joy, even in the midst of a trial, as the Apostle Peter describes:

> Through our faith, the mighty power of God constantly guards us until our full salvation is ready to be

revealed in the last time. May the thought of this cause
you to jump for joy, even though lately you've had to put
up with the grief of many trials (1 Peter 1:5-6 TPT).

In other words, a "God-inspired" life would always look like this:

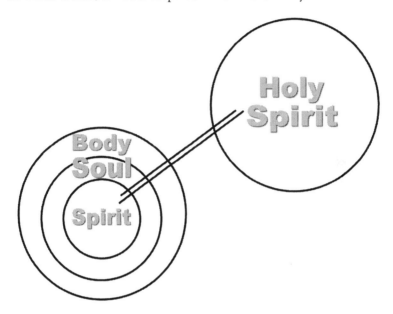

However, as delineated and explained in previous chapters of this
book, we live in a world that is oppressive and confusing—one controlled by an evil enemy,[11] who seeks to kill and destroy our minds,
wills, and emotions (our souls, the *nephesh*) and who tries to keep our
spirits from connecting to the power of the Holy Spirit. He does this
through lies, deceit, the temptation of sin and all the pain and misery
that arise from it.[12]

And when our souls have been greatly harmed in life, tainted by Satan's
lies, our sin, and other entanglements, they are divided and weak. Many
of our "parts" are suffering, still receiving Satan's messages. And when
these parts get "triggered," they "act up," demanding all the attention!

Consequently, as life continues, the *neshama,* this very essence of
God in us—the divine element that has given us our "potential" in the
first place—becomes covered over by a thick web of enemy "subterfuge."

Over time, this essence, breath, spirit, becomes so "covered up," so entangled, it is "suffocated" by the lies of the enemy. Our human spirit cannot get or maintain a strong connection to the Holy Spirit. It has fallen out of proper alignment. Hence the Psalmist cries, "Let my passion for life be restored, tasting joy in every breakthrough you bring to me!" (Psalm 51:12 TPT)[13]

There are two ways to perceive what is going on when our spirit, soul and body are out of sync with the Holy Spirit.

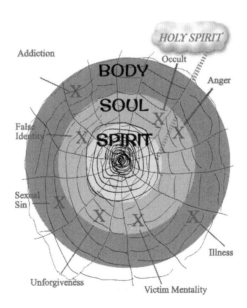

This is what the enemy has been trying to achieve all along! The *neshama* is still within. And if we have in fact been born again, it still has a connection to the Holy Spirit, though perhaps hanging by a thin strand. But the Spirit of God in us is no longer the filter through which our life passes. The damaged soul (*nephesh*) has become life's filter. It has become the core of who we are. And when that happens, we get into big trouble.

When Adam and Eve were ashamed, fearful, deceitful, murderous, etc., they were filtering life through their fallen souls, which was also a fallen "mindset," that is, their "flesh." Their spirits, once "alive" unto God, still held their God-given "potential." But when sin entered the picture, their spirits became "dead" unto Him, no longer properly "connected." As a result, they continued to fall short of their potential, the destiny God had in mind for them from the beginning. This is how their "connection" to God looked after they "fell":

The difference came when Eve chose to worship Lucifer instead of the One True God. At that moment she became controlled and directed by human reason apart from the Holy Spirit—which resulted in a life of sin and all the miseries arising from it. (See Chapter One.)

> Now the mind of the flesh [which is sense and rea-
> son without the Holy Spirit] is death [death that com-
> prises all the miseries arising from sin, both here and
> hereafter]. But the mind of the {Holy] Spirit is life and
> [soul] peace [both now and forever] (Romans 8:6 AMP).

The Neshama is a Light-Giving Revelation

"The spirit God breathed (*neshama*) into man is like a living lamp, a shining light searching into the innermost chamber of our being" (Proverbs 20:27 TPT).

Most often, a person needs to invite Jesus to come and heal a soul wound, which the enemy of his soul has kept "hidden." This is where most of the people I help are stuck. They can't seem to put their finger on those things which have been hidden.

But to be healed and then delivered, we must typically "find" the things "hidden"—those things that are covered over, veiled, deep within, that is, traumatic memories that have been forgotten—or DNA imprints embedded through generational iniquity.

For purposes of healing ourselves—or helping others get healed—we must learn to ask God to show us anything that would assist us along these lines. Of course, the more aware we become of our connection to God's spirit, the stronger that connection becomes, and the bigger our spirits (in union with the Holy Spirit) get. The more diminished our flesh becomes, the better we are at "hearing" what God is telling us and "seeing" what He is showing us.

This explains why *neshama* "training" is so important. One, it is the bridge to the gift of union with the Holy Spirit, which comes to us through Jesus.

> Then God exalted him to his right hand upon the
> throne of highest honor. And the Father gave him the
> authority to send the promised Holy Spirit, which is
> being poured out upon us today. This is what you're see-
> ing and hearing! (Acts 2:33 TPT).

Two, understanding the connection between our spirits and the Holy Spirit, gives us access to God's thoughts feelings, purposes, and power—which is the key to our inner healing and the subsequent joy that comes from that experience.

> Those who live in the Spirit are able to carefully evaluate all things, and they are subject to the scrutiny of no one but God. For 'Who has ever intimately known the mind of the Lord Yahweh well enough to become his counselor?' Christ has, and we possess Christ's perceptions (1 Corinthians 2:15–16 TPT).

> But for those who have been chosen to follow him, both Jews and Greeks, he is God's mighty power, God's true wisdom, and our Messiah (1 Corinthians 1:24 TPT).

In other words, because we have the breath of God in us, we can live in union with Him and know the thoughts, feelings, and purposes of His heart. He will tell us what we need to know; even those hidden things about our past will be revealed. When we live in a revelation of union with the Holy Spirit, our internal world radically changes!

However, an awareness of union with the Holy Spirit requires practice, focus, and time. I believe memory healing is a critical part of this training.

Neshama Training Helps Us Sense God's Love

I have seen God bless so many people through their memory healings, with sudden knowledge of things that had been previously hidden, a sort of "connecting the dots" experience, if you will. It was His way of saying, "Not only do I want to heal you and be real to you in your life right now, but I want to show you how much I have always loved you—how I have always been there for you, even when you didn't realize it. I have always had a plan and purpose for you, which is now being fulfilled!"

In my first book, *Finding the Secret Place: Eight Keys to Experiencing God's Presence*, I share how I came to know God at age 19. I had come to a point in life where nothing made sense. There was confusion, inner

WHAT IS THE *NESHAMA*?

According to Genesis, the breath of God, *neshama* in Hebrew, is the Spirit of God, a force that (1) creates blood and gives "life" to forms that are "without life." It is also the "spark" (2) that brings into human existence the soul (*nephesh*)—the mind, will, and emotions.[1] (3) Last, this spirit of God is a "deposit" that gives all humans the ability to become "born again"—at which time man's spirit becomes "alive" unto God by being "joined" to the Holy Spirit. By extension, this union of a believer's spirit to the Holy Spirit provides (4) the ability to be "inspired" by Him and to "grow up" into His image.] (5) For memory healing and deliverance purposes, the *neshama* is our life's perfect filter, helping us to process life properly, as it happens, but also as we reflect on past or future circumstances. In this sense, it is a lamp which gives revelation to those things in us and around us that have been hidden from us by the enemy.

conflict, and little peace. The watershed experience came when I witnessed how out of whack some of the people in my dad's church were, coupled with how dysfunctional my mom and dad seemed to be in terms of handling the situation. It was then that I knew I needed a real relationship with the Almighty, not a superficial one like so many of the people I knew. I repented, in tears, on my bed at home. I remember this distinctly. I just wanted to know God like some of my new friends at college and like Bernice, the lady I mentioned in Chapter Three.

Don't get me wrong, my dad loved God and sincerely served Him his entire life. He was a good man, not egotistical at all, very humble. However, to some of the church members' dismay, Dad was weak where it came to evangelism. It just wasn't his way! He was Presbyterian! As I have said before, I now realize that the real problem was not Dad's unwillingness to have altar calls or his inability to speak more forcefully

with people about the need for salvation. It was his limited understanding of how the Holy Spirit operates.

He simply had never been exposed to the workings of the Holy
Spirit. He had always been taught and believed that the gifts of the Spirit
were restricted to the time of the Gospels—and that the Holy Spirit
Movement[14] had divided many churches. So, he shied away from it
entirely. But without question, a fuller understanding of the Holy Spirit
would have given him the mind of Christ talked about in 1 Corinthians
Chapter Two. With God's words in his mind and in his heart and in his
conversations,[15] he would have had more confidence! He would have
"heard" what God was saying about the problems that were erupting
in the church. Also, God would have counseled him, through the Holy
Spirit, about how to handle the people, who were hurting and "acting
out" in the church.

As I continued in my own memory healings about a year or so ago, a
"disappointment" came to mind. I was disappointed that, as a child, my
dad never taught me one-on-one at home much about the Bible or the
need to have a viable relationship with God. Hence, I was "late" coming
to know Him, by my own estimation.

The associated memory I recalled occurred at age eight. My dad had
called Mom on the phone and said, "Send Emily over to the study, so I
can talk with her about joining the church tomorrow." All these years I
remember the emphasis to be on "joining the church," not "coming into
a relationship with God."

In my memory, I was engulfed in a big chair in Daddy's office at the
church. He was sitting across from me near the typewriter, telling me
that I would join the church the next day, and that this was going to be
the most important decision and event of my life. He quizzed me on the
questions that I would be asked, such as "Are you a sinner?" And "Do
you confess your sin and the need to be forgiven through faith in the
death, burial, resurrection and ascension of Jesus?" Of course, being the
compliant type anyway, I said "yes" to all the questions.

Now at some point in the memory "dialogue" with Daddy, I had
asked Jesus to come and be with me there in the big chair. Note: I didn't
literally "see" Him in my visual mind. Some people do! But I had a strong

impression that drove my imagination to "see" Him there. I was sitting in His lap! And He was holding me close, while Daddy was talking to me.

Then suddenly, I saw Jesus kneeling by Daddy's chair! And He had His hand on Daddy's arm, as though He were blessing him. Daddy had been looking at me the whole time. But Jesus's presence caught his attention, and he looked over at Him, still kneeling by His side. That's when Daddy stopped talking. He was overcome by the Presence, his eyes fixed on Jesus.

My sense in the memory encounter was that Jesus was healing my dad, restoring the joy of his salvation, taking his disappointments, and forgiving his failures. At that moment, I was able to forgive Daddy for being less than what I needed at the time. I began to realize that he truly was doing the best he could with what he had. I recalled that his own dad abandoned him through abuse, drunkenness, divorce, and premature death.

A few months after my memory encounter with Dad and Jesus, I was at a birthday party for a friend, where I happened to be chit-chatting with an older gentleman in his 80s by the name of Dr. Dean. Now Dr. Dean had a reputation for being an anointed prophet. I had heard my friends speak of him prior to this event. So, I wasn't entirely surprised when Dr. Dean blurted out, "How old were you when you came to know the Lord?"

"Well, I was 19," I said, the answer I always gave when asked that question.

"The Holy Spirit just told me you were eight," he said. "And the call on your life is so great that Satan has tried to take you out around eight to ten times. You might not be aware of them all," he continued with a relaxed air.

"Really!" I was taking it all in. I dismissed the part about my life hanging in the balance and addressed the age-of-salvation issue, instead. "I have always thought that I was nineteen. But I can see how it might be true that I was eight. Well, well. What a pleasant surprise!" I was thinking about the recent memory-encounter, which I eventually got around to telling Dr. Dean about.

To you, the reader, what I learned from the prophet that day might not seem like that big of a deal. But I was overwhelmed to think that my dad was the one who led me to the Lord! For too many years I thought he had failed.

Later, I couldn't help but think that the memory healing with me, Dad, and Jesus, just a few months prior, somehow triggered this chain of events. The Holy Spirit downloaded into Dr. Dean the truth about something that I had been addressing in my own spirit through the memory healing. It was as though Dr. Dean's "union" with the Holy Spirit interfaced, or intersected, with my "union." Then Dr. Dean was able to communicate to me God's heart, so I could know the truth about my dad, something that had been hidden.

Perhaps it's a small thing in the scheme of things. But God wants me to have it all. Nothing is too small or insignificant where it comes to me, His child!

"For the Lord God is a Sun and Shield; the Lord bestows [present] grace and favor and [future] glory (honor, splendor, and heavenly bliss)! No good thing will He withhold from those who walk uprightly" (Psalm 84:11 AMP).

Union with God Redeems Losses

Little four-year-old Barbara Jean was standing alone on the street corner beside a neighborhood park in Ridgewood, New Jersey. The park was situated about a half mile down the street from the apartment building where she and her family lived. Tears streaming, Barbara Jean looked up and down the street again and again, but her dad was nowhere in sight.

Surely, he did not expect her to cross the street alone! Mother would be furious at them both! Yet her keen sense, even at age four, told her that he might not return any time soon. He had gotten so angry with her earlier in the park that he had smacked her across the face, taking off, and leaving her on the corner.

Now she was in a state of panic and fear that would follow her for many years to come.

Today, almost sixty years later, Barbara Jean is a Ministry Coordinator for a large Assemblies of God Church. She has been a believer in Jesus for more than thirty years and is a thriving Christian.

But until she met Jesus, she was a rebel, in every sense of the word.

For example, at 16, she was sexually promiscuous and had an abortion. Perhaps being raised Catholic in NYC with a broken man for a

father—a heavy-handed Irish immigrant living under the stress of working several jobs to provide for a wife and six kids—made her rebellious,
she says. And full of fear, she adds.

Perhaps this same fear—a fear of losing control—would drive her
to become a top sales agent for a large life insurance company by her
mid-twenties.

By then, all seemed well to outsiders looking in. Barbara Jean was
happily married and successful beyond her years. Yet her inner world,
unseen by even those closest to her, was crashing in. Now she was unex-
pectantly pregnant again, and terrified to face the reality of having a
child and possibly jeopardizing her thriving career.

Immediately, she planned another abortion to avert this fear.

Thankfully, two individuals, a neighbor and a Christian friend at
work, convinced her to cancel the abortion—an hour before the sched-
uled appointment!

Three years later, with two small children in tow, Barbara Jean found
herself in another panic mode. This time her father was dying in a NYC
hospital a few hours away. Recklessly speeding down the interstate, she
was fearful that she would not arrive on time. To make matters worse,
she was having "homicidal and suicidal visions." Basically, she was terrified that she would harm her own children.

"God, don't let me crash the car!" Barbara Jean sobbed, as she continued weaving down the highway. The voices in her head didn't make
things any easier. They were saying, "You are not worthy to be a mother!
You have got to go—or you will kill them both!"

The panic was really setting in now. Amid the sobs, Barbara Jean
screamed at her three-year-old daughter to sing.

Barbara Jean: "Gerilyn! Sing! A song! Any song!"

Gerilyn: "I don't know a song."

Barbara Jean, emphatically: "Yes, you do! Sing!" This was an attempt
to block the voices and stay grounded in reality, while driving, she relates.

Gerilyn, feebly: "Mary had a little lamb."

Barbara Jean: "Louder!"

Gerilyn: "Little lamb, little lamb."

Barbara Jean: "Louder!"

Gerilyn screamed: "Mary had! a little! lamb! his fleece! was! White! as snow!"

Finally, they made it to the hospital. Barbara Jean's dad had rebounded. And the kids were hyper. And she needed a cigarette. So she said to her sister, "I'm taking the kids to the park."

Thank God for the park! It was a big park with a duck pond, trails, and swings. It was winter and cold, but the kids didn't mind. They could feed the ducks and swing, while Barbara Jean smoked.

She looked around. There was only one lady there with her little son. He and Gerilyn quickly made friends over by the swings, while Barbara Jean managed her 18-month-old a short distance away.

"My fafa was sick, and we were driving," Gerilyn said to the lady and boy. "My mom was crying, and she told me to sing Mary Had a Little Lamb. My fafa is dying."

It didn't take long for the lady to come near Barbara Jean. "Your dad is sick. Does he know Jesus as His Lord and Savior?"

"This day couldn't get any worse!" Barbara Jean mumbled under her breath. "A Jesus freak!"

"I don't know what my dad believes," she snapped, then turned away.

"My dad died twelve years ago from bone cancer," the young woman said.

Gerilyn and the woman's little son were on the horseys. She followed Barbara Jean.

Then, mysteriously, Barbara Jean heard another voice saying, "You were crying and screaming all the way here, asking for help. Just listen!"

To which the lady declared, "The devil is after you!"

Then she grabbed Barbara Jean by the arm and spoke with an authoritative voice, "But he can't touch you, in Jesus's name!"

Suddenly, tears began streaming down Barbara Jean's face. What this gal was saying was true! The voices, the fears, the horrid visions, the chaos and no good. She had everything—a successful career, a wonderful husband, beautiful children—yet she had nothing. And it was all a big dark secret. No one knew about her misery. She had such an ability to cover things up—so nothing odd could be seen or detected.

No one had known but God—and now this woman, a missionary on furlough, who had appeared from out of nowhere at just the right time. Barbara Jean flung herself into the woman's embrace—a flood of peace coming over her like never before.

Barbara Jean and I met about four years ago. She was in a group I led, where we read and studied my book, *Finding the Secret Place*. When I told Barbara Jean about how I was delving into the memory healing aspect of experiencing God and living in union with Him, coupled with learning to "exchange" wrong things for right things, that is, allowing God to "redeem our losses," she was intrigued and wanted to meet privately about it.

Later when we got together on the back patio of her home, she confessed she had dealt with fear her whole life.

"When did you first remember having such intense fear?" I asked.

"I was about four. I was in the park with my father," she began.

So, we asked Jesus to come and stand with little Barbara Jean on the corner down the street from her apartment building. It was a very sweet encounter. Her dad showed up, saw Jesus standing there with his daughter, and broke down in shame. Jesus, who towered over them both like a giant, said to him, "You are forgiven."

Then Jesus extended His arms, and Barbara Jean's dad fell into His embrace. Barbara Jean was able to see her dad for the first time as a man who had no tools, powerless over his ways. There were more tears, grown-up tears, there on the patio. Finally, Barbara Jean had forgiven her dad for the many losses she had experienced in childhood due to his violent anger and all the fear that had been induced from it. She didn't view him any more as "a dad who'd failed."

But there was more revelation to come. When we were finished with the memory healing, I said to Barbara Jean, "Wow, what's with all the parks? It seems like two of the most significant moves of God in your life occurred in parks!"

Barbara Jean looked at me with surprise. I had no idea what would come next.

"Oh my gosh, it was the *same* park!" Her eyes were brimming with tears of joy at the thought. God had been there all along. He had heard her four-year-old cries. Then He had drawn her back to the very place, where she had made her first conscious cry out to Him.

In the end, that same neighborhood park symbolized the losses *and* the redemption! God would use it as a visual illustration to show Barbara Jean how He had taken her full circle—how He had connected all the dots of her life. He had also restored her bad memory and set her on a new path, one filled with renewed joy and fresh revelation, along with an ability to overcome lingering fears!

"I will be glad and rejoice[16] in Your mercy and steadfast love, because You have seen my affliction. You have taken note of my life's distresses" (Psalm 31:7 AMP).

We Rejoice in the Light, Life and Love of God

> Those who walk in darkness have seen a radiant light shining upon them. They once lived in the shadows of death, but now a glorious light has dawned! Lord, you have multiplied the nation and given them overwhelming joy! They are ecstatic in your presence and rejoice like those who bring in a great harvest and those who divide up the spoils of victory! (Isaiah 9:2–3 TPT).

For almost two years, I led a group of women in a weekly Bible study/ prayer time. The purpose of the group was "to explore new biblical realities." What we had in common was that we wanted to take things to another level. We especially wanted to begin operating in higher levels of healing and deliverance. I didn't really know for sure where we were going with it, except that we were to follow the theme of God's Light, Life, and Love.

Early on, I developed a new prayer pattern whereby our prayer team would lift people "up" into the throne room where Jesus is. This could be someone in our immediate presence, but most often it was someone who was not. In our prayer imagination, we would take these people by the hand and "sit" them right at the feet of Jesus—where they were subject to His Light, Life and Love.

We were all coming to realize that being in God's presence tends to change everything. So, through our lifting-up prayers, we hoped to stir up, affect, and change the people we were praying for—through the realities of God's Light, Life, and Love pouring down upon them.

First, we asked God to shine His Light into the person's soul, that is his mind, his will, and his emotions—and to expose and drive out any darkness that was consuming him. Then we asked God to reveal any issues or problems at hand—and to let that person know how he might, with God's help, go about fixing them.

Then we thanked God for His revelation light and the work He was doing in response to our presence prayers. Last, we would "declare" out loud: "Darkness is being exposed and driven out! Revelation is being received! New thoughts are being introduced! In Jesus's name and because of His blood!"

We did the same thing with God's Life and Love. We asked Jesus to breathe His Life into our person—the same breath God breathed into Adam and Eve in Genesis 2:7, the *neshama*! We imagined that the breath, Spirit, life, and nature of God was filling him up and healing him at all levels—body, soul, and spirit.

Last we asked God to wrap this person up in a blanket of *agape*[17] love—which never fails, which transforms the spirit, which can be felt in the heart, and which drives out all fear, anxiety, and frustration. Then we declared that this person was full to overflowing with a fresh revelation of God's life and love, transformed by His nature, obedient to His ways and purposes, and calm and peaceful in his life circumstances.

Our group was especially eager to see how these presence prayers might affect those people in our lives who seemed a bit more resistant to the deep things of God. Do you know the old saying, "You can lead a horse to water, but you can't make him drink"? Well, that's exactly how we felt about some of our dearest loved ones.

At this point we were committed to praying and lifting them "up," but we were counting on God's Light, Life and Love to do all the work from that point on. We were also mindful of what Priscilla said as noted in Chapter Six: When a person has opportunity to interface with the "real" Jesus, things begin to happen!

And then God announced, "Let there be light," and light burst forth! And God saw the light as pleasing and beautiful; he used the light to dispel the darkness (Genesis 1:3–4 TPT).

Life came into being because of him, for his life is light for all humanity. And this Living Expression is the Light that bursts through gloom—the Light that darkness could not diminish! (John 1:4–5 TPT).

Whatever the revelation light exposes, it will also correct, and everything that reveals truth is light to the soul (Ephesians 5:13 TPT).[18]

Jesus said, "The thief comes only to steal and kill and destroy. I came that they may have and enjoy life, and have it in abundance [to the full, till it overflows]" (John 10:10 AMP).

Jesus repeated his greeting, "Peace to you!" And he told them, "Just as the Father has sent me, I'm now sending you." Then, taking a deep breath, he blew[19] on them and said, "Receive the Holy Spirit" (John 20:21–22 TPT).

Jesus said, "I have made Your Name known to them and revealed Your character and your very Self, and I will continue to make (You) known, that the love which You have bestowed upon Me may be in them [felt in their hearts] and that I [Myself] may be in them" (John 17:26 TPT).

Love is large and incredibly patient[20] (1 Corinthians 13:4 TPT).

Love is a safe place of shelter, for it never stops believing the best for others. Love never takes failure as defeat, for it never gives up (1 Corinthians 13:7 TPT).

There is no fear in love [dread does not exist], but full-grown (complete, perfect) love turns fear out of doors and expels every trace of terror! For fear brings with it the thought of punishment, and [so] He who is afraid has not reached the full maturity of love [is not yet grown into love's complete perfection] (1 John 4:18 AMP).

Breakthrough Comes in Unexpected Ways

Just about everyone in our presence-prayer group had a dysfunctional immediate or extended family member in mind to lift "up" into the Light, Life, and Love of God. In addition, we all had people in our families, who perhaps knew the Lord but had become misguided or confused in some way and needed a special touch.

One of the ladies in our group, Shar, had a burden for her unsaved husband. We lifted him up to the throne room frequently and fully believed that God was at work, even when she often couldn't see it—softening the heart of this man, who had refused to acknowledge Him for the length of their almost fifty-year marriage. I strongly felt that by the time I was ready to begin writing this chapter, Shar's husband would be saved, and we would all be rejoicing over God's goodness.

Around the time the Covid pandemic hit, our group had disbanded to pursue other ventures. I needed to get this book finished. Others had taken on new leadership and teaching responsibilities. My husband also needed my help to get a new space for his cigar shop renovated and decorated.

Then I heard God say, "I want you to wait a bit on finishing the book. You need time to 'grow up' into what you are writing about. Also, there are breakthroughs coming, which you will write about in the remaining chapters of your book. And I would like for you to do some teaching on Sundays at the cigar shop for a few months."

So, for four months I conducted a "service" at the shop called the

"Holy Smokes!" A few patrons and other people came, and several people I had known over the years watched through Facebook. It was definitely a period of growth, just as God had said. I was able to practice speaking in front of people about all the topics I cover in this book. At the same time, I crystalized my thinking about a lot of things God had instructed me to write, and I revised my thinking on some things, as well. I viewed all of these as forms of breakthrough.

But there was more to come. Right before the 2020 election, my eldest daughter called and said she was divorcing her husband of thirteen years. I was devastated. This had come from out of nowhere. It just didn't make sense. Seemingly, they were the couple who had it all.

But I guess things are often not what they seem. "Lord, what is this?" I questioned. He said, "This is part of your breakthrough and the result of your presence prayers. Those things that can be shaken must be shaken. Those things that are hidden must be revealed."[21]

Sometime after our group quit meeting on a regular basis, Shar's husband Terry had a heart attack. We all continued praying. Shar, of course, was faithful to attend to his every need. He soon recovered, but there was still no word on his conversion. I argued with the Lord: "Lord, you said I would write about Terry in Chapter Seven!"

A number of months later, a member of our prayer group called and said Shar's husband had passed away. Apparently, he had been very sick for several weeks before he succumbed. Unfortunately, I had not been aware of this. Also, I was heartbroken for Shar and feeling dejected that he had seemingly left her and this earth before receiving the Lord. "Lord, what is this?" I asked.

Within hours, the same group member called me back. She was elated! A mutual friend had just talked with Shar who reported that, during that two-week period of illness, she and Terry had bonded like never had before. Through their heart-felt discussions he assured her that he had repented and turned to Christ for his salvation. Praise God! It is never too late to come into the Light, Life, and Love of God!

So, dear friends, don't let this one thing escape your notice: a single day counts like a thousand years to the

Lord Yahweh, and a thousand years counts as one day. This means that, contrary to man's perspective, the Lord is not late with his promise to return, as some measure lateness. But rather, his "delay" simply reveals his loving patience toward you, because he does not want any to perish but all to come to repentance (2 Peter 3:8-9 TPT).

The Breeze Through the Trees

About three years ago, I was thinking and praying about the presence prayer process I have just described—whereby I bring a person into God's presence and then ask Him to shine His light on them, breathe His breath into them, and wrap them up in love. Specifically, I was wondering if the Lord could use these "realities" to stir up and bring to the surface some of my people's hidden or long-forgotten memories.

Would the recollection of such memories prompt them to let Jesus come and heal them there? Or would the Holy Spirit show them some "new thing"—something that would push them farther along the path to full salvation or spiritual maturity, just as it had done for me and others?

Almost immediately I saw a picture in my head of something that looked like a grove of trees swaying in the wind. I thought "That's weird." I don't literally "see'" things very frequently, so I figured this must be something I needed to investigate. Then, it occurred to me that "the trees" looked like something you might find microscopically in the brain.

I was wondering where I could look up some microscopic pictures of the brain, when I happened to look down at a long line of books I had accumulated on my desk top for research purposes. I have a long built-in desk that takes up practically a whole wall, so there were probably thirty books propped up with bookends right there in front of me for easy access.

The one that immediately caught my eye was Dr. Caroline Leaf's book *Switch on Your Brain: The Key to Peak Happiness, Thinking, and Health*. "Aha! Maybe there is something in this one," I thought, grabbing it. I noticed a couple of sticky notes hanging out, likely serving as bookmarks on pages I might need for future reference. I opened to the top sticky note page and saw a picture that was clearly taken through a microscopic lens. First glance, it looked like a grove of spindly trees, varying heights, all capped with fully-seeded dandelion heads. I was flabbergasted! It was almost the exact picture I had seen in my head, though mine was more like a video with the "trees" swaying back and forth. The paragraph preceding the picture read:

> Part of this activity is the movement of thought (existing memories), linked in some way to the incoming information, moving from the nonconscious metacognitive level to the conscious cognitive level. These thoughts in your brain look like trees in a forest. And as the signals sweep through these trees like a wind, research shows they will activate four to seven thought-trees (memories) that will then move into the conscious, and you will become aware of them. I call this the "breeze through the trees."[22]

The section of Dr. Leaf's book I had turned to was about her "21-day brain detox plan." What she was describing there is how "hidden, unconscious" memories can be brought into the conscious mind through an outside stimulation or signal of some sort. Scientifically, it has been proven that this "stimulation" works to blow through our existing conscious thoughts, that is, "the trees," which activates other unconscious memories, propelling them to the conscious level.

Now, after I read in context what Dr. Leaf was saying, I realized that she was not necessarily talking about God's Light, Life, and Love being the outside stimulation or signal. Rather, she was talking about a thought "activity" that would work to dredge up toxic thoughts and associated memories, so they could be dispelled.[23]

However, I couldn't help but think that the Holy Spirit was validating to me, through this lady's very scientific research, that our group's presence prayers were dredging up things in our people that would ultimately lead to their healings. In other words, I saw the Holy Spirit "shaking their trees," connecting dots, giving them pause, and prompting them to invite Jesus to come and take away the toxicity associated with their traumatic memories!

The River of God's Spirit Makes Us Overflow Joy

To experience the true joy of our salvation, we must experience revelation concerning the mysteries that have been hidden within us. One of these mysteries is how our individual God-given spirits can connect to the Holy Spirit, the life-giving force of God that Jesus made available to us after He was resurrected, on the day of Pentecost.[24] This connection, or union with the Godhead[25] through the power of the Holy Spirit, is like a river of Light, Life, and Love flowing through us.

In the Bible, rivers are metaphors for the Holy Spirit. *The Passion Translation* says the Hebrew word for river, *nahar*, comes from a root word that means "sparkle" or "to be cheerful." In the garden of Eden there was a river of God that flowed into four rivers. Since the number four in Hebrew represents "universality," that is, the "four corners of the earth," these rivers symbolize the Holy Spirit's ability to "refresh and water the whole earth."[26] This would include the Holy Spirit's ability to refresh all the people of God, making them "sparkle" and full of "cheer"!

Flowing from the Land of Delight was a river to water the garden, and from there, it divided into four branches. The first river, Overflowing Increase, encircles the gold-laden land of Havilah. The gold of that land is pure, with many pearls and onyx found there. The second river, Gushing, flows through the entire land of Cush. The third river, Swift Flowing, flows east of Assyria. And the fourth is the river Fruitfulness[27] (Genesis 2:10–14 TPT).

It gives me great joy to have this understanding—that within every person, even in unbelievers, there resides the life-giving breath that God breathed into them. This breath, spirit, light, *neshama,* is what gives each one the "potential" to grow up into the things of God, that is, to be joined to Him and to receive His nature and His favor.

Further, my joy increases as the awareness of my own union with the Holy Spirit expands. This happens as I spend more time in His Presence, basking in the fullness of His Light, Life, and Love, which flows through me like a gushing river—overflowing and touching everyone with whom I come in contact.

My friend, be aware of your union with the Holy Spirit. Live in the throne room, where you are free to bask in these realities. You will be full of bliss and joy! Your union with the Holy Spirit will affect others!

Also, remember this: The *neshama* within others—though perhaps weak and dim, covered up by a thick web of trauma, unbelief, lies, and deceptions—is nonetheless always seeking to find and connect with the True Light, Life, and Love of God.

As you and I continue "being" receptacles of God's Light, Life, and Love, many of these dim spirits will respond to His Light within us. They will become so attracted to this Light, they will break out of their constraints and join to the Holy Spirit, too!

Until then, let's develop a habit of living in the Presence of God ourselves, then lifting our needy, dysfunctional people "up." Let's imagine the Light shining on them, the Life and Love pouring into them! The Holy Spirit is responding to our prayers and declarations. He is blowing through their trees, shaking them free of things that are keeping them down and blind. What a joy to be used in such an effortless way. It's not about us at all! It's about Him!

> Then on the most important day of the feast, the last day, Jesus stood and shouted out to the crowds — "All you thirsty ones, come to me! Come to me and drink! Believe in me so that rivers of living water will burst out from within you, flowing from your innermost being, just like the Scripture says!" (John 7:37–38 TPT).

My Prayer and Declaration:

Jesus, thank you for joining Yourself to me through my union with the Holy Spirit. I am learning that "union" with You gives me holy "imagination!"[28] And I'm using that imagination[29] now to see You as You are—my transfigured Savior[30] and Redeemer,[31] full of Light,[32]

Life[33] and Love.[34] Jesus, as I stand before You, I trust You to do *as You will* unto me.[35] I lean into Your outstretched arms[36] and ask You to pour Your Light, Life and Love into me now.[37] I want You to change me from the inside out!

With the holy "imagination" and faith You have given me, I see Your Light consuming all my wrongness, that is, all my fleshly ideas and twisted perceptions. I am receiving revelation of new spiritual realities now! Your thoughts, feelings and purposes are coming into my mind. Healing and change at all levels of my being are occurring—spirit, soul, and body! Every cell[38] in my body is refreshed[39] and renewed! Hallelujah!

> Suddenly, he transported me into his house of wine—
> he looked upon me with his unrelenting love divine.[40]
> Revive me with your raisin cakes.[41] Refresh me again
> with your apples. Help me and hold me, for I am lovesick!
> I am longing for more—yet how could I take more? His
> left hand cradles my head while his right hand holds me
> close. I am at rest in this love (Song of Songs 2:4–6 TPT).

Personal Questions to Consider:[42]

Has your joy been stolen due to a dysfunctional relationship you currently have with someone else?

Does someone you know suffer from a "dysfunction"?[43] Can you use your holy "imagination" and take this person with you into the heavenly throne room now?

What might happen when you are both touched, that is, consumed, by His Light, Life and Love?

Chapter Eight

REPEAT

"But when the truth-giving Spirit comes, he will unveil the
reality of every truth within you. He won't speak on his own,
but only what he hears from the Father, and he will reveal
prophetically to you what is to come" (John 16:13 TPT).

Summary: There is a plan of God that points to your divided heart's
complete restoration and mine.[1] Beyond that, the plan involves the restoration and purification of the church.[2] Last, this plan promises that
all things divided will be restored,[3] whether "in heaven or on earth or
under the earth."[4] It is to this end that God placed *all things* inside a
judicial system based on the irrefutable principles of True Justice and
Righteousness[5] where He is the Judge of all.[6] (Chapters One–Four)
You see, the Creator foresaw the spiritual drama that would transpire
between us and Satan—the god of this world, who would attempt to
jeopardize the divine plans the one true God set for us in the beginning.
Yes, God knew that certain unchanging laws of the universe, supported
by a just and right legal system, would be needed to stop this spiritual adversary. Without such perimeters, this enemy could successfully
divide and conquer us as individuals, as a church, and as a human race.

Until the manifestation of "complete" restoration occurs, we are
enlisted people engaged in a legal battle between good and evil, God
and Satan. Therefore, we cannot bury our heads in the sand or hide in a
hole—lest we be deemed "guilty as charged."

First, we must individually face our adversary in heavenly court to set our personal records straight. In court, God is on our side. Jesus is our appointed court Mediator, and the Holy Spirit, our Counselor and Legal Aid. Together they defend us, providing us the best legal counsel and revelation possible concerning the truth about the most important laws of the Father's judicial system: repentance, forgiveness, rightness, judgment, and "sonship."

When we willingly submit to these laws, starting in the courtroom, our Merciful Judge, the One True God, the Father, (1) acquits us, freeing us from the adversary's accusations and condemnations, and (2) fully arms and equips us under the protective custody of the court. Yet this is just the beginning of what God has planned! Now that we have settled Satan's legal arguments, we are ready to go "beyond" the courtroom into the intimacy of the Father's passionate love—the "shining place"[7] of His Sanctuary, also called the Zion-realm. (Chapters Five–Eight) Daily REPEATING our engagement with the Father there in the "shining place" is how we become "manifest" sons. Now we are (3) clothed with the Father's Divine Nature, and (4) "perfected" in His Love. We (5) manifest the Anointed One, Christ, the Hope of much glory. We are restored.

It was the end of 1944. The Battle of the Bulge. Charlie the Chaplain, a 20-year-old Captain in the US Army, crouched as low as he could in the foxhole. His buddy did the same. They had staked out in the German-engineered hole, several hours prior, along with other troops in their unit—all scattered among holes previously dug at the perimeter of a wide-open field. They needed to rest. But the grinding of German tanks in the distance was closing in. Boom! Grenades were now exploding to the right and to the left of them.

The commanding officer shouted out the next orders. They were to make a run for it, across the field to the safety of allied troops on the other side, about a mile away.

"I will lift up mine eyes to the hills." Charlie began quoting his favorite Psalm out loud as he hurriedly removed a coin from his pocket and tossed it. Heads. He had won the toss and would exit the hole first. His buddy would follow right behind him. "My help cometh from the

Lord, who made heaven and earth," he continued, clutching his buddy's hand in a tight grasp, then bounding out of the hole.

Boom! A grenade had landed somewhere behind him. Where was his buddy? He could not look back to see. He zigzagged across the rocky field at a fast clip. "He will not suffer my foot to be moved." Boom! Boom! Now the grenades were starting to fly in all directions. "He that keepeth me shall not slumber nor sleep."[8]

I heard my dad tell this story from the pulpit several times in my younger years, and each time it had a profound impact on me. Probably because in the telling of it, he would get very emotional, with lots of long pauses, trying to hold back tears. God had spared his life. But his buddy never made it out of the foxhole. Did he freeze in fear? No one would ever know for sure the reason he didn't make it out in time. After the war, Dad would deliver the young man's identification tags to his widow, who lived somewhere in New Jersey, so the story went.

As a young child, I didn't know much about WWII—other than it was an evil war that had to be fought because a very evil man named Hitler had done a lot of very bad things to the Jews. Many good people like my dad's buddy died, as a result. But good would win over evil in the end, and Charlie the Chaplain would come home and go to college on the GI Bill. Then, during his senior year, he would become manager of the baseball team—at which time he would suffer yet another close call. A team member took a practice swing and accidently walloped my dad in the head, causing a severe concussion and brain hemorrhage. It took Dad the better part of a year to recover from that accident.

But the "call" on my dad's life, to serve God in the ministry, was indeed "irrevocable"[9] and would soon become reality. He attended seminary. Finally, in the mid-50s he became ordained in the Presbyterian Church. He and Mom married in 1958, and I arrived in 1959, during the first of five pastorates he served over the course of many years.

To Whom Much is Given, from Him Much is Expected

"For everyone to whom much is given, from him much will be required; and to whom much has been committed, of him they will ask the more" (Luke 12:48b NKJV).

The year before my dad died, I had been reading several passages in the Psalms out loud to him, when I realized that he was motioning for me to stop reading. He appeared almost desperate to tell me something, which ended up having to do with "knowing" God's will. With labored breath he said, "If you can't figure out what God's will is, then just do the best you can with what you've got." It struck me later, that of all the things he could have said, that was the most important thing he wanted me to know.

Dad's remarks to me that day now make me wonder if he had suffered from possible regrets and a deep-seated belief that he had in fact somehow missed the mark God had set for him in life. It also strikes me that he possibly never experienced that quiet confidence of "knowing" God's love at a deep, deep level. Further, I think the mindset he carried at the end of his life—the one that said "there was more, and I missed it"—could likely be traced all the way back to the child who had no loving and dependable earthly father. I think it can also be traced to that foxhole in Germany.

As the verse in Luke suggests, much would be expected of someone whose life had been spared, especially at the possible expense of someone else's. But what? What had God expected? At the end of his life, did my dad think he missed the destiny God had purposed for him since the beginning?

A Christian neighbor of mine once said something to me that was almost the same as what my dad said to me that day at the hospital. In reference to someone who had hurt me she said, "He probably did the best he could with what he had." I realized much later that her statement was true. "What" this person who hurt me "had"—due to his own early life experiences—was disappointment, hurt, volatility, insecurity due to embarrassment, and therefore "a need to cover up" and a need to "elevate himself above others," that is, pride.

What my dad "had" was similar, though the result was different—because he was extremely humble, almost to a fault—again likely due to his WWII experience and the college accident. He, too, was holding hurt and insecurity—but mixed with guilt and a need to "do works" because of a "religious" mentality. His mindset was that he had been spared, not once, but twice. God expected much—and he was willing to "serve" much. But this was the problem: My dad's "limited thinking" would not allow him to do what was *really* expected—to just be a "son" and experience all the good things God had for him.

If only Dad had been more "aware" of his union with the Holy Spirit. If only he had asked Jesus to come into his memories and help him to rewrite them—then "exchange" the things he was holding, such as guilt and lack of confidence, for the Divine Nature of the Father. Then, he would not have been restricted by a consciousness of guilt concerning mistakes or other things in life that were beyond his control. Instead, he would have reveled in being a beloved and favored son, always facing difficulties with an anointed perspective, God's perspective. Always loved. Always favored.

All in all, the Holy Spirit would have given my dad greater discernment and confidence. Then he would have understood my mother's limitations better—and loved her better—and he would have engaged with people in a more effective way, especially with his children. The reason: He would have been more fully aligned and "engaged" with the Creator and able "to dance" through life with Him—instinctively knowing how to follow His lead. This would have led to greater developments, more interesting pursuits, more fun! Last, he would not have faced the end of his life questioning whether he had done enough or been on the right track. He would have been content and satisfied to know that God's purposes in his life had been accomplished.

The Call to the Dance

"Of the Rock who bore you, you were unmindful; you forgot the God who travailed in your birth" (Deuteronomy 32:18 AMP).

There is a funny little word in this verse. I found it when studying Philippians 2:15-16.[10] It's "khul"—which can mean "to bring forth." But it can also mean "to dance, twist, and whirl."[11] Here in *the Amplified Bible* it is translated "travail."

The intersecting phrase between the Philippians Chapter Two and Deuteronomy Chapter 32 passages is "a perverse and crooked generation":

> He is the Rock, His work is perfect, for all His
> ways are law and justice. A God of faithfulness without

breach or deviation, just and right is He. They [Israel]
have spoiled themselves. They are not sons to Him, and
that is their blemish—a perverse and crooked generation! (Deuteronomy 32:4–5 AMP).

The big-picture meaning here is that God had travailed to bring forth
a perfect work in His people, but they had gotten out of step with Him. Of
course, He had desired to continue the dance. The symphony of His Light,
Life and Love was still playing softly in the background. And continuing
would be sure to get them back on track. But they stopped interfacing
with Him altogether, veering off the path and becoming "crooked."[12]

A few years back, I recalled a situation in my wilderness years, when
I was alone and trying to figure things out. It was a Friday night, and I
was "dancing"—by myself in the foyer of my house. Now this was the
type of dance where a woman partners with a man, who leads her in
"the steps," which could end up being any number of configurations. So
the lady had to pay close attention. More than that, she had to learn to
"feel" the next move, given the slightest bit of pressure put to her hand.
If she could learn to respond instinctively, the harmonic flow would be
seamless. And I was getting pretty good at it, because I had taken classes
for more than a year with a man I had been seeing on a regular basis.
However, I had broken up with this person two months prior to "figure
things out." So, for two months this had become the ritual: me, the
music, the dance, and an "imaginary" partner.

Now there is way more to this memory than the superficial details.
You can read more about my wilderness experience in *Finding the Secret
Place* if you like. But for purposes of understanding this story about me
dancing in the foyer, let me give you the backdrop details.

My husband and I had been separated and living apart for more
than a year, though not yet divorced. He also had another relationship.
But several months prior to this incident in the foyer, he had hinted at a
possible reconciliation between us. At the time, honestly, my heart told
me that I did not want to pursue it. I was much "happier" apart from
him. But my "moral" side kept telling me that I should at least give it a
try. So here I was, two months in, dancing alone.

Then my son came in the door. It was late. "Mom, are you OK? I don't like seeing you here all by yourself."

I assured him that all was fine. But deep inside I kept asking myself, "Why am I being alone?" Now it's important to note that I do not recall asking God His opinion about my situation, at all. I just knew that I had "given up" my relationship with the other guy—to be home, available, and ready to explore reconciliation if and when my husband showed up. So, there I was. Waiting for what was, on my husband's end, always an excuse—a "legitimate" delay of some sort. My patience was wearing thin.

And so, as I twirled around with my imaginary dance partner in the foyer that night, I "thought" I had done all I could do to give reconciliation a chance. Yes, I had done the best I could with what I had. Now, it was time to move on. And I did. That was the night I put the nail in the coffin on our marriage. I called my "guy" the next day and continued that relationship for another three years.

The Rewriting of Memories with a Father's Help

A few years ago, when I was thinking and yet again trying to "figure things out," I suddenly realized that one of the most defining moments in my entire life was that night in the foyer. "Lord, where were You?" I asked. When I looked back to the memory after many years, I knew He had been there, though I'd had no eyes to see Him at the time.

He replied, "I was dancing with you, trying to woo you back to Myself. But you wouldn't listen or respond!"

"Lord," I asked, sadly, "what if I had said 'yes' to the dance that night, been more agreeable to Your overtures?"

"You would have 'stepped into your destiny' a lot sooner," was His reply.

Later, after I had begun to understand the value of "rewriting" memories, the "rewrite" on this one came to me in the middle of the night. I got up and pounded it out on the computer:

Forty-six years old: I am dancing in the foyer, trying to wrap my head around being with my husband again. My mind is full of fear. How would it ever be different? I would be trapped again, in a loveless marriage. I am holding "empty promises" and "dread" and "fear."

"Jesus, come!" I say loudly.

Suddenly, I feel the touch of a warm hand, clasping mine. When I twirl around, I see Him. I am dancing with Jesus! He says, "Now, my daughter, you are part of the Father's dance!" We glide across the floor, effortlessly, His Life, Light, and Love flowing through me. "Look at you!" He exclaims. "You are following My lead perfectly!"

"I'm so sorry I tried to do this by myself!" I confess to Him.

"The Father is happy for your return! There are many things planned. You will see."

The fear, dread and "empty promises" I have been holding melt into His hands as we continue. Then He tells me that my son's healing will be tied to the recreation of this memory.

At that moment my son, Will, enters the scene. "Mom, you are so happy! Tell me how you happen to be so happy tonight!"

He doesn't see Jesus yet, but when the Savior says his name, "Will!" his eyes open in awe and wonder. "Come and join us in the dance," Jesus says to him.

Will comes over to us. We huddle with our arms around one another's shoulders. Then we do the "hora," the Jewish dance I learned in the sixth grade! While dancing, Jesus speaks to Will face to face. He understands his frustration and anger, especially toward his dad. But forgiveness is the key to joy and success, He reminds him.

Also, Jesus tells him, "I am sowing seeds of greatness in you now, My son. One day, when you are ready to depend on Me entirely, those seeds will bear much fruit. Everyone will be shocked at the outcome!"

He ends with, "Yes, today I invite you to dance, but one day I will invite you to come and sit with me on My throne."

Another rewrite, at the computer, the same night: Fast forward about ten years. I am visiting NYC, where both my girls live. The three of us are at Kate's apartment. Though I am now happily married to Larry, lately I have been grieving the losses of my first marriage—especially the negative effect it has had on my now-adult children. Tension has been building between me and Claire, in particular. I am voicing my disappointment to her—that she has deliberately disconnected herself from me. She won't talk. She shows up late, leaves early. She is always irritated with me. Everything I do. Everything I say.

Suddenly, from out of nowhere, my little Kate, who knew Jesus at three and sang songs about Him in a video that is forever etched in my memory, blows up and begins reminding me of all my failures as a mom—especially during those wilderness years before and after the divorce when I wasn't paying attention, when it was "all about me." I didn't take a picture of her at her college graduation. I didn't give her a card for her wedding. All through the divorce she had to be the parent in the relationship, etc, etc, etc.! Gosh, that hurt! So, I asked Jesus to come and be with me in that moment.

In the rewrite, Jesus is holding me up. I am resting "in" Him. Then He begins to remind me about my destiny. I am a "healer" of relationships. I will help many people find their way back to rightness, function, union with the Father.

"It is time for all the fractures and disappointments in that grieving woman to heal, so you can get on with My work," Jesus says.

Suddenly, the Holy Spirit, allows me to see something I have never seen before: I see the "me" Kate was just describing standing before me. And I am compelled to take her in my arms and tell her that she is loved. Because she is an important part of my story. And I want her to come along because she is part of who I am. But she must know her place. She will not dominate me. She will be a part representing who I once was. She will be part of the fabric but not the main attraction.

In the big picture, she and all the other "me's" are not distinguishable one from the other. They are simply part of the whole "me" going forward into the amazing destiny that is mine. And as I go "forward" into what God has planned, when "wrongness" rears its ugly head, I lean into "rightness." I know when I am "right" because I am living in harmony with myself, others, and my Father, who made me. I am whole, not fractured, complete, always dancing with Jesus.

In the recreated scene, Kate and Claire are also touched by Jesus. He is looking at them, Love flowing, His arms extended. Mesmerized, they move toward His embrace. I walk over. We all melt into each other and into Him. As we abide together in union with His Light, Life, and Love,

He tells us that there were many dysfunctions. The enemy was seeking to destroy our relationships. But now things are different. The Spirit is present. And He is actively changing things. We are all "true" daughters, change agents—the Holy Spirit working through each one of us and bringing us into never-interrupted union with the Father. Our relationships will never be the same. We are healed!

> Lord, I have so many enemies, so many who are against me. Listen to how they whisper their slander against me, saying; "Look! He's helpless! Even God can't save him from this!" But in the depths of my heart I truly know that you, Yahweh, have become my Shield: You take me and surround me with yourself. Your glory covers me continually. You lift high my head when I bow low in shame. I have cried out to you, Yahweh, from your holy presence. You send me a Father's help. So now I'll lie down and sleep like a baby—then I'll awake in safety, for you surround me with your glory. Even though dark powers prowl around me, I won't be afraid. I simply cry out to you: "Rise up and help me, Lord! Come and save me!" And you will slap them in the face, breaking the power of their words to harm me. My true hero comes to my rescue, for the Lord alone is my Savior. What a feast of favor and bliss he gives his people! (Psalm 3:3–4 TPT).

Exchanging Shame and Fear for Honor and Sonship

"What is the opposite of *shame*?" I asked the group. There were many answers, some close, but not the one I had in mind. I had in fact "asked" my thesaurus the same question several years prior. I wanted to identify just the right "redemption" word for "shame" so I could insert it on the "Rightness/Wrongness" chart I was creating.

Honor. No one ever guesses this word, which is not surprising to me when I really think about it. I have helped a lot of people with shame issues. Most have suffered so deeply in this area, and have such low self-esteem as a result, they find it hard to wrap their heads around the fact that God wants to "exchange" their shame for *honor*. What this means is that God wants to *honor* you with a future that is analogous to "true sonship." It matters not to Him what your past looks like. He wants you to have the best future possible. Because you are His.

But the manifestation of this reality in our lives cannot occur unless we have revelation of it. That's why I was beyond excited when I realized how the story of the prodigal son in Luke Chapter 15 personifies perfectly the "exchange" of the "shame" thought pattern, for the other, that of "sonship." You likely know the story:

> Once there was a father with two sons. The younger son came to his father and said, 'Father, don't you think it's time to give me the share of your estate that belongs to me?' So the father went ahead and distributed among the two sons their inheritance. Shortly afterward, the younger son packed up all his belongings and traveled off to see the world. He journeyed to a far-off land where he soon wasted all he was given in a binge of extravagant and reckless living (Luke 15:11–13 TPT.)

As the story continues, the son, likely after many years of humiliation and despair concerning his bad decisions, "realized what he was doing" and decided to go back to his father's house.

> There are many workers at my father's house who have all the food they want with plenty to spare. They lack nothing. Why am I here dying of hunger, feeding these pigs and eating their slop? I want to go back home to my father's house, and I'll say to him, "Father, I was wrong. I have sinned against you. I'll never be worthy to be called your son. Please Father, just treat me like one of your employees (Luke 15:17–18 TPT).

The Greek word used for "realized what he was doing" literally means "returned to himself" or "came back to his true self."[13] I believe this means that he *began* the process of discovering his true self—that is, his "sonship"—when he "turned" back to his father's house. Certainly, admitting fault and going back home, that is, repenting, was the first step of this son's return to the correct mindset—though his thought pattern upon return to the father was still largely that of a slave. Can you imagine his shock when the father "raced out to meet him, swept him up in his arms, hugged him dearly and kissed him over and over with tender love?" Then this:

> Turning to his servants, the father said, "Quick, bring me the best robe, my very own robe, and I will place it on his shoulders. Bring the ring, the seal of sonship, and I will put it on his finger. And bring out the best shoes you can find for my son. Let's prepare a great feast and celebrate. For this beloved son of mine was once dead, but now he's alive again. Once he was lost, but now he is found! And everyone celebrated with overflowing joy (Luke 15:22–24 TPT).

I am convinced that the highest level of inner healing occurs when the truth of this parable is understood at a very deep level. This happens progressively, over time, as a hurting person, once full of shame and fear, spends time "at home" in the heart of the Father, learning and experiencing, day to day, what it means to be a "true son."

Even a doctrinally advanced Christian—or one who has been "slain in the Spirit" multiple times, for that matter—cannot be completely healed until he *knows and experiences* what it means to be a "true son." The truth of this statement is exemplified by the immature behavior of the elder son, who became angry and jealous and offended when the wayward brother was given such a grand reception.

> The older son became angry and refused to go in and celebrate. So his father came out and pleaded with him. "Come and enjoy the feast with us!" The son said, "Father, Listen! How many years have I been working like a slave for you, performing every duty you've asked as a faithful son? And I've never once disobeyed you.

But you've never thrown a party for me because of my faithfulness. Never once have you even given me a goat that I could feast on and celebrate with my friends like he's doing now. But look at this son of yours! He comes back after wasting your wealth on prostitutes and reckless living, and here you are throwing a great feast to celebrate—for him! The father said, "My son, you are always with me by my side. Everything I have is yours to enjoy. It's only right to celebrate like this and be overjoyed, because this brother of yours was once dead and gone, but now he is alive and back with us again. He was lost but now he is found!" (Luke 15:28–32 TPT).

Notice the elder son had "been working like a slave, performing every duty" for his entire life! And he had taken great pride in his apparent "faithfulness" to his father. But there was no joy in it! He had never become a "true son"!

"If the Son sets you free from sin, then become a true son and be unquestionably free!" (John 8:36 TPT).

"What is it, Lord?"

There is a reason why Jesus encouraged his disciples to renew their minds to such an extent that they would *become* "true sons." Because when a person has not hit the highest levels of revelation concerning "sonship" and the experience of honor associated, he is not completely free from sin and all the misery that arises from it.

I have discovered a secret. Becoming a true son and experiencing the freedom and honor that comes with that status is easier and quicker when we learn to ask our Father the right questions. With that said, "Why?" is never the question to ask!

"Why do my children have to mistreat me like this?" "Why am I always left out?" "Why is this so hard?" "Why don't we have more money?" "Why did you bring us out of Egypt to have us starve in the desert?" "Why is my husband constantly hurting me by doing this or saying that?" "What have I done to deserve this?" "Why am I depressed?" "Why did my brother have to die?"

These questions clearly make the situations at hand all about me. Consequently, my current "fallen" mentality, gets reinforced. I need my Father's mindset to break out of what I am going through, so I can get on with what it is He has for me!

It came to me one day that my "best" prayer is this: Simply, "Lord, what is it?"[14] This was the same question the children of Israel asked concerning the mysterious little seeds that appeared every morning on the ground. Turns out "it" was "manna"[15]—which could be ground into bread. And "it" was just what they needed while they were traipsing through a less than ideal territory on the way to the promised land.

Even today, when we consume our "What is it?"—without griping and complaining, just listening and receiving—the little cake God gives each day is so satisfying. It reveals something deep, from His heart. And over time, we are surprised to find that our daily intake has changed our minds and brought us into alignment with Him. As it turns out, the repetition of going to that "private place reserved for the lovers of God"[16] has proved to be quite transforming.

This is why I wake up every morning asking, "Lord, what is it? What do You want to tell me today?"

I usually hear Him say things like this:

"I love you! There is nothing you can do or not do to make Me love you more—and nothing you can do or not do to make Me love you less!"

"Everything I have is yours!"

When someone disappoints or offends me, I immediately ask, "Lord, what is this about?"

His reply: "It's about you learning to be my true daughter, living in union with me so I can live my life in you, so I can respond to all these people and situations on your behalf—instead of you trying to do it in your own strength!"

> Lord, direct me throughout my journey so I can
> experience your plans for my life. Reveal the life-paths
> that are pleasing to you. Escort me along the way; take

me by the hand and teach me. For you are the God of my increasing salvation; I have wrapped my heart into yours! (Psalm 25:4–5 TPT).

Then, by constantly using your faith, the life of Christ will be released deep inside you, and the resting place of his love will become the very source and root of your life. Then you will be empowered to discover what every holy one experiences—the great magnitude of the astonishing love of Christ in all its dimensions. How deeply intimate and far-reaching is his love! Endless love beyond measurement that transcends our under-standing—this extravagant love pours into you until you are filled to overflowing with the fullness of God! (Ephesians 3:17–19 TPT).

Helping People Get Out of Their Fallen Mindsets

In today's world there is a high percentage of people, even church people, who are still trapped in fallen mindsets. Even if they have done some legal work in the courts of heaven, many of these folks still need help escaping. As I see it, they have not yet advanced "beyond" the courts to the intimacy of the Father's "Shining Place,"[17] His Sanctuary, where over time the mindsets of "orphan mentality," "victim mentality," "works mentality," "offense," and "fear" are dissolved into "sonship." My ministry goal is to walk these people through the courts to get the legal stuff taken care of and then straight into the Daily Presence. Repeating this process is the only way to get completely freed from these mind-sets—which is the only way a person can become a "true son."

When ministering to someone I ask, "Lord, what is it You want us to do today?" I can't possibly know where to go to get to the issue at hand. But the Holy Spirit can tell me.

When I met my friend Quinzell, a young black man from Detroit, he had been grieving for more than a year concerning the murder of his brother—who had been shot during a civil dispute in another state. Since then, a major issue for Quin had been chronic nightmares—and an inability to sleep at night with any consistency at all. Also, he suffered from a nagging disappointment that he had not seen or spoken with his brother for several months prior to his passing.

In addition to all these problems, Quin had suffered from a lifetime of having no dependable father figure; his biological father had been largely unreliable and extremely abusive, verbally.

Quin and I had already completed a few healing sessions. As we progressed into the next Zoom call, I sensed he had come up against a spiritual block. Finally, I asked, "Lord, what is it?" He said, "Take Quin to the hospital room, so he can speak with his brother before he dies."

As Quin had explained to me previously, his brother, Demetrius, Meechie (pronounced MEE' chee) for short, had been left on the ground to die. However, he crawled to safety and was later transported to the hospital, where he died later that night.

So per the prompting of the Holy Spirit, Quin and I "created" a supernatural memory in the unseen realm—one that had never occurred until that time and place. The aftereffect was beyond anything we could have imagined. The love of the Father came and rested on Quin like it never had before.

This is how it happened: In the creation of the memory, Quin entered the hospital room where Meechie lay. Immediately, Quin saw him so vividly! And Jesus was there, too, at his bedside. Quin slowly approached, then touched his brother's hand, feeling its warmth. Then he clutched it. Meechie's eyes opened and engaged with Quin's.

"I love you, my brother," Quin said, breaking down into a sob of relief. "Oh, how I have wanted to tell you that, face to face, before you go! I'm so thankful the Father God has given me this.

"There are so many things I want to say. But the main thing I want you to know is that I will be a dad to your children. You have my promise. You go on home now. All is well."

Jesus placed His hand on Quin's. Then Meechie stirred, his gaze resting gently on Jesus's face.

"Be at peace," Jesus said.

With that, Meechie closed his eyes and slipped away into the Father's arms. Peace flooded Quin's heart like a river. My heart was overflowing, too. We were both crying like babies on that Zoom call!

It's been months now since the encounter Quin had with his dying brother. But he can still recall the emotions of that moment—when he engaged with Meechie in such a very real and meaningful way that he will never forget. It was as though it had really happened. And he and I believe it did—in the spirit realm.

Also, Quin will never forget the Father's love—for having arranged the whole thing through the power of the Holy Spirit. "He didn't have to do that for me. But He did, cause He knew I needed it. He used it to help me understand how much He loves me. It opened up my heart to His love," Quin explains.

Quin highlighted to me some other things that have happened to him in the last number of months—which he believes occurred supernaturally as a result of this created encounter. First, two prophets on different occasions reported that Meechie was given the opportunity to come back to life on earth. But he was so at peace in his Father's house, he declined the offer!

Next, Quin overheard two of his brother's five small children talking. The older one said to the younger, "We don't have a dad. He died." Quin piped in and said, "Now you know I discussed this with your dad, and he said I could be your dad. So, you can call me Dad!"

The older said, "OK, Dad!" To which the younger one said, "I wanna call you Dad, too!"

Then this: The baby was one year old when her dad died and doesn't remember him at all. She's three now. Also, to Quin's knowledge, she never knew his name—or said it out loud. Her grandmother gave her a brown doll recently. "What will you name her?" she asked.

"Meeshe," she said. Where did she get that name, everyone wondered? They looked it up. It's an Islamic girl's name that means "life" and "alive"!

The Keys that Unlock Hellish Mindsets

> When I saw him, I fell down at his feet as good as
> dead, but he laid his right hand[18] on me, and I heard

his reassuring voice saying: "Don't yield to fear. I am
the Beginning and I am the End, the Living One! I was
dead, but now look—I am alive forever and ever. And I
hold the keys that unlock death and the unseen world.[19]
Now I want you to write what you have seen, what is,
and what will be after the things that I reveal to you"
(Revelation 1:17–19 TPT).

Though we have fallen, hellish mindsets that cause us to act
like orphans, victims, religious workers, and receptacles of offense
and fear—Jesus Christ, our Savior and Deliverer, holds the keys to
unlock them.

That's why He gave us the Holy Spirit—so we can get a revelation
about (1) what is really going on inside our minds and (2) the fact that
Jesus already has the keys that can set us free from this bondage. Over
time, as we grow up into this understanding, we get set free, completely,
and become true sons.

But when the truth-giving Spirit comes he will unveil
the reality of every truth[20] within you. He won't speak
on his own, but only what he hears from the Father, and
he will reveal prophetically to you what is to come (John
16:13 TPT).

What did the Father ask the Holy Spirit to teach us concerning these
realities? In John Chapter 16, we find the answers.[21] One, the Father
asked the Holy Spirit to teach us the truth about our sin. As we have
discussed, sin is derived from a broken self-image, a fallen mindset.
Therefore, sin is believing lies about oneself. In this sense, every image
or thought of our imagination that fights against "sonship," or "living in
union" with the Father through the Holy Spirit is sin.[22] The symptoms
of sin are many and include all manifested behaviors and attitudes based
on these self lies.

Two, the Father wants us to know what true righteousness is—and
where it comes from. First, "right standing"[23] pertains to our "status"

with God or our "relationship" to God: Forgiven. Connected in sonship. So "right standing" is the "cancellation of debt" and the "acquittal" that comes through our (1) acknowledgment of sin, (2) repentance,[24] that is, saying we are sorry for it, and (3) faith that the blood of Christ paid for this necessary transaction.

Next, "uprightness of heart"[25] has to do with the "good fruit" that comes out of our connection to God—the "manifestation" of the "restoration to original harmony or innocence." In other words, "uprightness of heart" is about coming into the fullness of our salvation—through "understanding" our sonship and "experiencing" an enduring harmony with God, self, and others.

Both forms of righteousness are available to us because of the work Jesus did for us on the cross.

Last, the Father wants us to know what He did to judge Satan. First, He paid a ransom[26] to buy back what Satan stole, that is, people and spiritual gifts.[27] The ransom was the value of Jesus's shed blood. Then, after Jesus died on the cross, the Father sent Him to hell[28] to take "captivity captive"[29] and recover the keys to death and Hades.[30] Before He ascended into heaven, Jesus led all his prisoners in a procession of triumph![31]

Critical Race Theory and Other Hellish Mindsets

Without getting into all the deeply theological aspects of the above, perhaps we can agree that they fit into a storyline that occurred sometime between Jesus's death and ascension experiences. Also, the keys Jesus recovered in "the realm of the dead"[32] are used to set people free, so they can live according to God's original design and "manifest" as the Father's true sons—equipped with authority, power, and "repossessed" spiritual gifts.

But hear me out: Modern-day believers cannot expect to walk in high levels of true authority, such as what Jesus intended for these last days, unless we are free of mindsets that block our intimacy with the Father and keep us from becoming his "manifest" sons.

"Victim mentality" has been around for a long, long time. There are many forms of it. My mother suffered from a victim mentality because what other people did and said affected her immensely—shutting her down and stymying her spiritual growth. Currently, Satan is using a form of victim mentality called Critical Race Theory[33] to kill our country—and individuals within. He is using it to keep us divided and separated from others, along racial and political lines.

More than twenty years ago, long after the racial tension of the sixties, but long before Critical Race Theory became a trending topic of conversation, this ugly mindset[34] was brewing under the surface of "smooth" waters.[35] I had been an agent at a large life insurance company for about five years and had a friend and fellow agent, who was well admired in the office and a very successful agent. A few years prior, this lady had taken an early retirement from a large corporation, where she had served as a regional supervisor. So she had many contacts and referrals to people in that company, who needed help managing their retirement income streams.

This agent and friend was also a Christian and came to a little Bible study I conducted in my office. Oh, I forgot to mention, she was African American! Even when I think of her right now, I don't see her in those terms at all. She was a sister. Someone I admired. A friend in the Lord. A shining light. A lover of God. Her skin color mattered not to me or anyone else who knew her.

Back to my story: I left the company. Years passed, and I eventually heard through a much closer friend and confidante, also one of my Bible study members, that our mutual friend had passed away. What a shock. She was in her mid-sixties when she died—of cancer. My close friend went on to say, "You know she suffered from a lot of bitterness. She was 'prejudiced' against us. She didn't think we could or would ever understand her perspective."

I was flabbergasted. "No, I did not know that!" I said in almost disbelief. But my friend's words I trusted to be absolutely true because she had been very well acquainted with this lady over the years.

I didn't know what to call it at the time, but now I realize my deceased friend likely suffered from this very common malady we call "victim mentality"—though one she managed to keep well hidden from most people. Victims blame their losses on other people. In their twisted way of thinking, they have a "right" to feel the way they do. But in the end, the truth is this: it's not what other people thought about them—or what they *perceived* they thought—that mattered. What mattered was *what they thought about themselves.*

Do people who hold onto their "victim" mindsets think this will make them feel better? Are they convinced such thinking will work to change things? These are lies from the pit of hell! Holding on to a hellish mindset is "death." And this is the reason I am determined to help people break out of them.

> Now the mind of the flesh [which is sense and reason without the Holy Spirit] is death [death that comprises all the miseries arising from sin, both here and hereafter]. But the mind of the [Holy] Spirit is life and [soul] peace [both now and forever] (Romans 8:6 AMP).

> For God sees us all without partiality (Romans 2:11 TPT).

> And we no longer see each other in our former state—Jew or non-Jew, rich or poor, male or female—because we're all one through our union with Jesus Christ with no distinction between us (Galatians 3:28 TPT).

Healing Dysfunctional Relationships Through Sonship

From the dining-room table, I saw my son kneel on the floor in the family room, where one of the grandchildren was reclining at the end of the couch. Then I saw him proceed to smother Grant, age seven, in hugs and kisses, telling him how much he loved him and how proud he was of him.

Now when I go visit my son's family, I usually stay for a few weeks. So I see it all. At this particular time in the visit, I'm sure I had already seen my son blow a fuse or two with the children. They are very typical kids, not always the best behaved. But this is what I know to be true: The demonstration of affection that I witnessed from the other room that day is very typical of how my son interacts with his children. No matter what, they know he loves them, dearly.

I couldn't help but be reminded of the Father's love for us, His Children. Then I remembered a prayer in the book of Numbers that so very well describes this love. It's called "the Priestly Prayer" and is purported to be the only prayer in the Bible written by God Himself.

"The Lord bless you and keep you; the Lord make His face to shine upon you, and be gracious unto you; the Lord lift up His countenance upon you, and give you peace" (Numbers 6:24–26 NKJV).

In Warren Marcus's book *The Priestly Prayer of the Blessing*, he describes the deeper meaning of this prayer through a thorough analysis of the Hebrew text. As a Messianic Jewish person himself, Marcus's claim is that the text we read in our English Bibles simply cannot do justice to the prayer that God instructed the High Priest, Aaron, to pray over the children of Israel every day.

The gist of Marcus's book is that the Father's love for us compels Him to "kneel" before us, getting down on our level, embracing us, placing a hedge of protection about us, allowing us to know and "see" His entire being and experience His transforming revelation light, favoring us with fellowship and friendship, lifting us up and bringing *everything that He is* to our aid, establishing us in peace and restoring us to a position that is even better than our original state![36]

One of the main points I want to make in this book is that fallen, imprisoned mindsets prevent even Christians from seeing God the Father in the manner Marcus describes. But if one can open himself up to the possibility, the mind can change, and victories can be won. Not only do we see our Father the way He really is, a loving, generous Father, but we begin to see ourselves the way He sees us, dearly loved with supernatural "potential" to grow up into the image of Jesus. These two revelations combined define "sonship."

In keeping with the Numbers 6 passage, the New Testament is clear: God's love, called *agape* in the Greek, is the most transforming frequency in the universe. One Greek scholar defines *agape* as derived from *ago*, "to lead as a shepherd leads his sheep," and *pao*, "to rest."[37]

As we grow up into our sonship, His love "rests" on us, "abides" in us. Also, "growing up" in God's love inspires us to "overcome" the things we deal with in life that are not what He had in mind.

I will never forget attending with a dear friend a banquet honoring a group of Christians, who had left the homosexual/lesbian lifestyle to follow Christ. As we were seated around the dinner table, I couldn't help but ask the question, "What changed for you? What was the defining moment when you changed your thinking and decided to give it up and embrace a new life?" The answer I kept getting, repeatedly, was this: "When I realized how much God loved me."

I have to admit, that was the very thing that changed my thinking—and my behavior, too—which, by the way, came *after* the encounter with the people at the banquet! It happened when I found the shells on the beach a few years later. That's when I realized how much God loved me—despite my tendency to consistently place Him second or third in my life, behind other relationships. I wrote a poem about this, which inspired my first book, *Finding the Secret Place*.

This discussion of God's love gets me to thinking. What if more husbands and wives suddenly *realized* how much God loves them, to the extent that their fallen mindsets change? Would there be fewer divorces? More patience? More compassion? Then, what if brothers and sisters in that family suddenly realized how much God loves *them*? Would there be less in-fighting, less jealousy? Greater kindnesses? More harmony?

And what if these same individuals went to church with "open faces"—no longer hiding behind "veils,"[38] that is, no longer trying to be people they are not—orphans, victims, people full of fear, etc.?[39] And what if more people in this same church were then inspired to take off *their* veils and let the light of God's face shine upon *them*? And *their* divisions were healed? And the love of God rested on *them* and enlarged *their* spirits? And all of this was happening because more and more people in the body were *realizing that they had been "fathered by God Himself"*?[40]

Overcomers and The Tree of Life

> For he died for us, sacrificing himself to make us holy and pure, cleansing us through the showering of the pure water of the Word of God. All that he does in

us is designed to make us a mature church for his pleasure, until we become a source of praise to him—glorious and radiant, beautiful and holy, without fault or flaw
(Ephesians 5:27 TPT).

I am reminded of the parable of the soils and the people who bore
fruit. Some of the people Jesus described in this story had a 30 percent
return on their investment. Others had a 60 percent return. But some
had 100 percent return. Why is that?

I believe the difference in return was the difference between those
who were completely restored vs. those who were not. Those who had
greater results were not the strivers, the victims, the orphans, the jealous elder brothers, that is, the divided persons. No, they were the sons,
the "manifest" sons of God[41] who were no longer divided within, who
had "come back to themselves, completely," who saw themselves the way
God saw them, and who saw others the same way.

As a result, the Love and the Glory of God "rested" on them. And
the Light and Life of God poured through them. God worked through
them and did all the heavy lifting. He lived his life through them and
accomplished His purposes for them! [42]

How do we get to this state of being Jesus was describing? Perhaps
we go no farther than these words of Jesus to the churches:

"To the one who overcomes I will give access to feast on the fruit of the
Tree of Life that is found in the paradise of God" (Revelation 2:7 TPT).

I believe Jesus is clear. We must go back to the Garden, that is, returning to our original sonship, and feasting daily from The Tree of Life.

But there's a hitch. Apparently, going back to paradise and eating
of the fruit involves "going under" a fiery sword as described here in
Genesis Chapter Three:

"He drove them out of the garden and placed fearsome angelic sen-
tries east of the garden of Eden, with a turning[43] fiery sword to guard
the way to the Tree of Life" (Genesis 3:24 TPT).

Could this be the Sword of the Spirit we have been using to "divide
soul and spirit" in our memory healings? I believe that it is! This fiery,
turning sword "guarding" the Tree of Life is the same sword described

in Hebrews 4:12. Both swords point us in the direction of our rightful identity! But to embrace that identity we must be willing to go through the soul surgery processes we have discussed in previous chapters.

So we "trust" the "sword" to shine its light deep within, identify spirit "intruders" attached to our souls, remove them, then bind them up. We call Jesus to come! His words touch our traumatized parts. They respond with repentance and forgiveness and the breaking of curses. The intruders go to the pit! And with each healing, there is less division, more wholeness, more freedom. New spiritual realities pour into our minds and hearts through the Holy Spirit's comfort and the washing of the Word. We are being changed, restored to sonship, made whole. We are overcomers!

I wish I could say this process is always quick and easy. It isn't. We must repeat it, as needed, until complete healing occurs.

We cannot give up! Jesus doesn't call us "overcomers" for no good reason!

Overcomers and the New World Order

Many of the people I have described in this book are overcomers. They are overcomers because the things in them that are not of God are being consumed bit by bit—by the light of His fiery sword.[44] This is happening because of their growing awareness of union with the Father and the resulting strengthening of intimacy. They are "continually, repeatedly, and habitually conquering."

This is the "last days" result: The "fruit" overcomers ingest from The Tree of Life ultimately gives them the authority to be seated with Jesus in the throne room[45]—where one day they will participate with Him in the healing[46] and ruling of the nations,[47] the New World Order as described in Isaiah 65 and Revelation 21:

> Then in a vision I saw a new heaven and a new earth. The first heaven and earth had passed away, and the sea no longer existed. I saw the Holy City, the New Jerusalem, descending out of the heavenly realm from the presence of God, like a pleasing bride that had been prepared for her husband, adorned for her wedding. And I heard a

thunderous voice from the throne saying, "Look! God's tabernacle is with human beings. And from now on he will tabernacle with them as their God. Now God himself will have his home with them—God-with-them will be their God! He will wipe away every tear from their eyes and eliminate death entirely. No one will mourn or weep any longer. The pain of wounds will no longer exist, for the old order has ceased (Revelation 21:1–4 TPT).

In Chapter Six, I touched on the agenda being pushed by the rulers and principalities of this world, as far as a counterfeit "New World Order" is concerned. Their concept of the New World includes population control, a world court ruled by The Illuminati elite, "passion and faith and tradition" ruled by "reason," and "personal rights" balanced with social "duties."

In 1991 George H. W. Bush spoke of this New World Order under the guise of "goodness and light" when he addressed Congress during the Gulf War. He said:

> What is at stake is more than one small country, it is a big idea—a new world order, where diverse nations are drawn together in common cause to achieve the universal aspirations of mankind: peace and security, freedom, and the rule of law. Such is a world worthy of our struggle, and worthy of our children's future!

In his book, *The New World Order*, published in 1991, Pat Robertson warned that "the new world order, if allowed to proceed as planned, will radically alter the life you lead and the freedoms you now enjoy."[48]

Dear reader, the day of reckoning as described in Robertson's book and other books is upon us. The church and its people must get equipped. Biblical prophecy is clear that we are to play a significant role in God's version of the New World Order, that is, "the restoration of all things!" However, those of us who are still divided, fatherless, and plagued by debilitating mindsets will not be able to participate. Further, Jesus will not return until the church is fully restored!

So run! Run, my friend! First, run into the courtroom of heaven. Get clean. Exchange your *wrongness* for Jesus's *rightness*. Then go beyond— to the highest realm of glory that is offered us, the Zion-realm[49]—where we are free to fellowship and feast with The Lord Yahweh and the overcomers assembling there in His army. This is where our ultimate healing occurs, where our dysfunctions with self, God, and others dissolve completely away, where God's perfect love rests upon us, and we become His Light, Life, and Love to the world.

> "And on this mountain, he will destroy the shroud wrapped around all the people, the veil spread over all nations. It is the gloom of death! He will swallow it up in victory forever!" (Isaiah 25:7–8 TPT).

The triumph of God's New World Order as described in the Bible is certain. Likewise, the church's participation at a never-seen or experienced supernatural level is certain and required. The time is now for people of faith to rise up and "manifest" as sons, returning 100 percent on the Father's investment!

Indeed, there will be a struggle. The enemy will not give up easily. But if we go about our assignments, allowing Jesus to live His life in us, our families and our spheres of influence will be inspired to participate. Revival will break out all over the world. God's team will win!

> And everything I have taught you is so that the peace which is in me will be in you and will give you great confidence as you rest in me. For in this unbelieving world, you will experience trouble and sorrows, but you must be courageous, for I have conquered the world! (John 16:33 TPT).

My Prayer and Declaration:

Yeshua, I do not want You to have died in vain where it comes to the life I have left to live here on earth. So take me now to the highest realm[50] where You reign over all of the universe.[51] I arise[52] and go with You now, trusting that you will lead me to the governmental seat You have designated for me in Your kingdom.[53] This is where You will give me revelation concerning my assignment. In obedience, I sit down upon this seat of authority where I am firmly established among other members of the remnant church, all of whom are gathering as the "end time" army. You dwell in the midst of us! And in Your Presence, we have all things! We have revelation of all the lies we have believed about ourselves. And we have the power to overcome. We are no longer victims or orphans. You, Yahweh, are our Father, and our minds are in perfect alignment with Yours.[54] We are no longer divided, jealous, offended, or prideful. We are whole, stable, restored. We shine, and Your glory rests upon us.[55] People and nations are drawn to us because Your LIGHT shines through us! We are Your priests and kings,[56] Your prisoners of hope[57] and love,[58] and we extend the olive branch of peace to all.[59]

> Now you are ready, my bride, to come with me as we climb the highest peaks together. Come with me through the archway of trust. We will look down from the crest of the glistening mounts and from the summit of our sublime sanctuary. Together we will wage war in the lion's den and the leopard's lair as they watch nightly for their prey (Song of Songs 4:8 TPT).

> But the lovers of God walk on the highway of light, and their way shines brighter and brighter until they bring forth the perfect day (Proverbs 4:13 TPT).

Personal Questions to Consider:[60]

To what extent has *Invite Jesus into Your Traumatic Memories* given you hope that your "divided" things can be restored?

How has your understanding of God's judicial system changed?

What is God showing you about a future that is good, not evil?

Afterword

"For I know the thoughts and plans that I have for you, says the Lord, thoughts and plans for welfare and peace and not for evil, to give you hope in your final outcome" (Jeremiah 29:11 AMP).

Upon entering my drunk friend's house, she immediately collapsed to the living room floor. Then she rolled around on the carpet for a bit, giggling and laughing.

My husband Larry had called me from our restaurant just 20 minutes prior, asking if I would come pick her up and take her home.

I had a fleeting thought of leaving her there in the floor to sleep it off. But suddenly her silly demeanor shifted. Now she was glaring at me, pointing an accusing finger.

"You have light coming out of you," she said, with a rather smug tone.

"And I feel love coming out of you."

Ok, well, that's good, I thought. Though she was clearly annoyed with me about it.

Then this: "I just need for you to go away and let me live my life the way I want to. You are judging me."

At this point in the living room encounter, I decided to get down in the floor and roll around, too. How could I otherwise connect with the real April—the one who wants to love Jesus but who at this moment was being controlled by an evil spirit? I was determined to get through to that woman. In a recent memory healing, Jesus had come and said to her, "April, you are a ballerina."

"April, remember what God said!" I blurted out in a loud voice, hoping she would hear. "You are a ballerina! You are His! He has plans for you!"

Obviously, this was not the time for an extended inner healing session. I just said these things and then began pushing back on the darkness in her as hard as I could. I spoke out loud so the demon would hear what I was saying: "The blood of Jesus and the mighty name of Jesus are more than enough to overcome you!" It was an addiction spirit plaguing her, along with a horde of other likely culprits, such as fear, shame, abuse, and self-destruction.

A few weeks ago, I was reading through some old journals and discovered an entry dated March 31st, 2018. "You have light coming out of you," I read. Wow, I didn't remember that part of the story at all. It had been almost four years. I did recall rolling in the floor! And trying to cast out the demon!

At that moment it occurred to me that I had received a Facebook post from April a while back—celebrating three years of sobriety. I looked back through my phone to try to determine what that date was. August 3rd. I did the math. It was almost four months to the day after we rolled around in the floor that April went to AA and never looked back! After that she got involved in church and has been steadily growing in her relationship with the Lord ever since!

A few weeks after I read the journal entry, I saw April and reminded her about the incident in the living room floor. She, of course, had no recollection of it. But she believed me and thanked me for my determination to help her get out of the pit she had been trapped in for so long.

Remembering my friend's story as I am wrapping up the writing of *Invite Jesus into Your Traumatic Memories* is a good reminder of so many things I have touched on in this book. God has plans, even for the imprisoned people around us who are still trapped in pits of hopelessness, seemingly with no means of escape.

All too often, we just see the "insurmountable" problems. But God sees the plans! In April's case His plans involve a successful business— and a podcast that encourages and inspires abused women to seek help. Currently, April interviews people like herself who are "overcoming" the obstacles that lead to such healing. She does this on an almost weekly basis.

By the way, what do you see on the front cover of this book? I've waited until now to tell you. But if you look closely, you will see Hebrew letters peeking through the clouds. It's Jeremiah 29:11!

"For I know the thoughts and plans that I have for you, says the Lord, thoughts and plans for welfare and peace and not for evil, to give you hope in your final outcome" (Jeremiah 29:11 AMP).

Let me leave you with a few thoughts about this hope that God has promised. It is closely connected to understanding and experiencing our *union* with Him, through Jesus and the power of the Holy Spirit. I can't emphasize this enough: it's our union with Him that gives us such hope! Because our union with Him is what changes things—for ourselves and for others we encounter. Our union with Him in the heavenly realm brings about His plans for peace, hope and prosperity, everywhere we go! As Jesus says, "Apart from Me you can do nothing" (as translated from the NIV).[1]

The goal is to practice *awareness* of this union.

Every day I practice thinking about my union with Him: "Lord, my spirit is joined to Yours! Thank You for this gift, this opportunity, this potential! Lord, I dwell with you in the heavenly realm! I am seated with You! I am advancing and finding my hope fulfilled![2]

"Lord, You love me! Your perfect love rests on me, in me! You are downloading Your love into me right now! Lord, through me, You love my husband! You love my children! You even love my enemies![3]

"Lord, many of the people I know and love are trapped. But, Lord, You use me to help them get out of the pit! When your love touches them through me, even through these things I am saying right now, things happen—good things!"[4]

This kind of practice can go on and on throughout my day.

It's with practice that our awareness becomes second nature. Then amazing things begin to occur without our even trying—like in my case where the demon saw light and love in me. I didn't even have to "try." Wow, it still makes me smile when I think of this. Jesus really is living His life in me, through my spirit's union with the Holy Spirit. Because I have practiced believing it. The more I practice union, the more I see the manifestations of it.

And as I go about living this life of union, I am increasingly a prisoner of His hope and His love.[5] There is just no way around it. I'm hooked. But the pressure is off. It's not about me! It's about Him! It's about what

He is doing in me and through me! And the outcome is all good!

I love being captive to Him.[6] No more dead works. No more relying on what I think I can do or say to change things. Jesus living His life in me is my only hope for any kind of change that will matter in the end.[7]

Friend, I pray you have enjoyed the journey of inviting Jesus into your memories. I pray you have experienced the peaceful effects of these realities. And I pray you are looking forward to the continuance of engagement with Him in your present, then moving forward with Him into your amazing future. Take a few deep breaths! God is with you and in you and leading you down a path that leads to the perfect day!

Continue to walk in it!

> "But the lovers of God walk on the highway of light, and their way shines brighter and brighter until they bring forth the perfect day" (Proverbs 4:18 TPT).

Endnotes

A Note from the Author

1. "Be well balanced and always alert, because your enemy, the devil, roams around incessantly, like a roaring lion looking for its prey to devour. Take a decisive stand against him and resist his every attack with strong, vigorous faith" (1 Peter 5:8-9 TPT). Antidikos is Greek for "enemy, adversary, opponent as in a suit of law," Strong's Concordance (G#476).

2. The legal aspects of the courts of heaven as pertains to believers in Christ will be dealt with in later chapters.

3. "For you should be professors instructing others by now; but instead, you need to be taught from the beginning the basics of God's prophetic oracles! You are like children still needing milk and not yet ready to digest solid food. For every spiritual infant who lives on milk is not yet pierced by the revelation of righteousness. But solid food is for the mature, whose spiritual senses perceive heavenly matters. And they have been adequately trained by what they've experienced to emerge with understanding of the difference between what is truly excellent and what is evil and harmful" (Hebrews 5:12–14 TPT). The Passion Translation notes: The Greek word for "children" is nepios, Strong's Concordance (#G3516), which means "still unfit to bear arms," that is, unprepared for battle. The Greek word for "not yet pierced" is apeiros (G#552), which means "inexperienced or unpierced."

4. "And now you must repent and turn back to God so that your sins will be removed, and so that times of refreshing will stream from the Lord's presence. And he will send you Jesus, the Messiah the chosen one for you. For he must remain in heaven until the restoration of all things has taken place, fulfilling everything that God said long ago through his holy prophets" (Acts 2:19–21 TPT).

5. "God is love. Those who are living in love are living in God, and God lives through them. By living in God, love has been brought to its full expression in us (The Passion Translation footnote says, 'love has reached its goal/destiny within us') so that we may fearlessly face the day of judgment, because all that Jesus now is, so are we in this world" (1 John 4:16 TPT).

6. "And now you must repent and turn back to God so that your sins will be removed, and so that times of refreshing will stream from the Lord's presence. And

he will send you Jesus, the Messiah, the chosen one for you. For he must remain in heaven until the restoration of all things has taken place, fulfilling everything that God said long ago through his holy prophets" (Acts 3:19–21 TPT).

7. THE MIGHTY FLAME OF THE LORD MOST PASSIONATE: The Passion Translation footnote says, "The phrase in Hebrew is 'a most vehement flame;' and is actually two Hebrew words. The first is 'a mighty flash of fire,' and the second is 'Yah,' which is the sacred name of God himself. The Hebrew shalhebet-yah could be translated 'The Mighty Flame of the Lord Most Passionate!'"

Boxes

Who is Satan?

1. "Look how you have fallen from your heavenly place, O shining one, son of the dawn! You have been cut down to the ground, you who conquered nations. You said in your heart, 'I will ascend into heaven and exalt my throne above the stars of God. I will rule on the mountain of the congregation, on the highest place of the sacred mountain. I will rise past the tops of the clouds and rival the Most High God!" (Isaiah 14:12-14 TPT). Note: This passage likely refers to a future "casting out" of Satan, as there is a reference to the ruling of nations. See Revelation, Chapter 12. Some scholars view this passage as relating to several different scenarios at the same time, such as Nebuchadnezzar and the fall of Babylon, Satan's fall from heaven, and even Adam and Eve's fall in the garden.

2. See Chapter One.

3. See Chapter One.

WHAT IS MEMORY HEALING?

1. See Chapter One.

2. "For you should be professors instructing others by now; but instead, you need to be taught from the beginning the basics of God's prophetic oracles! You are like children still needing milk and not yet ready to digest solid food. For every spiritual infant who lives on milk is not yet pierced by the revelation of righteousness. But solid food is for the mature, whose spiritual senses perceive heavenly matters. And they have been adequately trained by what they've experienced to emerge with understanding of the difference between what is truly excellent and what is evil and harmful" (Hebrews 5:12–14 TPT). *The Passion Translation* notes: The Greek word for "children" is *nepios*, *Strong's Concordance* (#G3516), which means "still unfit to bear arms," that is, unprepared for battle.

The Greek word for "not yet pierced" is *apeiros* (G#552), which means "inexperienced or unpierced."

3. "And now you must repent and turn back to God so that your sins will be removed, and so that times of refreshing will stream from the Lord's presence. And he will send you Jesus, the Messiah the chosen one for you. For he must remain in heaven until the restoration of all things has taken place, fulfilling everything that God said long ago through his holy prophets" (Acts 2:19–21 TPT).

Chapter One

1. "All rise! For God now comes to judge as he convenes heaven's courtroom. He judges every judge and rules over every ruler, saying, 'How long will you judges refuse to listen to the voice of true justice and continue to corrupt what is right by judging in favor of the wrong?'" (Psalm 82:1–2 TPT).

2. "For in the day of trouble He will hide me in His shelter; in the secret place of His tent will He hide me; He will set me high upon a rock" (Psalm 27:5 AMP).

3. "Your glorious throne rests on a foundation of righteousness and just verdicts. Grace and truth are the attendants who go before you" (Psalm 89:14 TPT).

4. "And now we are brothers and sisters in God's family because of the blood of Jesus, and he welcomes us to come into the most holy sanctuary in the heavenly realm—boldly and without hesitation" (Hebrews 10:19 TPT).

5. "It shall come to pass in the latter days that the mountain of the Lord's house shall be [firmly] established as the highest of the mountains and shall be exalted above the hills, and all nations shall flow to it. And many people shall come and say, Come, let us go up to the mountain of the Lord, to the house of the God of Jacob, that He may teach us His ways and that we may walk in His paths. For out of Zion shall go forth the law and instruction, and the word of the Lord from Jerusalem" (Isaiah 2:2–3 AMP).

6. Mom was not having a "nervous breakdown." But as a young person, I was fearful of things like this—things I had "heard" about in life but didn't yet understand.

7. HOW DO PEOPLE GET "TRIGGERED"? A trigger is a stimulus that reminds a person of a past traumatic event, usually causing an emotionally charged response such as anger, sadness, fear, or panic. The stimulus can be anything that serves as a reminder of the trauma—a smell, a sound, a sight of something, a word or phrase spoken, a particular circumstance, etc.

8. THE TERM "CROUCHING" OR "RESTING OUTSIDE THE

PORTAL" was associated with demons in one of the ancient Semitic languages, according to *The Passion Translation* notes for Genesis 4:7. From the context, it seems God is saying that a demon-beast is outside Cain's door due to his disobedience. He had given a poor sacrifice to God because his heart was not right with Him. "Why are you so angry and bothered? If you offer what is right, won't you be accepted? But if you refuse to offer what is right, sin, the predator, is crouching in wait outside the door of your heart. It desires to have you, yet you must be its master" (Genesis 4:6–7 TPT).

9. "Now, may the God of peace and harmony set you apart, making you completely holy. And may your entire being—spirit, soul, and body—be kept completely flawless in the appearing of our Lord Jesus, the Anointed One. The one who calls you by name is trustworthy and will thoroughly complete his work in you" (I Thessalonians 5:23–24 TPT).

10. "And we know that we are God's children and that the whole world lies under the misery and influence of the Evil One" (1 John 5:19 TPT).

11. SATAN'S REBELLION: "You were in Eden, the garden of God; every precious stone was your covering, the carnelian, topaz, jasper, chrysolite, beryl, onyx, sapphire, carbuncle, and emerald; and your settings and your sockets and engravings were wrought in gold. On the day that you were created they were prepared. You were the anointed cherub that covers with overshadowing [wings], and I set you so. You were upon the holy mountain of God; you walked up and down in the midst of the stones of fire [like paved work of gleaming sapphire stone upon which the God of Israel walked on Mount Sinai]. You were blameless in your ways from the day you were created until iniquity and guilt were found in you. Through the abundance of our commerce you were filled with lawlessness and violence, and you sinned; therefore I cast you out as a profane thing from the mountain of God and the guardian cherub drove you out from the midst of the stones of fire. Your heart was proud and lifted up because of your beauty; you corrupted your wisdom for the sake of your splendor. I cast you to the ground; I lay you before kings, that they might gaze at you. You have profaned your sanctuaries by the multitude of your iniquities and the enormity of your guilt, by the unrighteousness of your trade. Therefore I have brought forth a fire from your midst; it has consumed you, and I have reduced you to ashes upon the earth in the sight of all who looked at you. All who know you among the people are astonished and appalled at you; you have come to a horrible end and shall never return to being" (Ezekiel 28:13–19 AMP).

12. Spiritual mutations, that is, "alterations" of our Divine Nature Abilities, are

related to "iniquities"—the egregious sins (and resulting curses) passed by the fathers unto the children, into the third and fourth generations. This concept will be discussed in later chapters. "The Lord is long-suffering and slow to anger, and abundant in mercy and loving-kindness, forgiving iniquity and transgression; but He will by no means clear the guilty, visiting the iniquity of the fathers upon the children, upon the third and fourth generation" (Numbers 14:18 AMP).

13. Scripture supports the idea that evil spirits have specific, negative functions such as despair, hopelessness, fear, shame, guilt, and many others. (See "What are the demons' names?" earlier in this chapter). For example, in Isaiah 61:3, the prophet references a "spirit of despair" (NIV). The implication based on its context in this passage is that a person has been held "captive" by such a spirit. The Anointed One has come to "release" him from the prison in which this spirit has managed to confine him. Another scripture suggesting that the name of the spirit correlates to his function can be found in Luke 13:10–11. Jesus has encountered a woman who "was bowed together and could in no wise lift up herself (KJV). The culprit was "a spirit of infirmity" (KJV), "a disabling spirit" (ESV), or "a spirit of bondage" (TPT).

14. The Charismatic Movement (1948-1988) is an inclusive term covering the Latter Rain Movement, the Charismatic Renewal, and the Faith Movement, according to Dr. Bill Hamon's book, *Seventy Reasons for Speaking in Tongues*, Destiny Image, 2012.

15. *Strong's Concordance* (H#5175).

16. *Strong's Concordance* (H#5172). The noun and verb forms are spelled the same but have slightly different pronunciations and meanings.

17. Prince, Derek. "The Structures of Satan's Kingdom," recorded in Bromley, England, October 1988.

18. "For God doth know that in the day ye eat thereof, then your eyes shall be opened, and ye shall be as gods, knowing good and evil" (Genesis 3:5 KJV)" The Hebrew word for "gods" is *elohim, Strong's Concordance* (H#430), which means "divine ones," "divine beings."

19. *The Passion Translation* notes for this passage says "unstable" can mean "restless" or "disengaged."

20. A reference to Satan or Lucifer. At this point in the conversation, the serpent had been cast down from heaven, to the underworld. He who had sought to be the highest was now the lowest. He was in effect "the lord of the Dead." Ezekiel 28:17. For more detail, see Heiser, Michael. *The Unseen Realm: Recovering the Supernatural Worldview of the Bible*, pg. 91.

21. Through the Messiah, Yeshua, this cloud of separation was removed: I have blotted out like a thick cloud your transgressions, and like a cloud your sins. Return to me, for I have redeemed you (Isaiah 44:22 AMP).

22. *Harmartia, Strong's Concordance* (G#206), is the Greek word for "sin." It come from two words, *ha* (meaning "negative") and *meros* (meaning "portion or form.") Therefore, to sin is to be without your allotted portion, without form—a disoriented, distorted, bankrupt identity. See notes from 1 John 3:4, *The Mirror Translation*.

23. "And the man said, 'The woman whom You gave to be with me—she gave me [fruit] from the tree, and I ate.' And the Lord God said to the woman, 'What is this you have done? And the woman said, 'The serpent beguiled (cheated, outwitted, and deceived) me, and I ate'" (Genesis 3:12–13 AMP).

24. Genesis 3:14-24.

25. "You are a hiding place for me: You, Lord, preserve me from trouble. You surround me with songs and shouts of deliverance. Selah [pause, and calmly think of that]! I [the Lord] will instruct you and teach you in the way you should go; I will counsel you with My eye upon you. Do not be like the horse or like the mule which have no understanding, Whose trappings include bridle and rein to hold them in check, Otherwise they will not come near to you. Many are the sorrows of the wicked, But he who trusts in and relies on the Lord shall be surrounded with compassion and lovingkindness. Be glad in the Lord and rejoice, you righteous [who actively seek right standing with Him]; Shout for joy, all you upright in heart" (Psalm 32: 7–11 AMP).

26. Notes from *The Mirror Translation*: The word "sin" is the Greek word *harmartia* (from *ha*, which means "negative" or "without" and *meros*, which means "portion" or "form").

27. "So God created man in His own image, in the image and likeness of God He created him; male and female he created them" (Genesis 1:27 AMP).

28. "Thus says the Lord, Who stretches out the heavens and lays the foundation of the earth and forms the spirit of man within him" (Zechariah 12:1 AMP).

29. *Elohim* in Hebrew can mean the Creator-God of Genesis 1:1 or "beings who live in the spirit realm," *Strong's Concordance* (H#430).

30. "The one who doesn't love has yet to know God, for God is love" (1 John 4:8 TPT).

31. "God is a Spirit, and he longs to have sincere worshipers who worship and adore him in the realm of the Spirit and in truth" (John 4:24 TPT).

32. Note: The Hebrew word for "breath" is *neshamah* which can mean "breath or spirit (of God or man), blast, wind, and divine inspiration or intellect,"

Strong's Concordance (H#5397).

33. God "blew" into the body He had formed from dust: "God formed man of the dust of the ground and breathed into his nostrils the breath of life; and man became a living soul" (Genesis 2:7 KJV).

34. "Soul" is *nephesh, Strong's Concordance* (H#5315), which can mean "living being, seat of the appetites, seat of emotions and passions, activity of mind, will or character."

35. "But the person who becomes united to the Lord becomes one spirit with Him" (1 Corinthians 6:17 AMP).

36. "But those who embraced him and took hold of his name were given authority to become the children of God!" (John 1:12 NLT).

37. *The Amplified Bible* notes say verse 22 is "left unfinished, as if to hasten to avert the tragedy suggested of men living on forever in their now fallen state."

38. "But now [in spite of past judgments for Israel's sins], thus says the Lord, He Who created you, O Jacob, and He Who formed you, O Israel: Fear not, for I have redeemed you [ransomed you by paying a price instead of leaving you captives]; I have called you by your name; you are Mine" (Isaiah 43:1 AMP).

39. "Your God says to you: 'Comfort, comfort my people with gentle, compassionate words. Speak tenderly from the heart to revive those in Jerusalem and proclaim that their warfare is over. Her debt of sin is paid for, and she will not be treated as guilty. Prophesy to her that she has received from the hand of Yahweh twice as many blessings as all her sins'" (Isaiah 40:1-2 TPT).

40. "God said, Let Us [Father, Son, and Holy Spirit] make mankind in Our image, after Our likeness, and let them have complete authority over the fish of the sea, the birds of the air, the [tame] beasts, and over all of the earth, and over everything that creeps upon the earth" (Genesis 1:26 AMP).

41. "The authority of the name of Jesus causes every knee to bow in reverence! Everything and everyone will one day submit to this name—in the heavenly realm, in the earthly realm, and in the demonic realm. And every tongue will proclaim, in every language: Jesus Christ is Lord Yahweh, bringing glory and honor to God, his Father!" (Philippians 2:10–11 TPT). See *The Passion Translation* note: "As translated from the Aramaic. The Greek text uses the word *kurios*, which is not the highest name for God. Yahweh (Hebrew) or Jehovah (Latin) is the highest name. *Kurios* is a title also used for false gods, landowners, merchants, and nobles. The Greek language has no equal to the sacred name (the tetragrammaton—YHWH,) Yahweh. Only Hebrew and Aramaic have that equivalent."

42. Satan will "bruise His heel" by putting Jesus to death on the cross. The

shedding of Jesus's blood was the first blow to Satan (the "bruise" which bought us back from Satan's grip) but the ultimate victory will come when Jesus returns and sends Satan to the lake of fire. (Revelation 20:7–10).

43. "She will give birth to a son and you are to name him 'Savior,' for he is destined to give his life to save his people from their sins" (Matthew 1:21 TPT). (See TPT footnote for the Hebrew definition of Jesus).

44. This close examination of the name Yeshua is needed because the word we most commonly recognize and use for this Savior is the Greek word, Jesus, which loses a degree of accuracy in the translation.

45. Taken from "The Hebrew Meaning of 'Jesus,'" www.hebrew-streams.org.

46. Ibid.

47. WHAT SECRET DOES "GOD'S ESSENCE" NAME HOLD FOR US WHO BELIEVE IN HIM? God's four-letter name, YHVA, Yahweh, is called the "Essence Name" of God and stands for "being" and "existence." The four Hebrew letters that comprise this name—in various combinations—represent all the Hebrew tenses of past, present, and future. One more tense is also represented with these same letters—the imperative command form that was used when God created the world. He said, "Be Light!" This is the imperative form of the verb "to be." Our past, present, and future all have God's Essence Name attached! Also, we have ability to speak things into existence when God's Essence Name is attached, just as God Himself "spoke" the world into existence. (Example: "Be healed!")

48. Ben-Gigi, Danny, "God's Secrets Only Hebrew Can Reveal," page 139. (See Chapter Two, Footnote #43 for more information about the Essence Name.)

49. *Strong's Concordance* (H#3467).

50. Taken from "The Hebrew Meaning of 'Jesus,'" www.hebrew-streams.org.

51. "The Son of Man has come to give life to anyone who is lost" (Matthew 18:11 TPT). "I will seek that which was lost and bring back that which has strayed, and I will bandage the hurt and the crippled and will strengthen the weak and the sick, but I will destroy the fat and the strong [who have become hardhearted and perverse]; I will feed them with judgment and punishment" (Ezekiel 34:16 AMP).

52. "[For I always pray to] the God of our Lord Jesus Christ, the Father of glory, that He may grant you a spirit of wisdom and revelation [of insight into mysteries and secrets] in the [deep and intimate] knowledge of Him. By having the eyes of your heart flooded with light, so that you can know and understand the hope to which He has called you, and how rich is His glorious inheritance in the saints (His set-apart ones)" (Ephesians 1:17–20 AMP).

53. **Going Deeper:** Visit www.emilygardnerfoppe.com to download and print additional question-and-answer material pertaining to this chapter and subsequent chapters. The material presented will (1) provide a review of this chapter and (2) take you deeper into the discussion.

Boxes:

HOW MANY DEMONS ARE THERE?

1. "Your hand-to-hand combat is not with human beings, but with the highest principalities and authorities operating in rebellion under the heavenly realms. For they are a powerful class of demon-gods and evil spirits that hold this dark world in bondage" (Ephesians 6:12–13 TPT).

2. "I won't speak with you much longer, for the ruler of this dark world is coming. But he has no power over me, for he has nothing to use against me" (John 14:30 TPT).

3. "The dragon's massive tail swept across the sky and dragged away a third of the stars of heaven and cast them to the earth. And the dragon crouched before the woman who was about to give birth—poised to devour the baby the moment it was born" (Revelation 12:4 TPT).

4. "Then I looked, and I heard the voices of myriads of angels in circles around the throne, as well as the voices of the living creatures and the elders—myriads and myriads! And as I watched, all of them were singing with thunderous voices: 'Worthy is Christ the Lamb who was slaughtered to receive great power and might, wealth and wisdom, and honor, glory, and praise!'" (Revelation 5:11–12 TPT).

WHAT ARE THE DEMONS' NAMES?

1. A whole chapter in the Book of Job, Chapter 41, is dedicated to describing Leviathan and his reckless behavior. In addition, the Prophet Isaiah reveals that "in that day [the Lord will deliver Israel from her enemies and also from the rebel powers of evil and darkness]. His sharp and unrelenting, great, and strong sword will visit and punish Leviathan, the swiftly fleeing serpent, Leviathan, the twisting and winding serpent; and He will slay the monster that is in the sea" (Isaiah 27:1 AMP).

WHAT IS HELL AND WHERE IS IT LOCATED?

1. Ezekiel 14:17

2. "Yet you shall be brought down to Sheol, to the innermost recesses of the pit (the region of the dead)" (Isaiah 14:15 AMP).

3. SATAN'S PLACE OF CONFINEMENT: "Then I saw an angel descending

from heaven; he was holding the key of the Abyss (the bottomless pit) and a great chain was in his hand. And he gripped and overpowered the dragon, that old serpent [of primeval times], who is the devil and Satan, and [securely] bound him for a thousand years. v.7 And when the thousand years are completed, Satan will be released from his place of confinement" (Revelation 20:1–2, 7 AMP).

4.   SATAN'S ETERNAL TORMENT: "Then the devil who had led them astray [deceiving and seducing them] was hurled into the fiery lake of burning brimstone, where the beast and false prophet were; and they will be tormented day and night forever and ever (through the ages of the ages). v. 12 I [also] saw the dead, great and small; they stood before the throne, and books were opened. Then another book was opened, which is [the Book] of Life. And the dead were judged (sentenced) by what they had done [their whole way of feeling acting, their aims and endeavors] in accordance with what was recorded in the books. v.15 And if anyone's [name] was not found recorded in the Book of Life, he was hurled into the lake of fire" (Revelation 20:10, 12, 15 AMP).

DO ALL EVIL BEINGS EXIST IN HELL?

1.   "Someone I'm acquainted with, who is in union with Christ, was swept away fourteen years ago in an ecstatic experience. He was taken into the third heaven, but I'm not sure if he was in his body or out of his body—only God knows. And I know that this man (again, I'm not sure if he was still in his body or taken out of his body—God knows) was caught up in an ecstatic experience and brought into paradise, where he overheard many wondrous and inexpressible secrets that were so sacred that no mortal is permitted to repeat them" (2 Corinthians 12:2–4 TPT). *The Passion Translation* notes that most scholars agree this is the highest realm of the immediate presence of God.

WHAT IS THE SECRET PLACE AND WHERE IS IT FOUND?

1.   See *Finding the Secret Place: 8 Keys to Experiencing God's Presence*, by Emily Gardner Foppe.

2.   The Hebrew word for "secret place" is *cether, Strong's Concordance* (H#5642), meaning "covering, shelter, hiding place, secrecy."

3.   "He offers a resting place for me in his luxurious love. His tracks take me to an oasis of peace, the quiet brook of bliss" (Psalm 23:2 TPT).

4.   "He who dwells in the secret place of the Most High shall remain stable and fixed under the shadow of the Almighty [Whose power no foe can withstand]" (Psalm 91:1 AMP).

5.   "You have said, 'Seek My face [inquire for and require My presence as your vital need],' My heart said to You, 'Your face (Your presence), Lord, will I seek, inquire for, and require [of necessity and on the authority of Your Word]'"

(Psalm 27:8 AMP).

6. "Surely the Lord God will do nothing without revealing His secrets to His servants the prophets" (Amos 3:7 AMP).

7. "I will cry to God Most High, who accomplishes all things on my behalf (for He completes my purposes in His Plan)" (Psalm 57:2 AMP).

8. "And let the beauty and delightfulness and favor of the Lord our God be upon us; confirm and establish the work of our hands – yes, the work of our hands, confirm and establish it." (Psalm 90:17 AMP).

9. A stronghold is a thinking pattern based on lies and deceptions. See Chapter Two.

WHAT IS THE PURPOSE OF THE HEAVENLY COURTROOM SETTING VS. THE SECRET PLACE?

1. "My little children, I write you these things so that you may not violate God's law and sin. But if anyone should sin, we have an Advocate (One Who will intercede for us) with the Father—[it is] Jesus Christ [the all] righteous [upright, just, who conforms to the Father's will in every purpose, thought, and action]. And He [that same Jesus Himself] is the propitiation (the atone sacrifice) for our sins, and not for ours alone abut also for [the sins of] the whole world" (1 John 2:1–2 AMP).

2. "Righteousness and justice are the foundation of Your throne; mercy and lovingkindness and truth go before Your face" (Psalm 89:14 AMP).

3. "Therefore, you have no excuse or defense or justification, O man, whoever you are who judges and condemns another. For in posing as judge and passing sentence on another, you condemn yourself, because you who judge are habitually practicing the very same things [that you censure and denounce]. [But] we know that the judgment (adverse verdict, sentence) of God falls justly and in accordance with truth upon those who practice such things. And do you think or imagine, O man, when you judge and condemn those who practice such things and yet do them yourself, that you will escape God's judgment and elude His sentence and adverse verdict?" (Romans 2:1–3 AMP).

4. "For there [is only] one God, and [only] one Mediator between God and men, the Man Christ Jesus, who gave Himself as a ransom for all [people, a fact that was] attested at the right and proper time" (1 Timothy 2:5–6 AMP).

5. "And I will ask the Father, and He will give you another Comforter (Counselor, Helper, Intercessor, Advocate, Strengthener, and Standby), that He may remain with you forever —the Spirit of Truth, whom the world cannot receive (welcome, take to its heart), because it does not see Him or know and recognize Him. But you know and recognize Him, for He lives with you [constantly] and will be in you" (John 14:16–17 AMP).

6. JESUS'S BLOOD IS OUR CONFIDENCE TO ENTER THE SECRET PLACE WHERE GOD IS: "Therefore, brethren, since we have full freedom and confidence to enter into the [Holy of] Holies [by the power and virtue] in the blood of Jesus, (v.22) Let us all come forward and draw near with true (honest and sincere) hearts in unqualified assurance and absolute conviction engendered by faith (by that leaning of the entire human personality on God in absolute trust and confidence in His power, wisdom, and goodness), having our hearts sprinkled and purified from a guilty (evil) conscience and our bodies cleansed with pure water" (Hebrews 10:19, 22 AMP).

7. John 14:16–17 references the Holy Spirit as *parakletos*, or "defense attorney," *Strong's Concordance* (G#3875). Jesus is our Mediator. He is also referred to as "defense attorney" or "advocate" in this passage: "My little children, I write you these things so that you may not violate God's law and sin. But if anyone should sin, we have an Advocate (*parakletos*) (One Who will intercede for us) with the Father—[it is] Jesus Christ [the all] righteous [upright, just, Who conforms to the Father's will in every purpose, thought, and action]" (1 John 2:1 AMP).

8. "The Secret Place" is considered synonymous with "the Sanctuary" and "the Mountain of God," also called "the Zion-Realm." On the other hand, "the Throne Room" is closely related to "the Courtroom" of heaven. We are seated with Christ in "the Throne Room" when we are motivated to use the "authority" He has given us to overcome evil.

WHAT IS GOD'S "GIFT" OF "AUTHORITY" TO HIS CHILDREN?

1. "Yet what honor you have given to men, created only a little lower than Elohim, crowned like kings and queens with glory and magnificence. You have delegated to them mastery over all you have made, making everything subservient to their authority, placing earth itself under the feet of your image-bearers" (Psalm 8:5 TPT). Note from TPT: The Hebrew word *Elohim* is the same name used for the Creator-God in Genesis 1:1 who "spoke" things into being.

2. "And he will send you Jesus, the Messiah, the chosen one for you. for he must remain in heaven until the restoration of all things has taken place, fulfilling everything that God said long ago through his holy prophets" (Acts 2:20 TPT). *The Passion Translation* notes explain, "The word restoration in Greek is *apokatastasis*, which infers the restoration of creation to the state of existence before the fall, but also Davidic covenant being restored. Luke's choice of the Greek word found only here in the New Testament is noteworthy. It is a medical term that means *restoration of perfect health*."

3. "Why are you so angry and bothered? If you offer what is right, won't you be accepted? But if you refuse to offer what is right, sin, the predator, is

crouching in wait outside the door of your heart. It desires to have you, yet you must be its master" (Genesis 4:6-7 TPT).

Chapter Two

1. Deep healing does not occur though "osmosis"—meaning "a passive transport, not requiring energy to be applied." From *Simple English Wikipedia*.

2. "For the Light of Truth was about to come into the world and shine upon everyone" John 1:9 TPT).

3. (1) "The eternal God is your refuge and dwelling place, and underneath are the everlasting arms; He drove the enemy before you and thrust them out, saying Destroy!" (Deuteronomy 3:27 AMP). (2) "So the young son set off for home, from a long distance away, his father saw him coming, dressed as a beggar, and great compassion swelled up in his heart for his son who was returning home. So the father raced out to meet him. He swept him up in his arms, hugged him dearly, and kissed him over and over with tender love" (Luke 15:20 TPT).

4. "Jesus repeated his greeting, 'Peace to you!' And he told them, 'Just as the Father has sent me, I'm now sending you.' Then, taking a deep breath, he blew on them and said, 'Receive the Holy Spirit.'" (John 20:21-22 TPT). The Greek word for "breathed" is *emphysao, Strong's Concordance* (G#1720). *The Passion Translation* footnote says: "The Greek word used here does not appear elsewhere in the NT, however, it is the same word found in the Septuagint for God "breathed" into Adam's nostrils the breath of life (Genesis 2:7)."

5. I have designed a RIGHTNESS/WRONGNESS CHART which can be downloaded from my website. www.emilygardnerfoppe.com. (See the QR Code on the back cover.)

6. "Once your life was full of sin's darkness, but now you have the very light of our Lord shining through you because of your union with him. Your mission is to live as children flooded with his revelation-light! And the supernatural fruits of his light will be seen in you—goodness, righteousness, and truth. Then you will learn to choose what is beautiful to our Lord" (Ephesians 5:8–10 TPT).

7. "There is a divine mystery—a secret surprise that has been concealed from the world for generations, but now it's being revealed, unfolded, and manifested for every holy believer to experience. Living within you is the Christ who floods you with the expectation of glory! This mystery of Christ, embedded within us, becomes a heavenly treasure chest of hope filled with the riches of glory for his people, and God wants everyone to know it!" (Colossians 2:26–28 TPT).

8. "I have been crucified with Christ [in Him I have shared His crucifixion] it is no longer I who live, but Christ (the Messiah) lives in me; and the life I

now live in the body I live by faith in (by adherence to and reliance on and complete trust in) the Son of God, Who loved me and gave Himself up for me" (Galatians 2:20 AMP).

9. Definition from *The Oxford Dictionary* online: a self-righteously moralistic person who behaves as if superior to others.

10. "It is always better to come to terms with the one who wants to sue you before you go to trial, or you may be found guilty by the judge, and he will hand you over to the officers, who will throw you into prison. Believe me, you won't get out of prison until you have paid the full amount!" (Matthew 5:25–26 TPT).

11. "Christ's resurrection is your resurrection too. This is why we are to yearn for all that is above, for that's where Christ sits enthroned at the place of all power, honor, and authority! Yes, feast on all the treasures of the heavenly realm and fill your thoughts with heavenly realities, and not with the distractions of the natural realm" (Colossians 3:1–2 TPT).

12 "Repent" is the Greek word *metanoia, Strong's Concordance* (G#3341), which means "turn from error" or "take another mind."

13. "Turn" is the Greek word *epistrepho, Strong's Concordance* (G#1994), which means "be converted" or "turn back."

14. "Repent" is *metanoia*.

15. "Through our union with Christ we too have been claimed by God as his own inheritance. Before we were even born, he gave us our destiny that we would fulfill the plan of God who always accomplishes every purpose and plan in his heart" (Ephesians 1:11 TPT).

16. "Are you weary, carrying a heavy burden? Then come to me. I will refresh your life, for I am your oasis. Simply join your life with mine. Learn my ways and you'll discover that I'm gentle, humble, easy to please. You will find refreshment and rest in me. For all that I require of you will be pleasant and easy to bear" (Matthew 11:28–30 TPT).

17. REMINDER: Download the RIGHTNESS/WRONGNESS CHART from my website. I designed it specifically for your use, while studying, meditating, praying, and relaxing in God's Presence! www.emilygardnerfoppe.com (See the QR Code on the back cover.)

18. "We love Him because He first loved us" (1 John 4:19 AMP).

19. "The Lord appeared from of old to me [Israel], saying Yes, I have loved you with an everlasting love; therefore, with loving-kindness have I drawn you and continued My faithfulness to you" (Jeremiah 31:3 AMP).

20. "But in the depths of my heart, I truly know that you, Yahweh, have

become my Shield: You take me and surround me with yourself. Your glory covers me continually. You lift high my head when I bow low in shame. I have cried out to you, Yahweh, from your holy presence. You send me a father's help" (Psalm 3:3–4 TPT).

21. "So now I'll lie down and sleep like a baby—then I'll awake in safety, for you surround me with your glory. Even though dark powers prowl around me, I won't be afraid. I simply cry out to you: 'Rise up and help me, Lord! Come and save me!' And you will slap them in the face, breaking the power of their words to harm me" (Psalm 3:5–7 TPT).

22. "So don't ever be afraid, dearest friends! Your loving Father joyously gives you his kingdom realm with all its promises!" (Luke 12:32 TPT).

23. "Life came into being because of him, for his life is light for all humanity. And this Living Expression is the Light that bursts through gloom—the Light that darkness could not diminish!" (John 1:4–5 TPT).

24. "Then Jesus said, I am light to the world and those who embrace me will experience life-giving light, and they will never walk in darkness" (John 8:12 TPT).

25. "LIFT" YOUR PEOPLE UP INTO GOD'S PRESENCE AND IMAGINE THIS: "Those who walked in darkness have seen a radiant light shining upon them. They once lived in the shadows of death, but now a glorious light has dawned! Lord, you have multiplied the nation and given them overwhelming joy! They are ecstatic in your presence and rejoice like those who bring in a great harvest and those who divide up the spoils of victory! For you have broken the chains that have bound your people and lifted off the heavy bar across their shoulders, the rod the oppressor used against them. You have shattered all their bondage, just as you did when Midian's armies were defeated" (Isaiah 9:2–4 TPT).

26. Our mindsets are "fallen" and must be constantly renewed through the Word and the Spirit.

27. Footnote for Isaiah 28:20, *The Book of Isaiah, The Passion Translation*, 2018.

28. "I pray that the light of God will illuminate the eyes of your imagination, flooding you with light, until you experience the full revelation of the hope of his calling—that is, the wealth of God's glorious inheritances that he finds in us, his holy ones!" (Ephesians 1:18 TPT).

29. "So let us seize and hold fast and retain without wavering the hope we cherish and confess and our acknowledgement of it, for He Who promised is reliable (sure) and faithful to His word" (Hebrews 10:23 AMP).

30. "And now we are brothers and sisters in God's family because of the blood of Jesus, and he welcomes us to come into the most holy sanctuary in the heavenly realm—boldly and without hesitation. For he has dedicated a new, life-giving way for us to approach God. For just as the veil was torn in two, Jesus' body was torn open to give us free and fresh access to him! And since we now have a magnificent High Priest to welcome us into God's house, we come closer to God and approach him with an open heart, fully convinced that nothing will keep us at a distance from him. For our hearts have been sprinkled with blood to remove impurity, and we have been freed from an accusing conscience. Now we are clean, unstained, and presentable to God inside and out! So now wrap your heart tightly around the hope that lives within us, knowing that God always keeps his promises!" (Hebrews 10:19–23 TPT).

31. WHEN JESUS MINISTERS TO ME IN A MEMORY, THE POWER OF THE TRAUMATIC EXPERIENCE TO HARM ME IS DISSOLVED: "I have told you these things, so that in Me you may have [perfect] peace and confidence. In the world you have tribulation and trials and distress and frustration; but be of good cheer [take courage; be confident, certain, undaunted]! For I have overcome the world. [I have deprived it of power to harm you and have conquered it for you]" (John 16:33 AMP).

32. THANK YOU, GOD! YOU ARE CHANGING MY NATURE THROUGH THE EXCHANGES YOU MAKE: "Everything we could ever need for life and godliness has already been deposited in us by his divine power. For all this was lavished upon us through the rich experience of knowing him who has called us by name and invited us to come to him through a glorious manifestation of his goodness. As a result of this, he has given you magnificent promises that are beyond all price, so that through the power of these tremendous promises you can experience partnership with the divine nature, by which you have escaped the corrupt desires that are of the world" (2 Peter 1:3–4 TPT).

33. THE ESSENCE OF HIS NAME HAS THE POWER TO GIVE ME ALL I NEED: "I assure you most solemnly I tell you, that My Father will grant you whatever you ask in My Name [as presenting all that I AM]. Up to this time you have not asked a [single] thing in My Name [as presenting all that I AM]; but now ask and keep on asking and you will receive, so that your joy (gladness, delight) may be full and complete" (John 16:23–24 AMP).

34. THE REDEEMER EXCHANGES MY FEAR FOR AN ABSOLUTE CERTAINTY OF HIS LOVE FOR ME: "There is no fear in love [dread does not exist], but full-grown (complete, perfect) love turns fear out of doors and expels every trace of terror! For fear brings with it the thought of punishment, and [so] he who is afraid has not reached the full maturity of love [is not yet

grown into love's complete perfection]" (1 John 4:18 AMP).

35. **Going Deeper:** Visit www.emilygardnerfoppe.com to download and print additional question-and-answer material pertaining to this chapter. The material presented will (1) provide a review of this chapter and (2) take you deeper into the discussion.

Boxes

WHAT IS THE ZION-REALM?

1. "In the last days, the mountain of Yahweh's temple will be raised up as the head of the mountains, towering over all the hills. A sparkling steam of every nation will flow into it. Many peoples will come and say, 'Everyone, come! Let's go up higher to Yahweh's mountain, to the house of Jacob's God; then he can teach us his ways and we can walk in his paths!' Zion will be the center of instruction, and the word of Yahweh will go out from Jerusalem" (Isaiah 2:2–3 TPT).

2. "Rise up in splendor and be radiant, for your light has dawned, and Yahweh's glory now streams from you! Look carefully! Darkness blankets the earth, and thick gloom covers the nations, but Yahweh arises upon you and the brightness of his glory appears over you! Nations will be attracted to your radiant light and kings to the sunrise-glory of your new day" (Isaiah 60:1–3 TPT).

WHAT IS A SOUL TIE?

1. "Don't you know that your bodies belong to Christ as his body parts? Should one presume to take the member of Christ's body and make them into member of a harlot? Absolutely not! Aren't you aware of the fact that when anyone sleeps with a prostitute he becomes a part of her, and she becomes a part of him? For it has been declared: The two become a single body" (1 Corinthians 6:15–16 TPT).

2 "But the one who joins himself to the Lord is mingled into one spirit with him" (1 Corinthians 6:17 TPT).

3. "From the beginning God created male and female. For this reason a man will leave his parents and be wedded to his wife. And the husband and wife will be joined as one flesh, and after that they no longer exist as two, but one flesh" (Mark 10:6-8 TPT).

4. "For in the resurrected state neither do [men] marry nor are [womn] given in marriage, but they are like the angels in heaven" (Matthew 22:30 AMP).

WHAT IS A STRONGHOLD?

1. "Every good gift and every perfect (free, large, full) gift is from above; it comes down from the Father of all [that gives] light, in [the shining of] whom

there can be no variation [rising or setting] or shadow cast by His turning [as in an eclipse]" (James 1:17 AMP). *The Passion Translation* uses "the Father of lights."

2. "For the Word that God speaks is alive and full of power [making it active, operative, energizing, and effective]; it is sharper than any two-edged sword, penetrating to the dividing line of the breath of life (soul) and [the immortal] spirit, and of joints and marrow [of the deepest parts of our nature], exposing and sifting and analyzing and judging the very thoughts and purposes of the heart. And not a creature exists that is concealed from His sight, but all things are open and exposed, naked and defenseless to the eyes of Him with whom we have to do" (Hebrews 4:12–13 AMP).

3. "For the weapons of our warfare are not physical [weapons of flesh and blood], but they are mighty before God for the overthrow and destruction of strongholds" (2 Corinthians 10:4 AMP).

4. Then he said to me, 'This [continuous supply of oil] is the word of the Lord to Zerubbabel [prince of Judah], saying, 'Not by might, nor by power, but by My Spirit [of whom the oil is a symbol],' says the Lord of hosts" (Zechariah 4:6 AMP).

Chapter Three

1. Larson, Bob. *Jezebel*, Chapter Three, "Control Freak," 2015.

2. "Let those curse it who curse the day, who are skilled in rousing up Leviathan" (Job 3:8 AMP).

3. From *Restored to Freedom*, by Nelson Schuman, 2017.

4. WHAT IS A GENERATIONAL SPIRIT? It is an evil spirit that has entered a person's bloodline due to generational "iniquity"—the egregious sin (and resulting curses) passed by the fathers unto the children, into the third and fourth generations. The detail of this concept will be discussed in later chapters. "The Lord is long-suffering and slow to anger, and abundant in mercy and loving-kindness, forgiving iniquity and transgression; but He will by no means clear the guilty, visiting the iniquity of the fathers upon the children, upon the third and fourth generation" (Numbers 14:18 AMP).

5. Generational curses can "attract" to us the influences of outside parties and the negative emotions they carry and inflict upon us.

6. Nelson Schuman speaks of these as being related to the Spirit of Legion. People severely oppressed by Legion are typically victims—bitter, unforgiving, isolated, even self-mutilating.

7. Wright, Henry W. *A More Excellent Way*, Whitaker House, 2009.

8. From "Word Study – And He Gave to Moses His Bride," www.chaimbentorah.com, 2014.

9. Ibid.

10. Paraphrased from "Word Study – And He Gave to Moses His Bride," www.chaimbentorah.com, 2014.

11. "Beloved, don't be obsessed with taking revenge, but leave that to God's righteous justice. For the scriptures say: 'Vengeance is mine, and I will repay,' says the Lord" (Romans 12:19 TPT).

12. "If the Lord Yahweh rescued Lot, he knows how to continually rescue the godly from their trials and to reserve the ungodly for punishment on the day of judgment" (2 Peter 2:9 TPT). The TPC notes say: Or "to keep the unrighteous under punishment until the day of judgment," which implies that the wicked are living under God's punishment even before they are ultimately judged.

13. "*Dissociation* refers to the mind's ability to compartmentalize and separate from conscious awareness those experiences which are traumatic. The traumatic information will remain unconscious until the conscious mind has gained enough joy capacity to manage the distressing emotions and resolve any internal conflicts that arise from the traumatic information." *Prayer Warriors: A Prayer Book for Survivors of Severe Trauma and Those Who Care for Them*, by Jo Getzinger and Sara Manasseh, 2008, CARE, Inc., pg. 87.

14. Connie owns a coffee shop in N.C. She found my book *Finding the Secret Place: 8 Keys to Experiencing God's Presence* online about four years ago. Since then we have met three time face to face and talked on the phone a number of times. I encouraged her to do more memory healing about two years ago when she was battling breast cancer. She contacted someone locally who had been trained in inner healing of this sort and had very good success.

15. "When he had sipped the sour wine, he said, 'It is finished, my bride!' Then he bowed his head and surrendered his spirit to God." (John 19:30 TPT). For further study of the Hebrew word *kalah*, a homonym that can mean both "fulfilled [completed]" and "bride," See *The Passion Translation* notes for this verse.

16. Taken from footnotes in *The Passion Translation*, 2017.

17. "USE WHAT FAITH YOU HAVE NOW TO APPLY JESUS'S BLOOD TO YOUR LIFE AND CIRCUMSTANCES. Granted, it is a mystery how or why this works. But the Bible is clear. There is amazing power in Jesus's blood shed for us. It is the single greatest reason we can receive everything we need." Taken from Chapter Three, *Finding the Secret Place: 8 Keys to Experiencing God's Presence*, by Emily Gardner Foppe.

18. "Saved" is the Greek word *sozo* – "to preserve one who is in danger of destruction, to save or rescue" and "to save one suffering from disease, to make well, heal, restore to health," *Strong's Concordance* (G#4982).

19. "Reconciled" is *katallasso* in the Greek, *Strong's Concordance* (#G2644). It means "to change, exchange, as coins, for others of equivalent value."

20. "For today in Bethlehem a rescuer was born for you. He is the Lord Yahweh, the Messiah. You will recognize him by this miracle sign: You will find a baby wrapped in strips of cloth and lying in a feeding trough!" (Luke 2:11–12 TPT). *The Passion Translation* notes indicate verse 11 is translated literally from the Aramaic text.

21. Download the RIGHTNESS/WRONGNESS CHART for free on my website! (See the QR Code on the back cover.)

22. **Going Deeper:** Visit www.emilygardnerfoppe.com to download and print additional question-and-answer material pertaining to this chapter. The material presented will (1) provide a review of this chapter and (2) take you deeper into the discussion.

23. "Every gift God freely gives us is good and perfect, streaming down from the Father of lights, who shines from the heavens with no hidden shadow or darkness and is never subject to change" (James 1:17 TPT).

Boxes

WHAT IS THE SPIRIT OF RELIGION

1. "They may pretend to have a respect for God, but in reality they want nothing to do with God's power. Stay away from people like these!" (2 Timothy 3:5 TPT).

2. See *The Mirror Translation* notes from 1 John 3:12.

CHAPTER FOUR

1. www.upcounsel.com/difference-between-covenant-and-contract

2. "Thus says the Lord: If you can break My covenant with the day, and My covenant with the night, so that there should not be day and night in their season, Then can also My covenant be broken with David My servant, so that he shall not have a son to reign upon his throne, and [My league be broken also] with the Levitical priests, My ministers" (Jeremiah 33:20–21 AMP).

3. "For I desire and delight in dutiful steadfast love and goodness, not sacrifice, and the knowledge of and acquaintance with God more than burnt offerings. But they, like [less-privileged] men and like Adam, have transgressed the covenant; there have they dealt faithlessly and treacherously with Me" (Hosea 6:6–7 AMP).

4. "All the heavens and everything on earth belong to you, for you are the

Creator of all that is seen and unseen. The four corners of the earth were put in place by you. You made the majestic mountains that are still shouting their praises to your name. Breathtaking and awesome is your power! Astounding and unbelievable is your might and strength when it goes on display! Your glorious throne rests on a foundation of righteousness and just verdicts. Grace and truth are the attendants who go before you" (Psalm 89:11–14 TPT).

5. "A child has been born to us; a son has been given to us. The responsibility of complete dominion will rest on his shoulders, and his name will be: The Wonderful One! The Extraordinary Strategist! The Mighty God! The Father of Eternity! The Prince of Peace! Great and vast is his dominion. He will bring immeasurable peace and prosperity. He will rule on David's throne and over David's kingdom to establish and uphold it by promoting justice and righteousness from this time forward and forevermore. The marvelous passion that the Lord Yahweh, Commander of Angel Armies, has for his people will ensure that it is finished!" (Isaiah 9:6–7 TPT).

6. "For there [is only] one God, and [only] one Mediator between God and men, the Man Christ Jesus, who gave Himself as a ransom for all [people, a fact that was] attested to at the right and proper time" (1 Timothy 2:5 AMP).

7. "So Jesus is the One who has enacted a new covenant with a new relationship with God so that those who accept the invitation will receive the eternal inheritance he has promised to his heirs. For he died to release us from the guilt of the violations committed under the first covenant" (Hebrews 9:15 TPT).

8. "For the accuser of our brothers and sisters, who relentlessly accused them day and night before our God, has now been defeated—cast out once and for all!" (Revelation 12:10 TPT). "Accuser" is *kategoreo* in the Greek, *Strong's Concordance* (G#2723), and refers to one who "makes an accusation before a judge."

9. "The Lord is long-suffering and slow to anger, and abundant in mercy and loving-kindness, forgiving iniquity and transgression. But he will by no means clear the guilty, visiting the iniquity of the fathers upon the children, upon the third and fourth generation" (Numbers 14:18 AMP).

10. "Thus says the Lord of hosts: If you will walk in my ways and keep My charge, then also you shall rule My house and have charge of My courts, and I will give you access [to My presence] and places to walk among these who stand here" (Joshua 3:7 AMP).

11. "They conquered him completely through the blood of the Lamb—and the powerful word of his testimony" (Revelation 12:11 TPT). *The Passion Translation* footnotes say this is translated from the Aramaic. "The Greek is 'the word of their testimony.' It is the faithful testimony of Jesus that has the power to destroy the works of the devil."

12. See Deuteronomy Chapter 28 and Jeremiah Chapter 17.

13. "Now there was a day when the sons (the angels) of God came to present themselves before the Lord, and Satan (the adversary and accuser) also came among them" (Job 1:6 AMP).

14. "And to the one who conquers I will give the privilege of sitting with me on my throne, just as I conquered and sat down with my Father on his throne. The one whose heart is open let him listen carefully to what the Spirit is saying now to the churches" (Revelation 3:21–22 TPT).

15. "But about his Son, he called him God, saying, 'Your throne, O God, endures forever and ever and you will rule your kingdom with justice and righteousness, For you have cherished righteousness and detested lawlessness. For this reason, God, your God, has anointed you and poured out the oil of bliss on you more than on any of your friends.' And he called him Lord, saying, 'Lord, you formed the earth in the beginning and with your own hands you crafted the cosmos. They will both one day disappear, but you will remain forever! They will all fade like a worn-out garment, And they will be changed like clothes, and you will fold them up and put them away. But you are I AM. You never change, years without end!' And God has never said this to any of his angels: 'Take your seat next to me at my right hand until I force your whispering enemies to be a rug under your feet'" (Hebrews 1:8–13 TPT). *The Passion Translation* notes: "I AM" in the Aramaic is "you are as you are!"

16. "Your glorious throne rests on a foundation of righteousness and just verdicts. Grace and truth are the attendants who go before you" (Psalm 89:14 TPT).

17. "But rather you have come to Mount Zion, even to the city of the living God, the heavenly Jerusalem, and to countless multitudes of angels in festal gathering. And to the church (assembly) of the Firstborn who are registered (as citizens) in heaven, and to the God Who is Judge of all, and to the spirits of the righteous (the redeemed in heaven) who have been made perfect. And to Jesus, the Mediator (Go-between, Agent) of a new covenant, and to the sprinkled blood which speaks [of mercy], a better and nobler and more gracious message than the blood of Abel [which cried out for vengeance]" (Hebrews 12:22–24 AMP).

18. This is one of the main premises in Robert Henderson's book *Operating in the Courts of Heaven.*

19. "For the accuser of our brothers and sisters, who relentlessly accused them day and night before our God, has now been defeated—cast out once and for all!" (Revelation 12:10 TPT). "Accuser" is *kategoreo* in the Greek (*Strong's Concordance* G#2723) and refers to one who "makes an accusation before a judge."

20. "Therefore, since we are justified (acquitted, declared righteous, and given a right standing with God) through faith, let us [grasp the fact that we] have

[the peace of reconciliation to hold and to enjoy] peace with God through our Lord Jesus Christ (the Messiah, the Anointed One)" (Romans 5:1 AMP).

21. *Strong's Concordance* (G#1344).

22. *Strong's Concordance* (G#1343).

23. "It's true that some of you once lived in those lifestyles, but now you have been purified from sin, made holy, and given a perfect standing before God—all because of the power of the name of the Lord Jesus, the Messiah, and through our union with the Spirit of our God" (1 Corinthians 6:11 TPT).

24. *Hagiazo, Strong's Concordance* (G#37).

25. "Peter, my dear friend, listen to what I'm about to tell you. Satan has obtained permission to come and sift you all like wheat and test your faith. But I have prayed for you, Peter, that you would stay faithful to me no matter what comes" (Luke 22:31–32 TPT).

26. *Exaiteo, Strong's Concordance* (G#1809).

27. *Strong's Concordance* (H#2398).

28. "Look how you have fallen from your heavenly place, O shining one, son of the dawn! You have been cut down to the ground, you who conquered nations. You said in your heart, 'I will ascend into heaven and exalt my throne above the stars of God. I will rule on the mountain of the congregation, on the highest place of the sacred mountain. I will rise past the tops of the clouds and rival the Most High God!'" (Isaiah 14:12–14 TPT). Note: The name Lucifer, a Latin word meaning "light-bearer," appears in *The King James Version*. The Hebrew for "shining one" as translated here, is *heylel, Strong's Concordance* (H#1966).

29. "That doesn't surprise us, for even Satan transforms himself to appear as an angel of light! So it's no wonder his servants also go about pretending to be ministers of righteousness. But in the end they will be exposed and get exactly what they deserve" (2 Corinthians 11:14–15 TPT).

30. "For God's eyes are upon the ways of a man, and He sees all his steps" (Job 34:21 AMP).

31. "Then with meekness you'll be able to carefully enlighten those who argue with you so they can see God's gracious gift of repentance and be brought to the truth. This will cause them to rediscover themselves and escape from the snare of Satan who caught them in his trap so that they would carry out his purposes" (2 Timothy 2:25–26 TPT).

32. "In the beginning [before all time] was the Word (Christ), and the Word was with God, and the Word was God Himself" (John 1:1 AMP).

33. The prodigal son came to his senses. The Greek word is *erchomai*, which means "to come" and *eis heauton*, which means "to one's senses." The phrase

means "to return to self." *The Mirror* notes for Luke 16:17.

34. The word for "curse" in the Old Testament is *qelalah*, *Strong's Concordance* (H#7045), which means "vilification, execration" or "abatement of the blessing."

35. "And not a creature exists that is concealed from His sight, but all things are open and exposed, naked and defenseless to the eyes of Him with Whom we have to do" (Hebrews 4:13 AMP).

36. "And Yahweh keeps saying: 'Why such countless sacrifices—what use are they to me? I've had my fill of your burnt offerings of rams and your fattened animals. I find no delight in the blood of bulls, lambs, or goats!'" (Isaiah 1:11 TPT).

37. "Then Satan answered the Lord, Does Job [reverently] fear God for nothing? Have You not put a hedge about him and his house and all that he has, on every side? You have conferred prosperity and happiness upon him in the work of his hands, and his possessions have increased in the land. But put forth your hand now and touch all that he has, and he will curse You to Your face" (Job 1:9–11 AMP).

38. Dr. Francis Myles' revelation on how God uses restraining orders to help us fight the enemy will be explained further in Chapter Six. See also Dr. Myles' book *Issuing Divine Restraining Orders from the Courts of Heaven*, Destiny Image, 2019.

39. "Let those curse it who curse the day, who are skilled in rousing up Leviathan" (Job 3:8 AMP). "[But it is] because the arrows of the Almighty are within me, the poison which my spirit drinks up; the terrors of God set themselves in array against me" (Job 6:4 AMP). "You have granted me life and favor, and Your providence has preserved my spirit. Yet these [the present evils] have You hid in Your heart [for me since my creation]; I know that this was with You [in Your purpose and thought]. If I sin, then You observe me, and You will not acquit me from my iniquity and guilt." (Job 10:12–14 AMP). "I will not restrain my mouth; I will speak in the anguish of my spirit. I will complain in the bitterness of my soul [O Lord]!" (Job 7:11 AMP). "I even wish that it would please God to crush me, that He would let loose His hand and cut me off!" (Job 6:9 AMP). "That You inquire after my iniquity and search for my sin—although You know that I am not wicked or guilty and that there is none who can deliver me out of Your hand? Your hands have formed me and made me. Would You turn around and destroy me?" (Job 10:6–8 AMP).

40. Paraphrases from Job, Chapters 32–37: God is full of mercy and loving-kindness, power, justice and plenteous righteousness, the young man testifies. There are no words to address such a Being as He is. We cannot defend ourselves before Him, because we are in the dark and He is unapproachable light. We are to regard and respect Him. We cannot be wise in our own

understanding and conceit. God speaks again and again, but man does not listen. Sometimes God must withdraw blessing to cut pride off a man – to show him that his self-sufficiency will disappoint.

41. "Ransom" is *kopher*, *Strong's Concordance* (H#3724), meaning literally, a "cover" as "a coating" over something—figuratively, a "redemption-price, sum of money, bribe, satisfaction."

42. "Job uselessly opens his mouth and multiplies words without knowledge [drawing the worthless conclusion that the righteous have no more advantage than the wicked]" (Job 35:16 AMP).

43. "Will you also annul (set aside and render void) My judgment? Will you condemn Me [your God], that you may [appear] righteous and justified?" (Job 40:8 AMP).

44. "Where were you when I laid the foundation of the earth? Declare to Me, if you have and know understanding" (Job 38:4 AMP).

45. "[Since you question the manner of the Almighty's rule] deck yourself now with the excellency and dignity [of the Supreme Ruler, and yourself undertake the government of the world if you are so wise], and array yourself with honor and majesty" (Job 40:10 AMP).

46. "Therefore humble yourselves [demote, lower yourselves in your own estimation] under the mighty hand of God, that in due time He may exalt you" (1 Peter 5:6 AMP).

47. "Yet how much more will the sacred blood of the Messiah thoroughly cleanse our consciences! For by the power of the eternal Spirit he has offered himself to God as the perfect Sacrifice that now frees us from our dead works to worship and serve the living God" (Hebrews 9:14 TPT).

48. Satan is the "monarch" or ruler over all the sons of pride. "Sons" is *Strong's Concordance* (H#1121), *ben*, as in "unrighteous sons of men," or "unrighteous sons of God," (meaning "angels" or "supernatural beings") as seen in other passages. Example: "Now there was a day when the sons (the angels) of God came to present themselves before the Lord, and Satan (the adversary and accuser) also came among them" (Job 1:6 AMP).

49. From Job 41:34 AMP.

50. Taken from Job, Chapter 41.

51. "Then you will seek Me, inquire for, and require Me [as a vital necessity] and find Me when you search for Me with all your heart" (Jeremiah 29:13 AMP).

52. The Hebrew word for "hope" is *tiqvah*, *Strong's Concordance* (H#8615).

53. The Hebrew word for "fear" in this context is "the fear of God, respect, reverence, piety," *Strong's Concordance* (H#3374), *yir'ah*.

54. This would include your volitional sins and your iniquitous generational sins.

55. **Going Deeper:** Visit www.emilygardnerfoppe.com to download and print additional question-and-answer material pertaining to this chapter. The material presented will (1) provide a review of this chapter and (2) take you deeper into the discussion.

BOXES

WHAT IS INIQUITY?

1. "The Lord is long-suffering and slow to anger, and abundant in mercy and loving-kindness, forgiving iniquity and transgression; but He will by no means clear the guilty, visiting the iniquity of the fathers upon the children, upon the third and fourth generation" (Number 14:18 AMP). "Iniquity" is *avon* in Hebrew (*Strong's Concordance* H#5771), meaning "perversity, depravity, guilt."

2. "Moses says of Israel: They [Israel] have soiled themselves. They are not sons to Him, and that is their blemish—a perverse and crooked generation!" (Deuteronomy 32:5 AMP).

3. In a very general sense, sin is a condition that causes a person to live "without portion or form"—that is, to live with a disoriented, distorted, bankrupt identity. This definition comes from the breakdown of *harmartia,* the Greek word for sin—*ha* meaning "negative" and *meros* meaning "portion or form." See notes from 1 John 3:4, *The Mirror Translation.*

Chapter Five

1. "Why do you misunderstand what I say? It is because you are unable to hear what I am saying. [You cannot bear to listen to My message; your ears are shut to My teaching.] You are of your father, the devil, and it is your will to practice the lusts and gratify the desires [which are characteristic] of your father. He was a murderer from the beginning and does not stand in the truth, because there is not truth in him. When he speaks a falsehood, he speaks what is natural to him, for he is a liar [himself] and the father of lies and of all that is false" (John 8:44 AMP).

2. "Even if our gospel message is veiled, it is only veiled to those who are perishing, for their minds have been blinded by the god of this age, leaving them in unbelief. Their blindness keeps them from seeing the dayspring light of the wonderful news of the glory of Jesus Christ, who is the divine image of God" (2 Corinthians 4:3–4 TPT).

3. See Chapter One, under the subtitle "Disobedience, Disconnection, Displacement, Disenfranchisement, Dysfunction," specifically as it relates to the

Greek word for "sin," *harmartia*, which can be interpreted to mean "without proper form."

4. See Chapter Four, under the subtitle "Satan Still Seeks to Sabotage with His Bag of Curses and Afflictions."

5. "So, get rid of all uncleanness and the rampant outgrowth of wickedness, and in a humble (gentle, modest) spirit receive and welcome the Word which implanted and rooted [in your hearts] contains the power to save your souls" (James 1:21 AMP). Note: "Word" is *logos* in the Greek, *Strong's Concordance* (G#3056), meaning "a word, uttered by a living voice," "embodies a conception or idea," and "the sayings of God."

6. "I have told you these things, so that in Me you may have [perfect] peace and confidence. In the world you have tribulation and trials and distress and frustration; but be of good cheer [take courage; be confident, certain, undaunted]! For I have overcome the world. [I have deprived it of power to harm you and have conquered it for you]" {John 16:33 AMP).

7. "So, faith comes by hearing [what is told], and what is heard comes by the preaching [of the message that came from the lips] of Christ (the Messiah, Himself)" (Romans 10:17 AMP). "Preaching" can be "word spoken" or "utterance" in other translations. The Greek word is *rhema*, *Strong's Concordance* (G#4487), which is "that which is or has been uttered by the living voice," "thing spoken," and "word."

8. This state of being could be described as *shalom*, *Strong's Concordance* (H#7965), the Hebrew word for "prosperity, bliss, wholeness, completeness, health, peace, welfare, safety, soundness, tranquility, perfectness, fullness, rest, harmony, the absence of agitation or discord." *Shalom* comes from a root verb meaning "to be complete, perfect, and (paid in) full." See *The Passion Translation* notes for Isaiah 45:7.

9. "I had heard of You [only] by the hearing of the ear, but now my [spiritual] eye sees You" (Job 42:5 AMP).

10. See Chapter Two, subtitles "Repenting is Turning and Being Converted to a New Reality" and "Repentance is a Lifestyle of Embracing New Thoughts and Developing a New Mindset."

11. "And I will ask the Father and he will give you another Savior, the Holy Spirit of Truth, who will be to you a friend just like me—and he will never leave you. The world won't receive him because they can't see him or know him. But you know him intimately because he remains with you and will live inside you" (John 14:16-17 TPT). Note: The word used for "Savior" here is *parakletos* in the Greek, *Strong's Concordance* (G#3875). In all translations, it is used in reference to the Holy Spirit, who exhibits many characteristics

and helps us in a wide variety of ways. It can mean "one who is summoned, especially one called to aid, one who pleads another's cause before a judge, a counsel for defense, a legal assistant, an advocate, a helper, an aider—or an intercessor, consoler, comforter."

12. Nelson Schuman, author, speaker and founder of Restored to Freedom, frequently brings these general information statistics to the attention of his audiences.

13. See Chapter One, under the subtitle "Evil Intelligence, the Occult, and the Lord of the Dead."

14. "For through the eternal and living Word of God you have been born again. And this 'seed' that he planted within you can never be destroyed but will live and grow inside of you forever. For: 'Human beings are frail and temporary, like grass, and the glory of man fleeting like blossoms of the field. The grass dries and withers and the flowers fall off, but the Word of the Lord endures forever!' And this is the Word that was announced to you!" (1 Peter 1:23–25 TPT).

15. According to *The Passion Translation* notes for James 1:21, the verb usage (*sozo*) for "to continually deliver us" can refer to the ultimate salvation of our souls (personality, emotions, thoughts) and/or our eternal salvation.

16. "How to Be Delivered from Demons," Derek Prince, YouTube video, 1995.

17. "I am sent to announce a new season of Yahweh's grace and a time of God's recompense on his enemies, to comfort all who are in sorrow, to strengthen those crushed by despair who mourn in Zion—to give them a beautiful bouquet in the place of ashes, the oil of bliss instead of tears, and the mantle of joyous praise instead of the spirit of heaviness. Because of this, they will be known as Mighty Oaks of Righteousness, planted by Yahweh as a living display of his glory" (Isaiah 61:2–3 TPT).

18. "Stay away from all the foolish arguments of the immature, for these disputes will only generate more conflict. For a true servant of our Lord Jesus will not be argumentative but gentle toward all and skilled in helping others see the truth, having great patience toward the immature" (2 Timothy 2:23–24 TPT).

19. The Hebrew word for "darkness" is *choshek* (*Strong's Concordance* H#2822), which means "misery, destruction, chaos, ignorance, sorrow, wickedness."

20. "But the one who joins himself to the Lord is mingled into one spirit with him" (1 Corinthians 6:17 TPT).

21. "He must correct his opponents with courtesy and gentleness, in the hope that God may grant that they will repent and come to know the Truth [that they will perceive and recognize and become accurately acquainted with and acknowledge it]. And that they may come to their senses [and] escape out of

the snare of the devil, having been held captive by him, [henceforth] to do His [God's] will" (2 Timothy 3:25-26 AMP).

22. "How to Be Delivered from Demons," Derek Prince, YouTube, 1995.

23. The phrase "tormented by demons," "oppressed by demons" and even "demon-possessed" can be the same Greek word: *daimonizomai*, which means "to be under the power of a demon," *Strong's Concordance* (G#1139).

24. According to *The Passion Translation* note for Luke 13:11, "a spirit of bondage" is literally translated "a spirit of weakness."

25. "Then Satan answered the Lord, Does Job [reverently] fear God for nothing? Have You not put a hedge about him and his house and all that he has on every side? You have conferred prosperity and happiness upon him in the work of his hands, and his possessions have increased in the land. But put forth Your hand now and touch all that he has, and he will curse You to Your face" (Job:19–11 AMP).

26. With this said, not all demons that "bother" us become "attached" to us. Many times, a demon will taunt us "through" the words or actions of another person. Such was the case in Acts 16 when a young girl (herself tormented by a demon named Python) tormented Paul. He finally cast the demon out of her. When a case like this one arises, we must identify the demon as the "tormentor" (vs. the person through whom he is speaking or acting). Then we must learn to cast the demon out of the person or command him to leave our presence. Either way, a demon cannot operate in the presence of Jesus's blood appropriated, unless we allow him.

27. See Chapter Four for more on Justin's story.

28. "So consider carefully how Jesus faced such intense opposition from sinners who opposed their own souls, so that you won't become worn down and cave in under life's pressures" (Hebrews 12:3 TPT). *The Passion Translation* footnote says, or "those who were their own stumbling block," as translated from the Aramaic.

29. The mother of the young man who molested Justin appeared at the door of his home, about 10 years after the molestations occured. She had come to tell Justin's family of his demise due to AIDS. Her concern involved a "little book" of graphic illustrations that she had found in his belongings. In the book, were the names of various boys he had victimized, Justin included.

30. See "What is Iniquity?" in Chapter Four.

31. The Greek word for "sin" is *harmartia*. See Chapters One and Four.

32. The sin pattern starts with *chata'ah*, Hebrew for "to miss the mark" or "not share in the prize." This first level of sin is not necessarily intentional because the spirit behind it can come in from out of nowhere, by no fault of

one's own. However, when a purpose or intention is established and a new thought pattern emerges, Satan's words, or word pictures, settle in and eventually create a "stronghold" or "transgression." The Hebrew word for this level of entrenchment in sin is *pasha*, which suggests a level of intentional rebellion against God's ways. When a person's thoughts morph into a pattern of thinking that drives him to commit habitual perversions, the highest level of sin is manifested. This is called "inquity" or *avon* in the Hebrew.

33. 2 Corinthians 10:5 (TPT).

34. WHAT IS WARFARE PRAYER? "Got Questions.org" describes it as "a weapon to do battle with the spiritual force of evil, especially in regard to one's daily life, habits, and struggles" and "prayers prayed for the purpose of waging war against an unseen, spiritual enemy who is bent on making us unhappy by thwarting our dreams and desires."

35. WHAT IS A VICTIM MENTALITY? "Verywellmind.com" says individuals with victim mentality find themselves blaming other people for events or situation in their lives. They "feel as though bad things keep happening and the world is against them."

36. Most psychologists agree that a person's psyche is largely developed by around age eight.

37. Ritual sacrifices of children to appease the "gods" were common in the ancient cultures, including those that existed in South America. Mind-altering drugs were also used by people in ancient cultures, so they could enter states of consciousness that would promote "interaction" with the spirit world. "The Capacocha, Human Sacrifices in the Inca Empire," www.ticketmachupicchu.com

38. She is full of *shalom*, Hebrew for "prosperity, bliss, wholeness, completeness, health, peace, welfare, safety, soundness, tranquility, perfectness, fullness, rest, harmony, and the absence of agitation or discord." *Shalom* also comes from a root verb meaning "to be complete, perfect, and (paid in) full." The "payback" referenced here is in regard to what the enemy owes us for all he has stolen! See *The Passion Translation* notes for Isaiah 45:7.

39. Taken from Scott Bitcon's ministry of healing.

40. When Jesus comes to the parts of a person's past, His words are always compassionate and full of peace. Though the memory itself might be horrifying, Jesus miraculously transports this person a quiet, secure place where she is encapsulated by a blanket of love.

41. Jesus's way with a person there in the memory gives her needed revelation concerning those who have sinned against her. With the revelation received, she is able to forgive those persons and then receive her own forgiveness.

42. In memory healing, it is important to note that the "part" who is "holding" an emotion must herself "break" the curse of that emotion or state of mind–fear, anger, suicide, etc.—or the curse will not be broken. In other words, the minister of healing cannot "lord it (healing) over" the individual "part." She must "want" to be healed. She has to be willing to utter the words, "I break the curse of 'blank'" to get healing.

43. When the healed part "goes with Jesus," this is a form of "assimilation." This is one way to look at it: the wounded part no longer functions on her own, apart from the core. She no longer acts in conflict with the core. She is now a part of the "whole." This is psychological equilibrium.

44. Or "That which you forbid on earth must be that which is already forbidden in heaven, and that which you permit on earth must be that which is already permitted in heaven." Another translation, according to *The Passion Translation* notes.

45. "Jesus called his twelve disciples together and gave them authority to cast out evil spirits and to heal every kind of disease and illness" (Matthew 10:1 NLT).

46. I am indebted to my mentor in deliverance, Scott Bitcon, who taught me the "ins and outs" of dealing with demons! Scott shares years of ministry wisdom in his new online training series which contains "real-life" deliverance videos. See his website for more information: innerhealinganddeliverance.org.

47. "Then I saw an angel descending from heaven; he was holding the key of the Abyss (the bottomless pit) and a great chain was in his hand. And he gripped and overpowered the dragon, that old serpent [of primeval times], who is the devil and Satan, and [securely] bound him for a thousand years. Then he hurled him into the Abyss (the bottomless pit) and closed it and sealed it above him, so that he should no longer lead astray and deceive and seduce the nations until the thousand years were at an end. After that he must be liberated for a short time" (Revelation 20:1–3 AMP).

48. The spirit of incubus is a demon who preys on women, especially while they are sleeping. The Latin word *incubo* literally mean "a nightmare induced by such a demon." From "Everything You Need to Know About the Incubus Demon," by Chrissy Stockton, Updated April 3, 2021.

49. The word "blood" in the English translation of Genesis 4:10 is plural in the original Hebrew, that is, "bloods." *The Passion Translation* note says, "Blood crying is a symbol of the soul crying out for the right to live, demanding for the punishment of the murderer. Bloodguilt calls for justice, even from the ground." Also: "Blood spilled outside the body is always plural in Hebrew. This speaks of his descendants that could have lived—their blood, too cries out against Cain."

50. "So Yahweh said to Cain: 'Why are you so angry and bothered? If you

offer what is right, won't you be accepted? But if you refuse to offer what is right, sin, the predator, is crouching in wait outside the door of your heart. It desires to have you, yet you must be its master'" (Genesis 4:6–7 TPT).

51. "Behold, I'm standing at the door, knocking. If your heart is open to hear my voice and you open the door within, I will come into you and feast with you, and you will feast with me" (Revelation 3:20 TPT).

52. "Throughout our history God has spoked to our ancestors by his prophets in many different ways. The revelation he gave them was only a fragment at a time, building one truth upon another. But to us living in these last days, God now speaks to us openly in the language of a Son, the appointed Heir of everything, for through him God created the panorama of all things and all time. The Son is the dazzling radiance of God's splendor, the exact expression of God's true nature—his mirror image! He holds the universe together and expands it by the mighty power of his spoken word. He accomplished for us the complete cleansing of sins, and then took his seat on the highest throne at the right hand of the majestic One" (Hebrews 1:1–3 TPT).

53. "For here is the covenant I will one day establish with the people of Israel: I will embed my laws within their thoughts and fasten them onto their hearts. I will be their loyal God and they will be my loyal people. And the result of this will be that everyone will know me as Lord! There will be no need at all to teach their fellow citizens or brothers by saying, 'You should know the Lord Jehovah,' since everyone will know me inwardly, from the most unlikely to the most distinguished. For I will demonstrate my mercy to them and will forgive their evil deeds, and never remember again their sins" (Hebrews 8:10–12 AMP).

54. "Call to Me and I will answer you and show you great and mighty things, fenced in and hidden, which you do not know (do not distinguish and recognize, have knowledge of and understand)" (Jeremiah 33:3 AMP).

55. "So why would I fear the future? For your goodness and love pursue me all the days of my life. Then afterward, when my life is through, I'll return to your glorious presence to be forever with you!" (Psalm 23:6 TPT).

56. "Greater than the grandeur of heaven above is the greatness of your loyal love, towering over all who fear you and bow down before you! Farther than from a sunrise to a sunset—that's how far you've removed our guilt from us. The same way a loving father feels toward his children—that's but a sample of your tender feelings toward us, your beloved children, who live in awe of you. You know all about us, inside and out. You are mindful that we're made from dust" (Psalm 103:11b–14 TPT).

57. "Lord, you're so kind and tenderhearted to those who don't deserve it and so patient with people who fail you! Your love is like a flooding river

overflowing its banks with kindness. You don't look at us only to find our faults, just so that you can hold a grudge against us. You may discipline us for our many sins, but never as much as we really deserve. Nor do you get even with us for what we've done. Higher than the highest heavens—that's how high your tender mercy extends!" (Psalm 103:8–11a TPT).

58. "Your anointing has made me strong and mighty. You've empowered my life for triumph by pouring fresh oil over me. You've said that those lying in wait to pounce on me would be defeated, and now it's happened right in front of my eyes and I've heard their cries of surrender!" (Psalm 93:11 TPT).

59. "For I know the thoughts and plans I have for you, says the Lord, thoughts and plans for welfare and peace and not for evil, to give you hope in your final outcome" (Jeremiah 29:11 AMP).

60. "Yahweh, you are my soul's celebration. How could I ever forget the miracles of kindness you've done for me? You kissed my heart with forgiveness, in spite of all I've done! You've healed me inside and out from every disease. You've rescued me from hell and saved my life. You've crowned me with love and mercy. You satisfy my every desire with good things. You've supercharged my life so that I soar again like a flying eagle in the sky! You're a God who makes things right, giving justice to the defenseless" (Psalm 103: 2–6 TPT).

61. "I will cry to God Most High, who accomplishes all things on my behalf (for He completes my purpose in His Plan)" (Psalm 57:2 AMP).

62. **Going Deeper:** Visit www.emilygardnerfoppe.com to download and print additional question-and-answer material pertaining to this chapter. The material presented will (1) provide a review of this chapter and (2) take you deeper into the discussion.

Chapter Six

1. To "stand in the gap" is to intercede, or intervene, by stepping in between another person or entity and the powers of darkness coming against them (it), repenting on their (its) behalf, and pleading for God's mercy through the application of Jesus's blood, that is, helping to enforce the victory that God has already won.

2. "The one who indulges in a sinful life is of the devil, because the devil has been sinning since the beginning. The reason the Son of God was revealed was to undo and destroy the works of the devil" (1 John 3:8 TPT).

3. "This is because I have never spoken on My own authority or of My own accord or as self-appointed, but the Father Who sent Me has himself given Me orders [concerning] what to say and what to tell" (John 12:49 AMP).

4. "So Jesus answered them by saying, I assure you, most solemnly I tell you,

the Son is able to do nothing of Himself (of His own accord); but He is able to do only what He sees the Father doing, for whatever the Father does is what the Son does in the same way [in His turn]" (John 5:19 AMP).

5. "After this, the Lord Jesus formed thirty-five teams among the other disciples. Each team was two disciples, seventy in all, and he commissioned them to go ahead of him into every town he was about to visit. He released them with these instructions: The harvest is huge and ripe. But there are not enough harvesters to bring it all in. As you go, plead with the Owner of the Harvest to drive out into his harvest fields many more workers. Now, off you go! I am sending you out even though you feel as vulnerable as lambs going into a pack of wolves. You won't need to take anything with you—trust in God alone. And don't get distracted from my purpose by anyone you might meet along the way" (Luke 10:1–4 TPT).

6. "When the seventy missionaries returned to Jesus, they were ecstatic with joy, telling him, 'Lord, even the demons obeyed us when we commanded them in your name!'" (Luke 10:17 TPT).

7. "Though He scoffs at the scoffers and scorns the scorners, yet He gives His undeserved favor to the low [in rank], the humble, and the afflicted" (Proverbs 3:34 AMP).

8. Henry Blackaby popularized this concept in "Experiencing God." The message is built upon what Blackaby calls the "Seven Realities." (1) God is always at work around you. (2) God pursues a continuing love relationship with you that is real and personal. (3) God invites you to become involved with Him in His work. (4) God speaks by the Holy Spirit through the Bible, prayer, circumstances, and the church to reveal Himself, His purposes and His ways. (5) God's invitation for you to work with Him always leads you to a crisis of belief that requires faith and action. (6) You must make major adjustments in your life to join God in what He is doing. (7) You come to know God by experience as you obey Him and He accomplishes His work through you.

9. "For he (Jesus) must remain in heaven until the restoration of all things has taken place, fulfilling everything that God said long ago through holy prophets" (Acts 3:21 TPT).

10. "But to as many as did receive and welcome Him, He gave the authority (power, privilege, right) to become the children of God, that is, to those who believe in (adhere to, trust in, and rely on) His name" (John 1:12 AMP).

11. "Blessed (happy, fortunate, to be envied) is the man whom You discipline and instruct, O Lord, and teach out of Your law, that You may give him power to keep himself calm in the days of adversity, until the [inevitable] pit of corruption is dug for the wicked" (Psalm 94:12–13 AMP).

12. "God is love! Those who are living in love are living in God, and God lives

through them. By living in God, love has been brought to its full expression in us so that we may fearlessly face the day of judgment, because all that Jesus now is, so are we in this world" (1 John 4 TPT).

13. "All that he does in us is designed to make us a mature church for his pleasure, until we become a source of praise to him—glorious and radiant, beautiful and holy, without fault or flaw" (Ephesians 5:27 TPT).

14. "But He gives us more and more grace (power of the Holy Spirit, to meet this evil tendency and all others fully). That is why He says, God sets Himself against the proud and haughty, but gives grace [continually] to the lowly (those who are humble enough to receive it). So be subject to God. Resist the devil [stand firm against him], and he will flee from you. Come close to God and He will come close to you. [Recognize that you are] sinners, get your soiled hands clean; [realize that you have been disloyal] wavering individuals with divided interests, and purify your hearts [of your spiritual adultery]" (James 4:6–8 AMP).

15. According to the Department of Families and Services record, both mother and grandmother had been products of the foster care system. In Hannah's ancestral lineage, foster care could be traced back as many as seven generations.

16. Satanic Ritual Abuse (SRA) falls within the category of Organized Abuse and involves the use of certain identifiable rituals and symbols that make it unique. This would include the killing of animals or humans and the drinking of blood—combined with sexual and verbal abuse, incantations, and such. Oftentimes, someone posing as "Jesus" participates in abusive sexual acts.

17. Russ Dizdar's website: http://www.shatterthedarkness.net

18. By general definition, a "cabal" is a group of people who are "formal and disapproving: a small group of people who work together secretly" (*Merriam-Webster Dictionary*). The intimation is that a cabal is united in some close design, usually to promote their private views or interests in an ideology, a state, or another community—often by intrigue and usually unbeknown to those who are outside their group. The use of this term usually carries negative connotations of political purpose, conspiracy, and secrecy.

19. The origins of trauma-based mind control programming began over a millennia ago; but modern research can be traced to Tavistock Institute of Medical Psychology, London, and Kaiser Wilhelm Institute of Germany—where the Nazis studied multi-generational abuse of children during WWII. Their findings confirmed that abused children were receptive to external mind control. This led to Operation Paperclip, a secret program where the United States imported more than 1600 Nazi scientists after WWII, who worked through the CIA to develop a mind-control program now known as MK Ultra. Here is

a video clip of several MK Ultra victims official testimonies before Congress in 1996: https://dougriggs.s3.amazonaws.com/Trauma-based-mind-control.mp4

20. "Parts" are also called "alters."

21. https://dougriggs.s3.amazonaws.com/Trauma-based-mind-control.mp4

22. From "The 13 Families of the Illuminati," by Mike Rothschild (using Duck Duck Go as the search engine).

23. "Activities in more than 22 countries around the globe will remember missing children on May 25," press release by the International Center for Missing and Exploited Children (ICMEC), May 2013. This article cites numbers as reported by the U.S. Department of Justice.

24. www.missingkids.org/footer/media/keyfacts

25. Public interest and awareness of this problem continues to increase. In 2020, te organization's Cyber Tip Line received more reports than ever before, 21.7 million—up 25% from the previous year, with the vast majority regarding sexual abuse material, online enticement, child sex trafficking, and child sexual molestation.

26. www.missingkids.org/footer/media/keyfacts

27. Lanning, Kenneth V. "Investigator's Guide to Allegations of 'Ritual' Child Abuse," January 1992. This was also known as "The Lanning Report."

28. Woodward, Doug. "Surviving Trauma Based-Mind Control – SRA/CIA," April 16, 2021. Doug Woodward interviews Kay Tolman, who is a survivor of ritual abuse and trauma-based mind control. Kay's experience combines generational abuse (family lines that were heavily occult influenced) and governmental programming (CIA mind-control programs which existed from the 1950s to at least the mid-1970s, according to this source). Kay's experience is somewhat unique because she comes from royal blood lines (Stuart, Livingstone, and others). Also, her father was apparently a double agent in World War II and connected with Lockheed. Her maternal line was deeply entangled in witchcraft. Doug interjects historical facts about the whole process of trauma-based mind control, along with testimony from the congressional record (Church and Pike committees on Un-American activities in 1975-76). www.faith-happens.com

29. Robinson, B.A. "Allegations of Mind Control and Programming by Satanic Cults," updated May 3, 2005. Copyright 1996-2005 by Ontario Consultants on Religious Tolerance.

30. "How to Be Delivered from Demons," Derek Prince, YouTube video, 1995.

31. "2010 Australian X Factor Winner Altiyan Childs Exposes Freemasonry," on a channel called The Ronald Show, YouTube.

32. "Brad Pitt, Robert Downey, Jr. & Mel Gibson Claim Hollywood is an 'Institutionalized Pedophile Ring,'" *Clever Journeys*, April 10, 2021.

33. Riggs, Doug. "Two Satanic Ritual Abuse Survivors Speak Out," September 22, 2019. https://www.dougriggs.org/SRA-DID-Resources.html

34. Rice, John Paul. Hollywood producer for 20 years and producer of "The Hunger Games," talks about Hollywood pedophiles, their ties to human trafficking, and the international network of evil cabal members who control it all. He also discusses "A Child's Voice," the feature film he put together a few years ago, which was removed, "un"published, from Amazon just prior to the publication of this video, August 13, 2020.

35. Jay Myers Documentaries, "Adrenochrome, the Elite's Secret Super Drug," April 27, 2018. (The is a re-upload from a previously censored video.)

36. Ossebaard, Janet. "The Fall of the Cabal," 2021, www.fallcabal.com / www.valcabal.nl This is a 20-part series. Ossebaard is an award-winning researcher from the Netherlands.

37. 1 John 5:18

38. I did eventually learn "Joshua's" real name. I am using his alias name here as his immediate family continues to be under attack by his larger extended family and many others within the satanic network.

39. A religious sect that espouses Lucifer as the true creator of the universe and mankind.

40. *Born into Battle* can be downloaded at www.movethismountain.info.

41. From 2 Corinthians 11:14 TPT.

42. "That which you forbid on earth must be that which is already forbidden in heaven, and that which you permit on earth must be that which is already permitted in heaven." See *The Passion Translation* notes for Matthew 16:19.

43. The pit is a holding receptacle. See Revelation 20:1–3.

44. "In the same way, there were heavenly messengers in rebellion who went outside their rightful domain of authority and abandoned their appointed realms. God bound them in everlasting chains and is keeping them in the dark abyss of the netherworld until the judgment of the great day" (Jude 6 TPT).

45. "When a demon is cast out of a person, it roams around a dry region, looking for a place to rest, but never finds it. Then it says, 'I'll return to the house I moved out of,' and so it goes back, only to find that the house is vacant, warm, and ready for it to move back in. So, it goes looking for seven other demons more evil than itself, and they all enter together to live there. Then the person's condition becomes much worse than it was in the beginning. This describes what will also happen to the people of this evil generation" (Matthew 12:43–45 TPT).

46. "Woe to the earth and the sea, for the devil has come down to you with great fury, because he knows his time is short" (Revelation 12:12 AMP).

47. It is unclear as to whether "suffocation" comes about due to an actual loss of oxygen or if the induced panic attacks create a "feeling of suffocation."

48. "Covid: Surge in calls to Bristol suicide prevention charity," January 20, 2021.

49. Many psychologists explain that a person's need to eliminate "cognitive dissonance" or internal conflict causes this mind and behavior contradiction to occur.

50. According to Joshua's book, *Born into Battle*, "witchcraft" can be described as "the entering into contractual relationships with demonic entities via the use of ritual magic."

51. Telephone Interview, August 1, 2021.

52. Riggs, Doug. "Two Christian Satanic Ritual Abuse Survivors Speak Out," September 19, 2019.

53. Yes, God blessed Joshua 25 years ago with a wonderful and understanding wife, who has stood by him and fought for him all these years! She is a special education teacher. They have four children.

54. "And Moses said to the Lord, 'If Your Presence does not go with me, do not carry us up from here! For by what shall it be known that I and Your people have found favor in Your sight? Is it not in Your going with us so that we are distinguished, I and your people, from all the other people upon the face of the earth?' And the Lord said to Moses, 'I will do this thing also that you have asked, for you have found favor, loving-kindness, and mercy in My sight and I know you personally and by name'" (Exodus 34:14–17 AMP)

55. "He said to me, 'Son of man, eat what you find [in this book]; eat this scroll; then go and speak to the house of Israel'. So I opened my mouth, and He caused me to eat the scroll. And He said to me, 'Son of man, eat this scroll that I give you and fill your stomach with it.' Then I ate it, and it was as sweet as honey in my mouth. And He said to me, 'Son of man, go, get you to the house of Israel and speak to them with My words'" (Ezekiel 3:1–4 AMP).

56. We can also stand in the gap on behalf of groups of people, such as families, or entities, such as businesses or countries.

57. Dutch Sheets' book *Intercessory Prayer: How God Can Use Your Prayers to Move Heaven and Earth* is a great resource for understanding this and other aspects of effective prayer.

58. This is the link to Joshua's website, created to inspire prayer and raise awareness of human trafficking: http://www.movethismountain.info.

59. Russ Dizdar, founder of Shatter the Darkness, passed away in 2021 due

to Covid-19 complications. His ministry still operates under strong leadership. The ministry website can be located at shatterthedarkness.net.

60. In this video interview an SRA expert who worked closely with Russ Dizdar says there are as many as 100 million SRA victims worldwide: Heavener, David. "Russ Dizdar's Death Remains a Mystery," 10/25/21, Bitchute.

61. "We have become his poetry, a re-created people that will fulfill the destiny he has given each of us, for we are joined to Jesus, the Anointed One. Even before we were born, God planned in advance our destiny and the good works we would do to fulfill it" (Ephesians 2:10 TPT).

62. "He will even deliver the one [for whom you intercede] who is not innocent; yes, he will be delivered through the cleanness of your hands" (Job 42:7 AMP).

63. "And now we are brothers and sisters in God's family because of the blood of Jesus, and he welcomes us to come into the most holy sanctuary in the heavenly realm—boldly and without hesitation" (Hebrews 10:19 TPT).

64. "Christ's resurrection is your resurrection too. This is why we are to yearn for all that is above, for that's where Christ sits enthroned at the place of all power, honor, and authority! Yes, feast on all the treasures of the heavenly realm and fill your thoughts with heavenly realities, and not with the distractions of the natural realm. Your crucifixion with Christ has severed the tie to this life, and now your true life is hidden away in God in Christ. And as Christ himself is seen for who he really is, who you really are will also be revealed, for you are now one with him in his glory!" (Colossians 3:1-3 TPT).

65. "He raised us up with Christ the exalted One, and we ascended with him into the glorious perfection and authority of the heavenly realm, for we are now co-seated as one with Christ!" (Ephesians 2:6 TPT).

66. "He appointed the Twelve, whom he named apostles. He wanted them to be continually at his side as his friends, and so that he could send them out to preach and have authority to heal the sick and to cast out demons" (Mark 3:15 TPT).

67. "So I, Yahweh, will assign him a portion among a great multitude, and he will triumph and divide the spoils of victory with his mighty ones—all because he poured out his life-blood to death. He was counted among the worst of sinners, yet he carried sin's burden for many and intercedes for those who are rebels" (Isaiah 53:12 TPT). "Intercedes" is *paga, Strong's Concordance* (H#6293), that is, to "meet" or "make attack" against the power of darkness on another person's behalf, to turn the evil away, to *redirect* it.

68. "Who then is left to condemn us? Certainly not Jesus, the Anointed One! For he gave his life for us, and even more than that, he has conquered

death and is now risen, exalted, and enthroned by God at this right hand. So how could he possible condemn us since he is continually praying for our triumph?" (Romans 8:34 TPT).

69. "And in a similar way, the Holy Spirit takes hold of us in our human frailty to empower us in our weakness. For example, at times we don't even know how to pray, or know the best things to ask for. But the Holy Spirit rises up within us to super-intercede on our behalf, pleading to God with emotional sighs too deep for words" (Romans 8:26 TPT).

70. "We are co-workers with God and you are God's cultivated garden, the house he is building" (1 Corinthians 3:9 TPT).

71. "For how could anyone be disgraced when he has entwined his heart with you? But they will all be defeated and ashamed when they harm the innocent" (Psalm 25:3 TPT).

72. "But if you live in life-union with me and if my words live powerfully within you—then you can ask whatever you desire and it will be done" (John 15:7 TPT).

73. "Yahweh said to my Lord, the Messiah: 'Sit with me as enthroned ruler while I subdue your every enemy. They will bow low before you as I make them a footstool for your feet.' Messiah, I know God himself will establish your kingdom as you reign in Zion-glory. For he says to you, 'Rule in the midst of your enemies!' Your people will be your love offerings. In the day of your mighty power you will be exalted, and in the brightness of your holy ones will shine as an army arising from the womb of the dawn, anointed with the dew of your youth!" (Psalm 110:1-3 TPT).

74. **Going Deeper:** Visit www.emilygardnerfoppe.com to download and print additional question-and-answer material pertaining to this chapter. The material presented will (1) provide a review of this chapter and (2) take you deeper into the discussion.

BOXES

WHAT IS SATANIC RITUAL ABUSE
From *Born into Battle*, by "Joshua Collins," SRA Survivor

1. This section is taken from Joshua's book and is used with his permission.

WHAT IS EVIL INTELLIGENCE AND HOW DOES IT WORK TO DESTROY LIFE?

1. "Beware that no one distracts you or intimidates you in their attempt to lead you away from Christ's fullness by pretending to be full of wisdom when they're filled with endless arguments of human logic. For they operate with humanistic and clouded judgments based on the mindset of this world system, and not the anointed truths of the Anointed One" (Colossians 2:8 TPT).

2 A video clip of Madonna, who explains in 41 seconds how evil intelligence operates: "Telling You How and Why," from pray4america post on Rumble. com., June 6, 2021.

WHAT IS LUCIFERIANISM?

1. In Hebrew, "the shining one" is translated "Lucifer." The term "shining one" in Isaiah 14 is used to describe the Babylonian King who was opposing the ways of God by saying in his heart that he would exalt himself to the level of God or beyond. "And you said in your heart, I will ascend to heaven; I will exalt my throne above the stars of God; I will sit upon the mount of assembly in the uttermost north. I will ascend above the heights of the clouds; I will make myself like the Most High." (Isaiah 14:13–14 AMP).

2. Tsarfati, Amir. "The Illuminati and the One World Government," August 24, 2019. Tsarfati explains that the belief system of the Illuminati, also called Gnosticism, began in the second century—and became the biggest enemy of the Christian faith during that period. The Gnostics promoted the "twisted" belief that God had two sons, Sataniel and Jesus. Sataniel (aka Satan or Lucifer), was not given the right to rule the celestial world; so, he created the visible world, instead. He also created man, according to this false narrative. With all this said, Gnostics believe that Lucifer is the true god of this world and is therefore worthy of man's worship and sacrifices.

3. Pugh, Dr. Joye Jefferies. "Eden: The Knowledge of Good and Evil." Dr. Pugh's belief is that the Illuminati bloodlines go all the way back to Cain, the son of Eve, who was impregnated by Lucifer after the encounter he had with her in the garden. Therefore, these bloodlines are tied to the pagan gods who work in opposition to the Hebrew God of the Bible Christians serve. Illuminati blood must be kept "pure" to fulfill Lucifer's "enlightened" objectives.

4. Census data from March 2020.

5. Vegas, Luis. "The Georgia Guidestones: Lucifer's 10 Commandments," April 26, 2020.

6. To this day, no one has laid claim to the origin of these "Georgia Guidestones," with the company from which the stones were purchased sworn to "secrecy" and made to destroy the purchase agreement soon after the monument's erection. Vegas, Luis. "The Georgia Guidestones: Lucifer's 10 Commandments," April 26, 2020.

7. According to the Georgia Encyclopedia, the engraved messages on "The Georgia Guidestones," as they are called, can be subdivided into four major areas: governance and the establishment of a world government, population and reproduction control, the environment, and humankind's relationship to

nature and spirituality. McKenzie, Barbara. "The Georgia Guidestones and the Globalist Plan to Reduce Humanity to Half a Billion," December 13, 2020.

8. The rest of the commandments are as follows: 2. Guide reproduction wisely—improving fitness and diversity. 3. Unite humanity with a living new language. 4. Rule passion—faith—tradition—and all things with tempered reason. 5. Protect people and nations with fair laws and just courts. 6. Let all nations rule internally resolving external disputes in a world court. 7. Avoid petty laws and useless officials. 8. Balance personal rights with social duties. 9. Prize truth—beauty—love—seeking harmony with the infinite. 10. Be not a cancer on the earth—Leave room for nature—Leave room for nature.

9. Ossebaard, Janet. "The Fall of the Cabal," 20-part documentary.

Chapter 7

1. *Neshamah, Strong's Concordance* (H#5397), can mean "spirit." But of the 24 times it is used, there seems to be an emphasis on the "breath" of God that gives "life" to all breathing things—and, more particularly, the "breath" that gives "life" and "inspiration" to humans.

2. Genesis 2:7

3. "But the one who joins himself to the Lord is mingled into one spirit with him" (1 Corinthians 6:17 TPT).

4. "Groaning," *stenagmos*, can be interpreted to mean "an emotional sigh," *Strong's Concordance* (G#4726). It is associated with the Greek word *hupererentugkhano* in Romans 8:26, *Strong's Concordance* (G#5241), and is best translated 'super [hyper] intercede for us.'"

5. "But He said to me, My grace (My favor and loving-kindness and mercy) is enough for you [sufficient against any danger and enables you to bear the trouble manfully]; for My strength and power are made perfect (fulfilled and completed) and show themselves most effective in [your] weakness. Therefore, I will all the more gladly glory in my weaknesses and infirmities, that the strength and power of Christ (the Messiah) may rest (yes, may pitch a tent over and dwell) upon me!" (2 Corinthians 12:9 AMP).

6. "Now the mind of the flesh [which is sense and reason without the Holy Spirit] is death [death that comprises all the miseries arising from sin, both here and hereafter]. But the mind of the [Holy] Spirit is life and [soul] peace [both now and forever]" (Romans 8:6 AMP).

7. "For the life (the animal soul) is in the blood, and I have given it for you

upon the altar to make atonement for your souls; for it is the blood that makes atonement, by reason of the life [which it represents]" (Leviticus 17:11 AMP).

8. Jesus answered, "Nicodemus, listen to this eternal truth: before a person can perceive God's kingdom realm, they must first experience a rebirth." Nicodemus said, "Rebirth? How can a gray-headed man be reborn? It's impossible for a man to go back into the womb a second time and be reborn!" Jesus answered, "I speak an eternal truth: Unless you are born of water and Spirit-wind, you will never enter God's kingdom realm. For the natural realm can only give birth to things that are natural, but the spiritual realm gives birth to supernatural life! You shouldn't be amazed by my statement, 'You must be born from above!' For the Spirit-wind blows as it chooses. You can hear its sound, but you don't know where it came from or where it's going. So it is within the hearts of those who are Spirit-born!" (John 3:3-8 TPT).

9. See Chapter One.

10. Another word commonly associated with God's Spirit in the Old Testament. *Ruach, Strong's Concordance* (H#7307) is "Spirit or spirit, wind, breath, mind." *Ruach* is used in reference to a man's spirit only seven times out of almost 378 in the KJV. Example: "Thus says the Lord, who stretches out the heavens and lays the foundation of the earth and forms the spirit of man within him" (Zechariah 12:1 AMP).

11. "It wasn't that long ago that you lived in the religion, customs, and values of this world, obeying the dark ruler of the earthly realm who fills the atmosphere with his authority, and works diligently in the hearts of those who are disobedient to the truth of God. The corruption that was in us from birth was expressed through the deeds and desires of our self-life. We lived by whatever natural cravings and thoughts our minds dictated, living as rebellious children subject to God's wrath like everyone else" (Ephesians 2:2–3 TPT).

12. "Those who are motivated by the flesh only pursue what benefits themselves. But those who live by the impulses of the Holy Spirit are motivated to pursue spiritual realities. For the mind-set controlled by the flesh is death, but the mind-set controlled by the Spirit finds life and peace" (Romans 8:5–6 TPT).

13. *The Amplified Version* reads, "Restore to me the joy of Your salvation and uphold me with a willing spirit." *The Passion Translation* note for this verse says, "The Hebrew word for "joy" comes from two Hebrew roots: one means 'bright' and the other means 'lily [whiteness].' David wanted to taste a joy that was bright, pure, and as beautiful as a lily."

14. The Holy Spirit Movement, often called "The Charismatic Movement" or the "Charismatic Renewal Movement," began in many mainline denomination churches around 1948.The emphasis became the truth of the baptism in

the Holy Spirit with the ability to speak in a spirit language. Dr. Hamon, Bill. *Seventy Reason for Speaking in Tongues*, p. 211.

15. "But the word is very near you, in your mouth and in your mind and in your heart, so that you can do it" (Deuteronomy 29:14 AMP).

16. "Rejoice" in Hebrew is *giyl*, *Strong's Concordance* (H#1523). It means "to spin around under the influence of violent emotions." Violent emotion can relate to "exultation" and "gladness" and "trembling fear."

17. *Agape*, *Strong's Concordance* (#G26), is a Greco-Christian term referring to unconditional love, "the highest form of love, charity" and "the love of God for man and of man for God." H.G. Liddell; Robert Scott (October 2010). *An Intermediate Greek-English Lexicon: Founded Upon the Seventh Edition of Liddell* and *Scott's Greek-English Lexicon.*

18. *The Passion Translation* notes say, "or everything revealed becomes light."

19. From *The Passion Translation* notes: The Greek word for "blew," *Strong's Concordance* (G#1720), is found only here in the New Testament. However, the same word is found in the Greek Old Testament (called *The Septuagint*) in Genesis 2:7, where God "breathed" His "breath" into Adam. TPT notes continue: "The beginning of new creation life came from the breath of Jesus. The mighty wind of Acts 2 was for power. The breath Jesus breathed into his disciples in this verse was for life."

20. *The Passion Translation* notes say the Aramaic can be translated, "Love transforms the spirit."

21. "Then [at Mt. Sinai] His voice shook the earth, but now He has given a promise; Yet once more I will shake and make tremble not only the earth, but also the [starry] heavens. Now this expression, Yet once more, indicates the final removal and transformation of all [that can be] shaken—that is, of that which has been created—in order that what cannot be shaken may remain and continue" (Hebrews 12:27 AMP).

22. Leaf, Caroline. *Switch on Your Brain*, Baker Books, 2013, page 160.

23. Dr. Leaf is a practicing Christian. The whole premise of her book is that science explains the human body, soul and spirit connection—and the relationship these parts have to self, God, others, and the universe. Also, science dovetails perfectly with the Word of God!

24. Peter said, "Can't you see it? God has resurrected Jesus, and we all have seen him! Then God exalted him to his right hand upon the throne of highest honor. And the Father gave him the authority to send the promised Holy Spirit, which is being poured out upon us today. This is what you're seeing and hearing!" (Acts 2:32–33 TPT).

25. God in three Persons: Father, Son, and Holy Spirit.

26. From *The Passion Translation* notes for Genesis 2:10.

27. Here the translators of *The Passion Translation* omit the real river names, that is, Pishon, Gihon, Tigris, and Euphrates, instead naming them according to their Hebrew meanings.

28. "Perfect absolute peace surrounds those whose imaginations are consumed with you; they confidently trust in you" (Isaiah 26:3 TPT).

29. "He (Abraham) is our example and father, for in God's presence he believed that God can raise the dead and call into being things that don't even exist yet. Against all odds, when it looked hopeless, Abraham believed the promise and expected God to fulfill it. He took God at his word, and as a result he became the father of many nations. God's declaration over him came to pass: 'Your descendants will be so many that they will be impossible to count!'" (Romans 4:17b–18 TPT).

30. "Eight days later, Jesus took Peter, Jacob, and John and climbed a high mountain to pray. As he prayed his face began to glow until it was a blinding glory streaming from him. His entire body was illuminated with a radiant glory. His brightness became so intense that it made his clothing blinding light, like multiple flashes of lightning. All at once, two men appeared in glorious splendor: Moses and Elijah. They spoke with Jesus about his soon departure from this world and the things he was destined to accomplish in Jerusalem. Peter and his companions had become very drowsy, but they became fully awake when they saw the glory and splendor of Jesus standing there and the two men with him. As Moses and Elijah were about to return to heaven, Peter impetuously blurted out, 'Master, this is amazing to see the three of you together! Why don't we stay here and set up three shelters; one for you, one for Moses, and one for Elijah?' While Peter was still speaking, a radiant cloud of glory formed above them and overshadowed them. As the glory cloud enveloped them, they were struck with fear. Then the voice of God thundered from withing the cloud, 'This is my Son, my Beloved One. Listen carefully to all he has to say.' When the thunderous voice faded away and the cloud disappeared, Jesus was standing there alone. Peter, Jacob, and John were speechless and awestruck. But they didn't say a word to anyone about what they had seen" (Luke 9:28–36 TPT).

31. "Peter and the apostles replied, 'We must listen to and obey God more than pleasing religious leaders. You had Jesus arrested and killed by crucifixion, but the God of our forefathers has raised him up. He's the one God has exalted and seated at his right hand as our Savior and Champion. He is the provider of grace as the Redeemer of Israel. We are witnesses of these things, and so is the Holy Spirit, whom God freely gives to all who believe in him'" (Acts 5:29-32 TPT).

32. In Him was Life, and the Life was the Light of men. And the Light shines on in the darkness, and the darkness did not understand it or overpower it or appropriate it or absorb it [and is unreceptive to it] (John 1:4–5 AMP).

33. "Then may your awakening breath blow upon my life until I am fully yours. Breathe upon me with your Spirit wind. Stir up the sweet spice of your life within me. Spare nothing as you make me your fruitful garden. Hold nothing back until I release your fragrance. Come walk with me as you walked with Adam in your paradise garden. Come taste the fruits of your life in me" (Song of Songs 4:16 TPT).

34. "He brought me to the banqueting house, and his banner over me was love [for love waved as a protecting and comforting banner over my head when I was near him]" (Song of Solomon 2:4 AMP).

35. "Let him smother me with kisses—his Spirit-kiss divine. So kind are your caresses, I drink them in like the sweetest wine!" (Song of Songs 1:1 TPT).

36. "But you, Oh LORD, are a shield around me; you are my glory, the one who holds my head high" (Psalm 3:3 NLT).

37. "For he is the complete fullness of deity living in human form. And our own completeness is now found in him. We are completely filled with God as Christ's fullness overflows within us. He is the Head of every kingdom and authority in the universe!" (Colossians 2:9-10 TPT).

38. Our bodies have three billion cells!

39. "But your dead will live again! Their bodies will rise from the dead! It's time to awaken and sing for joy, you dwellers in the dust! As the glistening, radiant dew refreshes the earth, so the Lord will awaken those dwelling among the dead" (Isaiah 26:19 TPT).

40. Or "his banner over me was love" (AMP).

41. King David served raisin cakes to God's people in 2 Samuel 6:19. They were dancing and rejoicing and celebrating the return of the Ark of the Covenant to Jerusalem. The Ark, which represented God's Presence among the people, had been stolen over 100 years prior. *The Passion Translation* notes that the Hebrew word for "with raisin cakes" is a homonym that also means "fires." In other words, the people were rejoicing and celebrating the fact that God's Presence had returned—and that His passionate, fiery, all-consuming love was still a banner over them!

42. **Going Deeper:** Visit www.emilygardnerfoppe.com to download and print additional question-and-answer material pertaining to this chapter. The material presented will (1) provide a review of this chapter and (2) take you deeper into the discussion.

43. Note: Even illnesses can be viewed as dysfunctions. In the case of illness, imagine the healing Light, Light and Love of God pouring into the affected areas of the sick person's body when you take him with you "up" to Jesus. Perceive in your mind and heart that all his cells are healed, restored.

Boxes

WHAT IS THE *NESHAMA*?

1. Note: It could be argued that some animals bear this same gifting of mind, will and emotions to one degree or another. However, the Bible is clear that humans are the highest order of creation, having been made a "little lower" than heavenly beings, and therefore given authority over all of creation. Only humans have the capacity to know "right" from "wrong" and "good" from "evil." Animals cannot "long for eternity" or "know" their Creator.

Chapter Eight

1. "For this old pattern of worship was a matter of external rules and rituals concerning food and drink and ceremonial washings which was imposed upon us until the appointed time of heart-restoration had arrived" (Hebrews 9:10 TPT).

2. "For he died for us, sacrificing himself to make us holy and pure, cleansing us through the showering of the pure water of the Word of God. All that he does in us is designed to make us a mature church for his pleasure, until we become a source of praise to him—glorious and radiant, beautiful, and holy, without fault or flaw" (Ephesians 5:27 TPT). Note: The Greek word for "radiant" is *endoxos, Strong's Concordance* (#G1741), which can mean "gorgeous, honorable, esteemed, splendid, infused with glory."

3. "For he must remain in heaven until the restoration of all things has taken place, fulfilling everything that God said long ago through his holy prophets" (Acts 3:21 TPT).

4. "Then every living being joined the angelic choir. Every creature in heaven and on earth, under the earth, in the sea, and everything in them were worshiping with one voice, saying: 'Praise, honor, glory, and dominion be to God-Enthroned and to Christ the Lamb forever and ever!'" (Revelation 5:13 TPT).

5. "He is the Rock, His work is perfect, for all His ways are law and justice. A God of faithfulness without breach or deviation, just and right is He" (Deuteronomy 32:4 AMP).

6. "Far be it from You to do such a thing—to slay the righteous with the

wicked, so that the righteous fare as do the wicked! Far be it from You! Shall not the Judge of all the earth execute judgment and do righteously? And the Lord said, 'If I find in the city of Sodom fifty righteous (upright and in right standing with God), I will spare the whole place for their sake'" (Genesis 18:25–26 AMP).

7. "Lord, who dares to dwell with you? Who presumes the privilege of being close to you, living next to you in your shining place of glory? Who are those who daily dwell in the life of the Holy Spirit? They are passionate and whole-hearted, always sincere and always speaking the truth—for their hearts are trustworthy" (Psalm 15:1–2 TPT). Note: The Hebrew word for "sanctuary" is taken from a root word for "shining place."

8. "I will lift up mine eyes unto the hills, from whence cometh my help. My help cometh from the Lord, which made heaven and earth. He will not suffer thy foot to be moved; he that keepeth thee will not slumber. Behold, he that keepeth Israel shall neither slumber nor sleep. The Lord is thy keeper; the Lord is thy shade upon thy right hand. The sun shall not smite thee by day, nor the moon by night. The Lord shall preserve thee from all evil; he shall preserve thy soul. The Lord shall preserve thy going out and thy coming in from this time forth, and even for evermore" (Psalm 121 KJV).

9. "For God's gifts and His call are irrevocable. [He never withdraws them when once they are given, and He does not change His mind about those to whom He gives His grace or to whom He sends His call.]" (Romans 11:29 AMP).

10. "That you may show yourselves to be blameless and guileless, innocent, and uncontaminated, children of God without blemish (faultless, unrebuk-able) in the midst of a crooked and wicked generation [spiritually perverted and perverse], among whom you are seen as bright lights (stars or beacons shining out clearly) in the [dark] world. Holding out [to it] and offering [to all men] the Word of Life, so that in the day of Christ I may have something of which exultantly to rejoice and glory in that I did not run my race in vain or spend my labor to no purpose" (Philippians 2:15–16 AMP).

11. "And watch: if the daughters of Shiloh come out to dance in the dances, then come out of the vineyards and catch every man his wife from the daugh-ters of Shiloh and go to the land of Benjamin" (Judges 21:21 AMP).

12. Remember the Hebrew word for "iniquity" is *avon* which can also mean "crooked." See Chapters Four and Five.

13. "To return to oneself" comes from the Greek words *erchomai*, "to come," and *eis heauton*, "to oneself," *Greek English Lexicon* by C. Grimm Wilke. See note from Luke 15:10, *The Mirror Translation*.

14. The bread from Heaven that fed the Israelites for 40 years of wilderness

wanderings is the Hebrew word *man*, or "manna," *Strong's Concordance* (H#4478). It means "what is it?"

15. "The manna was like coriander seed and its appearance was like that of bdellium [perhaps a precious stone]. The people went about and gathered it and ground it in mills or beat it in mortars, and boiled it in pots, and made cakes of it; and it tasted like cakes baked with fresh oil. And when the dew fell on the camp in the night, the manna fell with it" (Numbers 11:7-9 AMP).

16. "There is a private place reserved for the lovers of God, where they sit near him and receive the revelation-secrets of his promises" (Psalm 25:14 TPT).

17. "O huge, magnificent mountain, you are the mighty kingdom of God! All the other peaks, though impressive and imposing, look with envy on you Mount Zion! For Zion is the mountain where God has chosen to live forever. Look! The mighty chariots of God! Ten thousands upon ten thousands, more than anyone could ever number. God is at the front, leading them all from Mount Sinai into his sanctuary with the radiance of holiness upon him. He ascends into the heavenly heights, taking his many captured ones with him, leading them in triumphal procession. And gifts were given to men, even the once rebellious, so that they may dwell with Yah. What a glorious God! He gives us salvation over and over, then daily he carries our burdens!" (Psalm 68:15–19 TPT).

18. The right hand speaks of power, authority, and blessing. See *The Passion Translation* notes for Revelation 1:17.

19. "The realm of the Dead" or "Hades." See *The Passion Translation* notes for Revelation 1:18.

20. *The Passion Translation* note says, "The Greek word for 'truth' is 'reality,' not doctrine. It is the application of truth that matters, not just a superficial knowledge."

21. "But here's the truth: It's to your advantage that I go away, for if I don't go away the Divine Encourager will not be released to you. But after I depart, I will send him to you. And when he comes, he will expose sin and prove that the world is wrong about God's righteousness and his judgments. 'Sin' because they refuse to believe in who I am. God's 'righteousness,' because I'm going back to join the Father and you'll see me no longer. And 'judgment' because the ruler of this dark world has already received his sentence" (John 16:7–11 TPT).

22. "We can demolish every deceptive fantasy that opposes God and break through every arrogant attitude that is raised up in defiance of the true knowledge of God. We capture, like prisoners of war, every thought and insist that it bow in obedience to the Anointed One" (2 Corinthians 10:5 TPT).

23. "For in the Son all sins are canceled and we have the release of redemption through his very blood" (Colossians 1:14 TPT). Redemption is "a liberation procured by the payment of a ransom," *apolytrosis, Strong's Concordance* (G#629).

24. "And now you must repent and turn back to God that your sins will be removed, and so that times of refreshing will stream from the Lord's presence" (Acts 3:19 TPT). "Repent," *metanoeo, Strong's Concordance* (G#3340), is "to change one's mind." "Turn back" is *epistrepho, Strong's Concordance* (G#1994), is "turn back to God" or "be converted."

25. "And by the blood of his cross, everything in heaven and earth is brought back to himself—back to its original intent, restored to innocence again" (Colossians 1:20 TPT). "Restored" is "brought back to a former state of harmony," *apokatallasso, Strong's Concordance* (G#604).

26. The price or payment made for our redemption, as when it is said that the Son of Man came "to give his life as a ransom for many" (Matthew 20:28 NLT). In the Old Testament, a slave was not liberated except when a ransom price had been paid. Even an original owner could not receive back his lost possession until he had bought it back with a price (Leviticus 25:47–54).

27. "Therefore it is said, When He ascended on high, He led captivity captive [He had a train of vanquished foes] and He bestowed gifts on men" (Ephesians 4:8 AMP).

28. "And he has generously given each one of us supernatural grace, according to the size of the gift of Christ. This is why he says: 'He ascends into the heavenly heights taking his many captured ones with him, and gifts were given to men.' He 'ascended' means that he returned to heaven, after he had first descended from the heights of heaven, even descending as far as the lowest parts of the earth. The same one who descended is also the one who ascended above the heights of heaven, in order to begin the restoration and fulfillment of all things" (Ephesians 4:7–10 TPT).

29. "You have ascended on high. You have led away captive a train of vanquished foes; You have received gifts of men, yes, of the rebellious also, that the Lord God might dwell there with them" (Psalm 68:18 AMP). *The Greek Septuagint* version translates this as, "You ascended on high, having taken captivity captive"—and suggests an "arresting at spearpoint" and a "repossession of mankind's gifts." See *The Mirror Translation* notes for Ephesians 4:8.

30. "When I saw him, I fell down at his feet as good as dead, but he laid his right hand on me and I heard his reassuring voice saying: 'Don't yield to fear. I am the Beginning and I am the End, the Living One! I was dead, but now look—I am alive forever and ever. And I hold the keys that unlock death and the unseen world'" (Revelation 1:17–18 TPT).

31. "He canceled out every legal violation we had on our record and the old arrest warrant that stood to indict us. He erased it all—our sins, our stained soul—he deleted it all and they cannot be retrieved! Everything we once were in Adam has been placed onto his cross and nailed permanently there as a public display of cancellation. Then Jesus made a public spectacle of all the powers and principalities of darkness, stripping away from them every weapon and all their spiritual authority and power to accuse us. And by the power of the cross, Jesus led them around as prisoners in a procession of triumph. He was not their prisoner; they were his!" (Colossians 2:14–15 TPT).

32. Or "the unseen world," which is Aramaic for Hades. See *A Greek-English Lexicon of the New Testament and Other Early Christian Literature, 3rd edition.*

33. From *Dictionary.com*: "Critical Race Theory refers to a way of analyzing systems, institutions, and power through a lens of race and racism. Central to CRT is the idea that many institutions are built on and enforce systemic racism and oppression of people of color, that this racism and oppression have a long history in the United States and the world (including slavery and its legacy), and that they are ongoing and driven by white supremacy."

34. My thoughts on CRT: The promulgation of this theory instills in people of color a mindset that says "I am victimized and disadvantaged"—and in white people one that says "I am evil and privileged."

35. The spirit of Leviathan hides below the surface of the deep in Job Chapter 41.

36. Warren, Marcus. *The Priestly Prayer of the Blessing: The Ancient Secret of the Only Prayer in the Bible Written by God Himself,* Charisma House, 2018.

37. See *The Mirror* notes on Ephesians 4:15.

38. "We can all draw close to him with the veil removed from our faces. And with no veil we all become like mirrors who brightly reflect the glory of the Lord Jesus. We are being transfigured into his very image as we move from one brighter level of glory to another. And this glorious transfiguration comes from the Lord, who is the Spirit" (2 Corinthians 3:18 TPT).

39. "Do not lie to one another, for you have stripped off the old (unregenerate) self with its evil practices and have clothed yourselves with the new [spiritual self], which is [ever in the process of being] renewed and remolded into [fuller and more perfect knowledge upon] knowledge after the image (the likeness) of Him Who created it" (Colossians 3:9–10 AMP).

40. "Those who are loved by God, let his love continually pour from you to one another, because God is love. Everyone who loves is fathered by God and experiences an intimate knowledge of him" (1 John 4:7 TPT).

41. "[But what of that?] For I consider that the sufferings of this present time (this present life) are not worth being compared with the glory that is about to be revealed to us and in us and for us and conferred on us! For [even the whole] creation (all nature) waits expectantly and longs earnestly for God's sons to be made known [waits for the revealing, the disclosing of their sonship]" (Romans 8:18–19 AMP).

42. "My old identity has been co-crucified with Messiah and no longer lives; for the nails of his cross crucified me with him. And now the essence of this new life is no longer mine, for the Anointed One lives his life through me—we live in union as one! My new life is empowered by the faith of the Son of God who loves me so much that he gave himself for me and dispenses his life into mine!" (Galatians 3:20 TPT).

43. The Hebrew word for "turning" is *haphak*, *Strong's Concordance* (H#2015), meaning "to turn, turn about, turn around, change, transform, be reversed, be converted."

44. "Whatever the revelation-light exposes, it will also correct, and everything that reveals truth is light to the soul. This is why the Scripture says, 'Arise, you sleeper! Rise up from your coffin and the Anointed One will shine his light into you!'" (Ephesians 5:13–14 TPT). Note: Some translations say, "Everything revealed becomes light."

45. "And to the one who conquers I will give the privilege of sitting with me on my throne, just as I conquered and sat down with my Father on his throne. The one whose heart is open let him listen carefully to what the Spirit is saying now to the churches" (Revelation 3:21–22 TPT).

46. "In the last days, the mountain of Yahweh's temple will be raised up as the head of the mountains, towering over all the hills. A sparkling stream of every nation will flow into it. Many peoples will come and say, 'Everyone, come! Let's go up higher to Yahweh's mountain, to the house of Jacob's God; then he can teach us his ways and we can walk in his paths!' Zion will be the center of instruction, and the word of Yahweh will go out from Jerusalem. He will judge fairly between the nations and settle disputes among many peoples. They will beat the swords they used against each other into plowshares and their spears into pruning hooks. No nation will take up weapons against another, nor will they prepare for war anymore. O house of Jacob, come let us walk in the wonderful light of Yahweh!" (Isaiah 2:2–5 TPT).

47. "Cling tightly to all you have until I appear. To everyone who is victorious and continues to do my works to the very end I will give you authority over the nations to shepherd them with a royal scepter. And the rebellious will be shattered as clay pots—even as I also received authority from the presence of

my Father, I will give the morning star to the one who experiences victory" (Revelation 2:25–28 TPT).

48. Robertson, Pat. *The New World Order*, Word Publishing, 1991, pg. 14.

49. Mt. Zion, one of seven significant mountains described in the Bible. See Chapter Two.

50. "Then suddenly, after I wrote down these messages, I saw a heavenly portal open before me, and the same trumpet-voice I heard speaking with me at the beginning broke the silence and said, 'Ascend into this realm! I want to reveal to you what must happen after his'" (Revelation 4:1 TPT).

51. "Because of this my praises rise to the King of all the universe who is indestructible, invisible, and full of glory, the only God who is worthy of the highest honors throughout all of time and throughout the eternity of eternities" (1 Timothy 1:17).

52. "Rise up in splendor and be radiant, for your light has dawned, and Yahweh's glory now streams from you! Look carefully! Darkness blankets the earth, and thick gloom covers the nations, but Yahweh arises upon you and the brightness of his glory appears over you!" (Isaiah 60:1–2 TPT)

53. Jesus said, "And to the one who conquers I will give the privilege of sitting with me on my throne. The one whose heart is open let him listen carefully to what the Spirit is saying now to the churches" Revelation 3:21–22 TPT).

54. "You will guard him and keep him in perfect and constant peace whose mind [both its inclination and its character] is stayed on You, because he commits himself to You, leans on You, and hopes confidently in You" (Isaiah 26:3 AMP).

55. What Yahweh thinks of us, His bride, in our "risen" state with Him: "Listen, my dearest darling, you are so beautiful–you are beauty itself to me! Your eyes glisten with love, like gentle doves behind your veil. What devotion I see each time I gaze upon you. You are like a sacrifice ready to be offered. When I look at you, I see how you have taken my fruit and tasted my word. Your life has become clean and pure, like a lamb washed and newly shorn. You now show grace and balance with truth on display. Your lips are as lovely as Rahab's scarlet ribbon, speaking mercy, speaking grace. The words of your mouth are as refreshing as an oasis. What pleasure you bring to me! I see your blushing cheeks opened like the halves of a pomegranate, showing through your veil of tender meekness. When I look at you, I see your inner strength, so stately and strong. You are as secure as David's fortress. Your virtues and grace cause a thousand famous soldiers to surrender to your beauty. Your pure faith and love rest over your heart as you nurture those who are yet infants" (Song of Songs 4:1–5 TPT).

56. "And You have made them a kingdom (royal race) and priests to our God, and they shall reign [as kings] over the earth!" Revelation 5:10 AMP).

57. "As for you also, because of and for the sake of the [covenant of the Lord with His people, which was sealed with sprinkled] covenant blood, I have released and sent forth your imprisoned people out of the waterless pit. Return to the stronghold [of security and prosperity], you prisoners of hope; even today do I declare that I will restore double your former prosperity to you." (Zechariah 9:11–12 AMP).

58. "Fasten me upon your heart as a seal of fire forevermore. This living, consuming flame will seal you as my prisoner of love" (Song of Songs 8:6 TPT).

59. "Then he said to me, This [addition of the bowl to the candlestick, causing it to yield a ceaseless supply of oil from the olive trees] is the word of the Lord to Zerubbabel, saying, Not by might, nor by power, but by My Spirit [of Whom the oil is a symbol], says the Lord of hosts" (Zechariah 4:6 AMP).

60. **Going Deeper:** Visit www.emilygardnerfoppe.com to download and print additional question-and-answer material pertaining to this chapter. The material presented will (1) provide a review of this chapter and (2) take you deeper into the discussion.

Afterword

1. Jesus said, "I am the sprouting vine and you're my branches. As you live in union with me as your source, fruitfulness will stream from within you—but when you live separated from me you are powerless" (John 15:5 TPT).

2. "But we long to see you passionately advance until the end and you find your hope fulfilled. So don't allow your hearts to grow dull or lose your enthusiasm, but follow the example of those who fully received what God has promised because of their strong faith and patient endurance" (Hebrews 6:11–12 TPT).

3. "You are always and dearly loved by God! So robe yourself with virtues of God, since you have been divinely chosen to be holy. Be merciful as you endeavor to understand others, and be compassionate, showing kindness toward all. Be gentle and humble, unoffendable in your patience with others. Tolerate the weaknesses of those in the family of faith, forgiving one another in the same way you have been graciously forgiven by Jesus Christ. If you find fault with someone, release this same gift of forgiveness to them. For love is supreme and must flow through each of these virtues. Love becomes the mark of true maturity" (Colossians 3:12–14 TPT).

4. As for you also, because of and for the sake of the [covenant of the Lord with His people, which was sealed with sprinkled] covenant blood, I have

released and sent forth your imprisoned people out of the waterless pit. Return to the stronghold [of security and prosperity], you prisoners of hope, even today do I declare that I will restore double your former prosperity to you (Zechariah 9:11–12 AMP).

5. There is a divine mystery—a secret surprise that has been concealed from the world for generations, but now it's being revealed, unfolded and manifested for every holy believer to experience. Living within you is the Christ who floods you with the expectation of glory! This mystery of Christ, embedded within us, becomes a heavenly treasure chest of hope filled with the riches of glory for his people, and God wants everyone to know it!" (Colossians 1:26–27 TPT).

6. "Fasten me upon your heart as a seal of fire forevermore. This living, consuming flame will seal you as my prisoner of love. My passion is stronger than the chains of death and the grave, all-consuming as the very flashes of fire from the burning heart of God. Place this fierce, unrelenting fire over your entire being. Rivers of pain and persecution will never extinguish this flame. Endless floods will be unable to quench this raging fire that burns within you. Everything will be consumed. It will stop at nothing as you yield everything to this furious fire until it won't even seem to you like a sacrifice anymore" (Song of Songs 8:6–7 TPT).

7. "So it is impossible for God to lie for we know that his promise and his vow will never change! And now we have run into his heart to hide ourselves in his faithfulness. This is where we find his strength and comfort, for he empowers us which sits in the heavenly realm beyond the sacred threshold, and where Jesus, our forerunner, has gone in before us. He is now and forever our royal Priest like Melchizedek" (Hebrews 6:18–20 TPT).

Made in the USA
Coppell, TX
30 March 2022

75765812R00146